2/20/04

To Marv –

Thanks for teaching me to love the written word.

You've been a great literary mentor –

Fondly –

Elly

GUERRILLA

RETAILING™

Unconventional Ways to Make Big Profits from Your Retail Business

By Jay Conrad Levinson,
Elly Valas
and Orvel Ray Wilson, CSP

THE GUERRILLA GROUPinc

We dedicate this book to that small band of entrepreneurs who bravely fight the retail wars, proving beyond doubt that guerrilla marketing really works.

Acknowledgements

I owe countless thanks to Orvel Ray Wilson, who has been my writing partner for many books, each one superb, and to Elly Valas, my newest writing partner. They did the heavy lifting on this book and I know that retailers around the world will be as grateful to my co-authors as I am.

—Jay Conrad Levinson

With special thanks to Bob Goldberg, Rosemary Jacobshagen and the North American Retail Dealer's Association (NARDA) and its members for opening their stores, lives and hearts, and for the opportunity to learn and teach, and to grow with them. In memory of my retail mentors: Jerry Gart, Zeke Landres and Harry Valas. With appreciation to Orvel Ray Wilson, for his support in making this book possible.

— Elly Valas

Deepest appreciation to Elly and, Jay, as well as to Aaron Wilson, Chris Boyer, Ryan Brady, Pat McNamara and all of the team at The Guerrilla Group who worked so hard to help make this book a reality. Special thanks to Denise, the love of my life, for putting up with our late nights and long hours while we were writing this book, and for her expert proofreading. Thanks as well to all our clients and friends, customers and suppliers who have shown us how wonderfully rewarding the world of small business can be.

— Orvel Ray Wilson

Contents

Contents ➤

GUERRILLA RETAILING

Introduction

So, You Want to Be a Retailer?

Whether you're trying to beat back Best Buy, ward off Wal-Mart, or open your own hometown hardware store, this book will show you how to survive, and *thrive* in today's hyper-competitive world of retail. After working with thousands of retailers all around the world, we've watched the losers come and go, while the winners grow and grow. We've catalogued their best practices, and organized them here for you step-by-step. Whether you're just developing your concept, or opening your tenth location, you'll find new ideas and tactics that can insure your success.

It's a jungle out there. There's never been a tougher time for retailers. You'll need all the help you can get just to survive. Luckily, you hold in your hands the world's most powerful arsenal for winning the retail wars.

You'll learn what to consider when choosing a name and identity for your business, and how to identify your best potential customers. You'll discover how to pick the right location, hire the right people and display the right merchandise. You'll learn how to retaliate against predatory pricing, while getting the maximum impact from your advertising. You'll learn about low-cost, high-payoff promotions that have been tested by award-winning retailers in dozens of industries. You'll learn how to build traffic, maintain margins, motivate salespeople and develop a following of loyal, repeat customers. We've even armed you with powerful analytical tools so you can diagnose and cure the most common business ailments without advice from an MBA.

No one is eagerly waiting for the next retail store to open and no one is going to throw a big party to celebrate your grand opening

1

unless you do. In the 1980s, developers threw up more than 1600 regional malls, so many in fact, that today they're having trouble finding sites for new ones. In the U.S. today, we already have nearly twenty square feet of retail space for every man, woman and child in the country. Compare that to only thirteen feet per person in 1980 and even today, only *two* feet of retail space per person in the United Kingdom. We are malled out, stored out and shopped out.

You've seen the hand painted signs in the windows, "Going Out of Business," and "Everything Must Go," or, more often, you make the trip to a favorite shop on a side street only to find the building empty and the windows papered over. These are tough times for retailers. The long-standing family businesses have been out-priced by the megastores and crowded out by urban renewal. Competition is fierce and margins are thin. Survival is difficult and profitability is illusive.

That is, unless you're a Guerrilla Retailer.

You've seen them, too, haven't you? They're the busy, exciting shops and stores where there's always a crowd and always something new and interesting to be found. You'll find them in downtown storefronts, backstreet shops and even (occasionally) in the regional mega-malls. They're at the swap meet, the flea market, or simply spread out on a blanket on the sidewalk. They break the conventional rules of merchandising. They may remain closed on Sunday, Labor Day and other big holidays. Or they might only open on Thursday evening and Saturday. Even so, they shatter the norms for sales per square foot and they make their owners delightful profits day-after-day, year-in and year-out.

No matter how the economy may swing, a never-ending stream of loyal, repeat customers adore these irregulars. Guerrillas not only love the musical ring of the cash register, but they enjoy the esteem of the community, the support of their vendors and the respect of their bankers.

How can this be? You hold the answer in your hand.

■ KNOW THE ENEMY

You are not paranoid. They really *are* out to get you. It's no secret that big box stores are capturing retail market share by storm. Since 1990, more than 13,000 locally-owned pharmacies have closed. The market share of independent bookstores has fallen from 58% in 1972 to just 15% today. Local hardware dealers are disappearing too; Home Depot and Lowe's have captured one-third of that market. Five companies account for 42% of all grocery sales. Blockbuster rents one of every three videos nationwide. A single corporation, Wal-Mart, now captures seven percent of all consumer spending, and is the world's largest employer.

More than 160 million consumers shop in discount stores each week, so if you're going to be a guerrilla retailer, it's best to know the enemy.

The terms "value retailers," "superstore," "big box retailer," and "category killer" are all used interchangeably. For these retailers, size *does* matter. Their retail model depends on big volume rather than big markups. To do a profitable volume, they must occupy a big space. Typically, they range in size from 90,000 to 200,000 square feet and are located as often as possible near highway interchanges. They all use the same windowless box store design, with several acres of single-floor layout and vast surface parking.

We have to give them credit. At Wal-Mart, "Everyday Low Prices" is more than just a slogan. Over the years, Wal-Mart has relentlessly wrung tens of billions of dollars in cost efficiencies out of the retail supply chain, then passed the larger part of those savings along to customers. The New England Consulting Group, in Westport, CT, estimates that Wal-Mart saved its U.S. customers $20 billion in 2003 alone. Factor in the price cuts that other retailers must make to compete and the total annual savings approaches $100 billion. It's no wonder that economists refer to a broad "Wal-Mart effect" that has suppressed inflation and set productivity gains rippling through the economy year after year.

However, Wal-Mart's seemingly virtuous business model is fraught with complications and perverse consequences, decimating whole communities of small town downtown merchants and driving down retail wages. The discounters' entrée into the community is often greeted with great fanfare from the Chamber of Commerce, blinded by the glitter of sales tax revenue and the promise of new jobs. Gifts from the city fathers include tax breaks, roads and infrastructure and environmental waivers.

Certainly the superstores are not the only culprits. The definition of "big" is relative, and has to be related to the product category. A superstore of diamonds needs only 5,000 square feet or so to be called a superstore, while a superstore of cars would cover acres and acres and acres. For the supermarket and grocery sector, a big-box superstore will typically be in the 50,000 to 100,000 square foot range. For warehouse operations such as Costco normally contain 120,000 square feet. In contrast, for book retailers, 25,000 to 50,000 square feet would qualify as a big-box. For other specialty retail categories like eyeglasses, a 5,000 square-foot store would qualify. The key point is that "big-box category-killer" stores are several times the size of the traditional outlets in their categories.

We can categorize these "superstores" into three subgroups: discount department stores, category killers and warehouse clubs.

Discount department stores include Wal-Mart, Kmart, Target and others who sell department store merchandise at lower prices.

Category killers are large niche retailers like Ikea, Toys R Us, Circuit City, Barnes & Nobel Books, Home Depot, Lowe's and Sports Authority that buy and sell in huge volumes at low prices. They create additional pressure on prices by eliminating the middleman and dealing directly with manufacturers.

Warehouse clubs, like Sam's Club, Costco and BJ's Wholesale, are membership shopping clubs. They offer a variety of goods, often including groceries, electronics, clothing, hardware and more, at wholesale prices. Unlike discount department stores, which may sell as many as 60,000 distinct items, warehouse clubs limit their range from 3,000 to 5,000 items. Their stores range in size from 104,000 to 170,000 square feet and serve markets up to 250,000 people.

Conglomerations of superstores in 250,000 to 750,000 square-foot centers are called "power centers."

Superstores have acquired their affectionate nickname "category killers" because they don't compete with existing businesses. They kill them off and monopolize the market.

When these behemoths move into a market, they typically over-staff the store with specially-trained teams of friendly, helpful salespeople, at least for the first few months of operation. Expanded staff and predatory pricing means that the first-time shopper has a positive experience and saves money. Customers are won early. Once the competition is demolished, the box store changes the product mix, raises prices and reduces staff. Some local stores just give up, while others try to adapt to fit a new market, but without access to venture capital, zoning variances or tax breaks, many fail.

As the category killer's smaller competition disappears, so do the helpful employees and prices start to rise.

"Predatory pricing" is another weapon wielded by the category killers. These "loss leaders" give the impression of wider savings. Car-bound customers find comparison-shopping inconvenient if not impossible. They're at the mercy of the bar-code scanner.

➤ The Fall of Department Stores

Troubled department stores are losing share to the mass merchants at one end of the scale, and specialty stores at the other. This reflects the larger economic issues buffeting retail in general, and the apparel business in particular, including deflation resulting from an oversupply of goods. Five years ago, department stores sold men's jeans at an average price of $40. Today, the same jeans sell for an average of only $34. At national chains like Sears, Roebuck & Co. or Kohl's Corp., the price is about $24. When the World Trade Organization further relaxes trade barriers with China in 2005, the U.S. market will be flooded with even more cheap clothing. All of this promises to put greater pressure on everyone to lower prices.

In spite of current economic trends, this is a great time to be in retail.

➤ Twenty Important Trends in Retail

1. Experts are forecasting continued success for Wal-Mart and their ilk, as shoppers become ever more bargain-conscious.

2. We also see continued growth for the super center format. Total super center sales will nearly triple by 2010.

3. Even so, there are opportunities for conventional retailers to survive in a world dominated by the big boxes.

4. No more one-size-fits-all. Guerrilla retailers will have to take more of a portfolio approach to the market in order to appeal to more discriminating shoppers. Even customers who used to shop at sporting goods superstores like Sports Authority are turning to specialty shops that sell only soccer stuff, or only snowmobiles, or the ultimate example: Golf For Her, a retail boutique created by entrepreneur Kris Foy in Broom-field, Colorado.

5. Department stores are in a death spiral. Escalating competition from discounters on one side and specialty stores on the other will continue to squeeze this category, which will face more consolidation and retrenchment.

6. Malls will get mauled. Many will have to change almost beyond recognition in order to survive. The good news for guerrillas is that customers who are tired of hiking through the sameness of mall after mall will be more likely to go to a destination store for just the right product and superior service.

7. Reconcept rather than just remodel. Compressed lifecycles for products, retail concepts and brands mean the end of large, mass-merchandised specialty chains.

There used to be a restaurant on Highland Avenue in Downers Grove, Illinois, called The Highland Grill. Great food, great service, in the upscale burgers-steaks-and-fries grill-food format, very successful, always jammed. Then suddenly, BAM, they're closed! Two and half months later they re-open as Parker's Ocean Grill with completely new décor, new menu, but the *same* staff. We asked, "What happened?"

The manager explained, "We're part of an eight-restaurant chain, Select Restaurants, Inc., headquartered in Cleveland, Ohio, and we've learned that every four or five years, we have to gut the place and do something completely different *before* we get stale and our customers get bored with us."

Today they operate 17 restaurants.

8. The Experience Economy excels. Guerrilla retailing concepts will mix content and commerce as never before. The Rainforest Café couldn't make it on the quality of their food alone. REI and their two-story climbing walls create an atmosphere of high adventure, even before you get your new gear outdoors.

9. Click & Brick. E-tailing's impact will extend beyond its relatively limited share (currently about 3%) of total retail sales. By 2008, it will be 12%. Forrester Research predicts U.S. online sales will grow to $204 billion by 2007.

10. Smart shopping. Consumers will embrace technologies that give them better information about products and more control over the shopping process. Roughly half of U.S. consumers already shop on the Internet at least occasionally. A larger proportion uses the web to research options before going to a brick-and-mortar store to make the purchase. The most successful operators combine information-rich on-line catalogues with storefront offerings. Guerrilla retailers will set up a computer terminal with Internet access and invite their prospect to check out competing products right there in the store instead of leaving to shop elsewhere.

11. Smart stores. Retailers will adopt technologies that enhance the productivity of store space and associates. Some solutions, including kiosks and self-checkout terminals, will im-

prove staff productivity and make shopping more convenient. Guerrilla retailers will provide floorwalkers with wireless handheld computers that can check inventory, schedule installations, or even write invoices from anywhere on the sales floor. Rental-car agencies and even some restaurants already use wireless floorwalkers. Soon you'll see a computer display mounted on your grocery cart that beeps an alarm when you pass an item that's on sale, driving multiple-item, impulse and companion-item purchases.

12. Mobile sales will remain elusive. Starbucks Coffee, in Seattle, Washington, has experimented with micro-marketing. A coupon appears on the screen of your cell-phone when you're in the neighborhood. But the sale of products and services via cell phones and other mobile devices will be limited through the end of the decade.

13. The global land rush continues. Despite growing world tensions, retailers and other businesses will remain committed to international operations.

14. Retailers will act more and more like suppliers. As retailers grow they will seek alternative sources of products, leading many suppliers to find their retail customers becoming their biggest competitors. Wal-Mart is already contracting for apparel directly with factories in China, two years in advance.

15. Retailers will become brand managers. Exclusive brands will be an important differentiation strategy for guerrilla retailers. You'll see more and more one-brand only stores like Victoria's Secret, Talbot's, J. Crew, Eddie Bauer, Abercrombie & Fitch, The Gap and Orvis.

16. Suppliers will start to act more like retailers. Retailers will look to key suppliers to become category consultants, setting

strategy for the category, managing inventory and selling space by location, almost as if they were operating leased departments.

17. Brand sharing. Retailers will plug into each other's shopper data base and leverage location by leasing space for a store-within-a-store. Department stores often feature Ralph Lauren, Calphalon, or Nautica stores-in-a-store. Starbucks is setting up shop in your local Barnes & Noble, as well as in Albertson's, right next to the Krispy Kremes.

18. Über retailers. Some giant retailers will leverage their brand identities, customer relationships and size to fulfill virtually all the needs of certain categories of shoppers. Cabela's has followed this strategy to wildly-profitable success specializing in hunting, fishing and outdoor gear.

19. Suppliers become retailers. Some suppliers will seek to sell directly to the consumer, as in The Nike Store and The Sony Store. BOSE sells their acoustic noise-canceling headphones directly to consumers in airports as well as their own stores.

20. Customers will call the shots. More and more, customer relationships will be *the* key competitive asset for guerrilla retailers.

The battle has begun. You are massively outnumbered, outspent and out-gunned, and unless you fight back with everything you've got, you don't stand a chance. You must become a Guerrilla.

➤ Small is Beautiful

Retailers are learning that when it comes to store size, bigger isn't necessarily better. Grocery chains such as Publix (and you could add Marsh, Harris Teeter and some others) with its 29,000 square foot store in Jacksonville, Florida, are finding that smaller units can create dollar volumes similar to bigger boxes.

Customers in the smaller stores are different. They make more trips to the store, buy more prepared foods and will walk to the store more often than those shopping in a 55,000 square foot unit.

First, there were only small stores. Then someone looked at the economics and said, "Look, I only have to pay one store manager." With this and all the other economies, large stores were born. This was followed by the concept of one-stop shopping, which was never supported by the consumer. Now, many large format retailers are having difficulty finding available store sites.

Large stores create an impersonal shopping experience that appeals to a different consumer than the one who is loyal to the local market. Not everyone wants to drive for 20 minutes to shop. Different customers require different types of merchandise. People will adapt as necessary, but some really do like the feeling that they are taking control of their shopping dollar by driving to the big box and surviving alone in the "wilderness of oversized servings." Others very much prefer personalized service and a special shopping experience.

There is certainly a place for both in this world. A big box must focus intently on the operations, while a smaller store can (and must) focus on the customer. Management of the box stores has pushed far too many administrative tasks down to the store level, causing distraction and lack of focus. This has led to the inability to deliver the type of management required to serve, please and cater to customers, not to mention the amount of time distracted from coaching and inspiring their associates. These are the key vulnerabilities that guerrilla retailers should exploit.

Many retailers are hard at work seeking a niche, creating points of differentiation and creating a value for their customers. Learning, finding out what works and expanding new and different formats can be exciting. These store formats may require a completely different skill set for reasons other than size. Imagine the need for an executive chef as your store's manager, depending on the format. There's a broad, unmet demand out there for different skills and talents for which size and dollar volume may be irrelevant.

These days, retail stores, for the most part, were not designed for the customer. Instead, they were developed to generate maximum *sales* with the least expense. There is nothing wrong with that, but guerrillas know that *profit,* not sales, is the only legitimate measure of small-business success.

Small guerrilla operators need to focus on adding value, and the extra special touches that the box stores can't provide. The talent level of your employees must be at the top of the scale. In a small store, everyone has to carry their own weight. Small stores get no economies of scale, so every mistake is magnified.

The good news is that small stores with talent and creativity can generate profit margins that the big stores only dream about. Plus they're experiencing the rewards of working with customers that can actually make it fun to work in retail.

Despite industry practice, stores should be designed as small as possible, while still meeting their merchandising and customer needs. Whole Foods Market, the world's largest retailer of natural and organic foods with more than 140 stores throughout the country, averages about the same per-store sales as Kroger or Safeway, but their stores are about half the size. This *sales-per-square-foot efficiency* compounds the profitability they earn from higher gross margins.

Successful small stores usually have high customer counts and low sales per transaction. On average, quick shoppers spend nearly as much in five to ten minutes as a "browser" will spend in ten to twenty minutes. The speed of spending is far higher for the shorter trips.

A great majority of customers shop the large-format stores *as if* they were a smaller store. Eighty to 90% of the shopping trips never get beyond the first twenty percent of the floor. By spreading 20,000 feet of shopping over a 60,000 foot box, you have just moved many of the items a shopper might have purchased outside of their ambit.

Soon, these big 130,000 square-foot stores are no longer going to be the big push, because, the population is getting older. People are not going to want to walk through big stores. Guerrilla retailers have to capitalize on this very important trend. These customers want to feel like they are special. In a big box store, they feel like a number. Their parents told them stories about what it was like going to the neighborhood market when they were growing up. They called the butcher by his first name and he knew what cut to give them and how thick they liked it.

A small store also has an advantage over a larger store when it comes to personnel. It can better spend its time on training and cross training. Employees tend to stay longer in a smaller store because they feel they are part of something special. In the future, retailers across the country will give in to their customers, and bring back a smaller store format with a focus on quality instead of variety.

> Still Room

There is still plenty of room for remarkable retailers. These guerrillas have a clear vision and a well-defined mission. They constantly strive to provide a unique shopping experience. They have Disney-ized the shopping trip by combining service, technology and theatre into a transcendent experience.

Shopping has become more and more experiential, so that the quality of the *experience* has become more important than the quality of the merchandise. Consumers will pay more for an item that's artfully displayed, beautifully lit and professionally presented in pleasant and exciting surroundings.

Retail has become *shoppertainment*. Successful guerrillas have turned their shops and stores into theaters, where the sales associates are the cast and the fixtures and merchandise provide the set. They tell a story or capture an era, seduce and excite you.

If you don't have a story to tell, a theme, or a well-defined, well-executed niche, if you're not remarkable, your days as a retailer are numbered.

If you isolate your uniqueness, defend your quality, provide expert advice and make shopping fun, you'll do a Snoopy dance on the way to the bank with each day's receipts.

$$Chapter\ 1$$

What Do We Mean by "Guerrilla"?

The strategy of course comes from guerrilla warfare; how do you fight back when you're outnumbered, outgunned and outspent by the competition?

Just as a lightly armed, fast-moving band of rag-tags can paralyze an army, the retail guerrilla relies on *information* and *surprise* to gain a tactical advantage.

Information is the new currency of the 21st Century. By information, we mean knowing more about your customers, your market and your products than anyone. Guerrillas constantly walk the floor, managing their business from the only perspective that matters: the customer's point-of-view. They ask casual questions and organize formal focus groups. They listen. It's really no mystery. If you really listen, your customers will always tell you *exactly* what you need to do to be successful.

By surprise, we mean going the extra mile, adding the extra touch, doing the unexpected. They often do the very *last* thing their competitors, or even their *customers*, expect. They under-promise and over-deliver. They tell the truth at all times, at all costs.

Guerrillas are dedicated to building customer loyalty, while also earning handsome profits. Profit is the only legitimate measure of your success. No one every went broke making a profit.

➤ Be Exceptional

No one today has resources to waste on inefficient marketing tactics like random cold calling or half-hearted follow-up. Consumers have more choices than ever, and will no longer settle for shoddy quality or unresponsive service. You have to be positively *exceptional* to maintain their loyalty. To win the business in today's brutal battlefield, you must become a Guerrilla.

Guerrilla Retailing is not so much a collection of techniques as it is an attitude, an approach, a philosophy of doing business. Guerrilla Retailing is about combining psychology and technology for getting maximum results at minimum cost. Some of it is common sense, but not all of it is common practice. Guerrillas build a constituency of dedicated followers by consistently maintaining the highest standards of quality, service and business principles.

Guerrillas rely on *time, energy and imagination* instead of the brute force of a big-budget marketing campaign. These are the three arenas where no one can outspend you.

■ A CREDO FOR GUERRILLAS

How do you explain it? Two identical storefronts in a strip mall; one sees tenant after tenant move in, open their doors and then fail, while its neighbor thrives year after year, generating generous profits for their owners. We've worked with successful retailers all over the world, from appliance stores in Atlanta to a tailor's shop in Bangkok, and as different as these stores may be, the successful ones all exhibit this set of winning characteristics. They're easy to remember because each word ends in "ent."

➤ Investment

Guerrillas consider the money they spend on their team, their facilities and their marketing to be an investment, not an expense. Just like buying blue-chip stocks, you should expect to get your principle back, plus interest. Guerrillas understand the need to invest whatever it takes to meet changing market and consumer conditions.

There are only two kinds of marketing: good marketing and bad marketing. Good marketing pays for itself and returns a dividend. It drives customers into your store and profits into your bank account. Everything else is bad marketing.

More important than money, guerrillas invest *time, energy* and *imagination.*

Planning and researching your market, your competitors and your customers' needs takes valuable time. But the time and money you invest in those relationships is a smart investment in the long run, if you manage it carefully. Be on the lookout for opportunities to leverage your selling capital for a greater return. For example, can the customer buy something, and also give you a merchandising suggestion, an introduction to another supplier, a referral, or a testimonial letter?

Rewarding customers for doing business with you is a particularly conservative investment. Don't expect overnight miracles. You might not hear from them again for months. But just like your blue-chip stocks, over the years they'll be worth a fortune.

The average retail business in America only invests between three and four percent of gross sales revenue back into marketing. At the launch, it's not unusual for start-ups to spend more than ten percent of revenues getting their name out and customers in. Guerrillas measure the effectiveness of every dollar spent on marketing.

And do something every day to invest in yourself. Constantly improve your knowledge of the product, the market and the customer. Read the trade journals that serve your industry religiously. Subscribe to them all. Two retail publications that we can recommend are The National Retail Federation's magazine *Stores and The Independent Retailer*, published by the North America Retail Dealer Association. Ask yourself, "What could I improve?" Ask your customers. Listen to their answers. Act on them. Organize focus groups of customers and ask, "How are we doing?" If you really listen, your customers will tell you exactly what you need to do to succeed.

➤ Consistent

Poor selling done consistently will be more effective than great selling done sporadically. The guerrilla who is consistent will outsell the better armed, better equipped, better organized corporate regulars, because prospects will trust them.

In the mind of the prospect, consistency is interpreted as credibility, longevity and success. This creates a feeling of trust. Guerrillas earn the confidence of their prospects and soon prospects become customers.

Most buying decisions are made unconsciously and modern psychology has shown us how to reach into the unconscious mind of prospects. Repetition is the key. At the risk of repeating ourselves, we'll say that again. Repetition.

Repetition is required on two fronts, selling the message to prospects customers and selling the message to the sales staff. Guerrillas repeat their offer to the same people over and over again. Even when prospects say, "no," and particularly when they say, "yes." They repeat their presentations and their specials and their seasonal offers. They repeat their message and their benefits.

And they repeat their sales training routinely. Weekly. Daily. Constantly. The most successful sales retail organizations in the world train and train and re-train. They train the truck drivers and the telephone receptionists and the service techs. Everyone hears the company's mission and values echoed in meetings, in the hallway, in the cafeteria and on posters in the break rooms.

Repetition. It's how the world knows who you are and what you're about. By maintaining the same identity over time, guerrillas attract business the others have left behind in their hasty retreat.

Do not capriciously change your prices, your products or your guerrilla approach. Just about the time you're bored stiff with your products, your presentation and your advertising campaign, the community you serve is just getting to know you and associating your name with those needs. By being consistent, the guerrilla becomes the second most likely source for their customers and when the competition screws up they automatically inherit their customers as well.

➤ Confident

Guerrillas know that they're selling quality. Unless your offering is top quality, guerrilla retailing will only accelerate your demise. Guerrillas believe in their products and their people. They depend on the rest of the organization to deliver on every promise, every time and then some. If they can't feel that kind of complete trust, they're working for the wrong outfit. They never bad-mouth anyone, even the competition. When something goes wrong, they take personal responsibility.

In an exit-poll survey, 10,000 shoppers in 50 states were asked, "Why did you buy that item here?" Of their responses, "selection" was ranked forth after third-ranked "service." Only 14% said price was most important (it ranked 9th overall). The second most frequent answer was "quality." At the top of the list, ranked as the most frequently cited reason for buying from a particular store was "confidence." They felt confident that their needs would be met and the dealer would stand behind their purchase. Guerrillas do everything they can to communicate their own absolute confidence in their company, their offering and themselves. That confidence is contagious and spreads to prospects and customers.

➤ Patient

Customers may not need your offering today, but they will sooner or later. Needs are cyclical. For example, if you've just eaten a big meal, you don't feel much like ordering pizza. Your appetite has been sated for the time being. But in a few hours, you'll begin to feel hungry again. Guerrillas are always on the lookout for the next *need cycle*, and strive to be there when the need arises again. They keep in touch with customers long after the competition has given up on them.

Not all purchases are made the first time the customer comes into the store. The larger the purchase, the more time consumers may take to carefully consider their buying decisions. So the guerrilla sticks with it. Every contact makes some kind of impression, so it takes a lot of contact time with prospects before they will be primed to do business with you. It may require several impressions of your company, your product or your idea to move the mind of a prospect from total apathy to purchase readiness.

➤ Assortment

Guerrillas offer a wide variety of goods and services and can adapt their offering, their terms, even their delivery schedule to meet the customers needs. The more flexible they can be, the better. The old days when Henry Ford could offer "any color you want, as long as it's black," are long gone. The more options you offer, the more people you can serve and the more you can sell. But guerrillas also stick to what they do well and sell what they do best.

➤ Subsequent

Guerrillas succeed by fighting for successive sales and concentrate most of their efforts selling to current customers. They wage their sales campaign simultaneously on three fronts, The Universe, Their Prospects, and Their Customers. But they marshal their resources to concentrate primarily on the third group.

The first arena, The Universe, includes everyone in your service area. Everyone.

Figure 1-1

Guerrillas invest 10% of their efforts reaching out at random to this massive audience, getting the message out and establishing their identity in the marketplace. They strike up conversations with people on airplanes and commuter trains. They get themselves interviewed on radio talk shows. They leave stacks of business cards on the counter by the cash register in the restaurant where they eat lunch. People who have an embryonic interest will pick them up and move into the next sphere.

This next group is smaller, a subset of the first and includes all of their Prospects.

Guerrillas know that someone is a prospect if they have a potential need for their offering, now or in the future. They haven't met. They're not in the guerrilla's file box, yet. Guerrilla Retailers devote 30% of their energy to moving people from the Universe into the domain of Prospects by letting them know that they exist and gathering as much information as possible.

Harvey Mackay, author of the best-seller, *Swim With the Sharks Without Being Eaten Alive*, shares the secret of his successful envelope business. His salespeople complete a questionnaire of 66 items of interest on every prospect, and not just business questions. Mackay's people find out your kids' names, your church affiliation, even your favorite sports teams and they use this information to build a close human bond.

The third domain in fig. 1-1 is the smallest, at the core of the other two and includes all of your Customers.

This includes everyone who has purchased anything from your store, ever. Guerrillas invest 60% of their selling time in reaching out to those people who have already bought. Yes, it's unconventional. That's why it works. Current customers are the most likely source of referral business and the *only* source of repeat sales. Guerrillas spend most of their time on the smallest group.

Guerrillas are in this for the lifetime value of a customer. For example, a shopper spends about $100 a week in the grocery store and on any Saturday the store is crawling with customers. So what if someone gets upset and goes somewhere else? Who cares? For the guerrilla, that's that's the fifteen-hundred-dollar question, because $100 a week, 50 weeks a year, over the 10 years that a customer shops in that store, is a lot of groceries. Assume a gross profit margin of only 3% and that's $1,500.00 in pure profit walking out the door. If someone stole $1,500 from your cash register, you'd be fuming, looking to put them in jail. But we watch retailers drive customers away all the time and no one even *thinks* of calling the police.

Let's look at some *really* interesting numbers. If someone has a good experience with your company store, they'll tell three people. If they have a bad experience, they'll tell nine people. One in five will tell more than *twenty* people. Word of mouth is one of the most potent weapons in the guerrilla arsenal. Guerrillas use it with great care to build and protect a reputation for service, quality and excellence.

➤ Convenient

Guerrillas know that they have to be user friendly. They have to be easy to reach, easy to talk to and easy to do business with. Their store hours mirror their customers shopping patterns. They answer their own phone. They return their calls. They give out their numbers at home, at the office and in the car, and they carry a pager. They have the phones manned at night and on weekends, even if only by an answering service. They are in touch.

A true guerrilla would never hand the customer an order form to fill out. They take care of all of the paperwork themselves. They do everything immediately.

➤ Excitement

Guerrillas are enthusiastic. They have a good word for everyone. They are militantly optimistic. They never complain about the weather, the economy or the people they work for. Their passion spreads like a wildfire. People love to do business with people who love their business.

➤ Different

It is better to be different than to be better. The best way to avoid head-on competition is to *never* go head-to-head with other stores in your market. Guerrillas are passionate about differentiating their stores from others. All things being equal, *price* becomes the battleground and you will never be able to beat the boxes on price. So plan your product mix so that things are *never* equal. What can you offer that is different, that provides more value, that is in scarce supply, that makes you unique?

Guerrillas are passionate about differentiating their stores from others. They work diligently to provide a fresh, unique customer experience. Because they understand the relationship between risk and reward, guerrillas seldom take the easy way out. They will make retail destinations out of unconventional buildings and try every memorable, humorous stunt to attract the attention of their customers. They will pioneer new products, seek new markets and go to extremes in to assure customer satisfaction.

➤ Commitment

The guerrilla is deadly serious about serving customers, making money and building a future for themselves and their company. They do not see retail selling as a step along the way, but as one of the most demanding and highly-paid professions. When they lose business to a competitor, they hunt down the cause and correct it. They will risk everything except quality and they treat every customer as if their business depends on him or her, because it does.

If your competitors don't hate you, you're not trying hard enough. If you're not 100% committed to your customers, your product and your organization, you'll never survive as a guerrilla. Get out and make room for someone who is. If it's your own business and you'd rather work on R&D or operations, hire someone who thinks about your customers constantly and make them your designated guerrilla.

These are the characteristics that guide the guerrilla's field tactics. They protect you from detection and assault.

Post these "ents" on your bulletin board. Sell by them. Live by them.

Chapter

What Kind of Retailer Do You Want To Be?

You too can be a guerrilla retailer once you learn the secrets of marketing, selling and managing people. You will learn how to develop a business plan that outlines your goals, defines your special niche and targets the customers you want to serve.

Retailers who do a better job of strategic planning than their competitors gain significant competitive advantage. The planning process can seem daunting at first, but it will energize you and fuel your success. It will help you organize what needs to be done and to anticipate the resources you'll need to reach your goals.

No one plans to fail, but many have failed to plan with dire consequences.

➤ MISSION AND VISION

Vision is the force that has led man to discover new continents and travel into space. It's the palpable drive that makes us set seemingly impossible targets and reach new heights.

In 1961, John F. Kennedy was able to mobilize the nation when he committed to landing a man on the moon before the end of the decade.

Steve Jobs changed the face of the world when he envisioned a personal computer on every desk in America.

Dick Schulze led his locally owned Sound of Music into the superstore giant Best Buy after he imagined himself becoming the nation's leading electronics retailer and having stores across the country. In 1983, he offered to share his vision with members of the Board of Directors of the North American Retail Dealers Association, just after he changed the name of the company to Best Buy. A year later, he was the keynote speaker at the association's annual convention delivering an address he titled, "How I'm Going to Eat Your Lunch," in which he outlined his plans for large-format stores, public financing and a national expansion plan.

Your Mission Statement outlines the fundamental direction of the company. It tells employees and customers what to expect, what the values and guiding principles of the business are and where the growth of the company will come from.

When drafting your Mission Statement, be careful that it doesn't limit your potential and that it doesn't make promises you can't keep. Since it will be used to guide your decision-making at every step of the way, it's a good idea to have your staff, customers, suppliers and other stakeholders review a draft before you cast it in concrete.

Valas Stores, Inc., founded in 1941 in Denver, Colorado, was one of the earliest consumer electronics retailers. They pioneered technologies like big screen television, VCRs and microwave ovens. Their mission statement read like this:

MISSION AND PHILOSOPHY

"It is the Company's philosophy to offer our customers a wide selection of innovative products within the product lines we market.

"We provide value to our consumers as well as technical expertise, both at the time of purchase and after the sale.

"The Company provides flexible, varied credit programs for our customers.

"The Company provides opportunities to our employees to profit, acquire new skills and advance within the organization.

"Through its involvement in various activities, the Company returns to the community some of the profits gained there.

"Our history, compassion and integrity have been keys to our success. We will continue to maintain our credibility with our suppliers, our consumers and our employees.

"We will strive for corporate profitability to enable us to grow and expand."

This mission statement kept the company from making costly mistakes. For example, in the early 1980s, Kerry Olson, one of the store's best sales associates tried to convince the company's management that they should start selling personal computers. After several weeks of wrangling and debate, the owners finally agreed to let her use a dark corner of the store to test the market for this odd new product. They told her to buy a couple of computers and a couple of printers and see what she could do.

A week later, Kerry came back to the weekly management meeting to talk about selling computers once again. When her managers said they thought they'd resolved that issue in the previous meeting, she asked them to re-read the company's mission statement.

The management team was reminded that, "It is the Company's philosophy to offer our customers a *wide selection* of innovative products *within the product lines we market.*" Kerry knew that just throwing a couple of pieces of equipment into an unused display area wouldn't work. She wanted a complete commitment.

The company spent the next three months merchandising an entire computer department, hiring a department manager and training the sales staff. The computer division soon accounted for 30% of the company's sales. Kerry Olson's radical views about the future of personal computers made her a pest and a heroine.

➤ Goals and Objectives

After you have defined your mission and your vision so that you can see where you're going, who your customers will be and what products you will be selling, you can begin to establish more concrete goals and objectives. Some of the most common include:

Performance Objectives:
- Market share
- Sales revenue
- Number of units of product sold per year

Financial Objectives:
- Gross margin
- Inventory turnover
- Gross margin return on inventory
- Return on assets
- Net profit margin
- Owner's equity

Productivity Objectives:
- Sales per square foot
- Sales per employee
- Sales per sales associate

Community Objectives:
- Provide employment opportunities
- Give consumers additional choices
- Contribute to the tax base
- Become a resource in the community
- Develop the ability to support charitable endeavors

Personal Objectives:
- Create wealth
- Self-gratification
- Promote an interest or hobby
- Status and respect

Successful guerrilla retailers develop goals that help promote the company's mission and vision. Goals must be specific and time bound so that you can measure and monitor your progress.

Guerrilla Retailers might have goals like:

- Beat industry averages by increasing gross margin to 1% by the end of the second quarter.

- Add an additional product category this year.

- Open a new location within three years.

- Recruit, hire and train three new sales associates before the holiday selling season.

- Establish sales goals every month to improve productivity of sales associates.

- Attend three new trade shows or product markets this year to look for expansion opportunities.

- Increase executive compensation 5% in the current fiscal year while still showing a 3% bottom line profit.

➤ Strategies and Tactics

Strategies are carefully designed action plans for reaching the company's goals and objectives. If goals determine where you want to go, strategies are the maps that get you there. They detail the steps you need to take to succeed at meeting the targets you've set for your business.

Let's say that your goal for this year is to increase your sales volume by $150,000. What are the strategies you might have to use? Remember, each strategy must include a detailed tactical action plan.

Hire one new sales associate

- ❑ Review job description for sales associates
- ❑ Write and place help wanted ad
- ❑ Initial screening of applicants
- ❑ Interview most qualified applicants
- ❑ Check references
- ❑ Conduct second interview with best candidates
- ❑ Tender offer

Train new sales associate

- ❑ Review job description
- ❑ Explain sales goals, commission system
- ❑ Discuss customer service policies
- ❑ Share sales philosophy and sales process
- ❑ Conduct training on computer system
- ❑ Arrange for product training with key vendors
- ❑ Arrange for associate to "shadow" other associates
- ❑ Review progress
- ❑ Offer additional training opportunities where necessary
- ❑ Celebrate new sales associate's success

Develop new promotion

- ❑ Detail steps of action plan necessary to develop new promotion

Conduct sales contest

- ❑ Detail steps of action plan to conduct sales contest

Add new product line

- ❑ Detail steps of action plan needed to add product line

Add new strategies with each new action plan as your vision unfolds.

chapter

Who Is Your Customer?

One of the most important decisions retailers make is defining their target customer. It's also one of the most difficult. There are very few products that can be marketed across all ages, all income ranges and all ethnic groups representing all demographic populations.

Even basic commodities like cereal are segmented. *Cream of Wheat* doesn't generally appeal to the *Cap'n Crunch* crowd.

Only compete in markets where you will win. Some basic precepts for "Wal-Mart-Proofing" Your Business:

Target customer

Box-stores target the wide middle of the market, where shoppers are driven primarily by price and location. Find a way to serve the under-served, unrecognized or unwanted shoppers.

Differentiation

Instead of competing on common ground, alter the value criteria to maximize your own competitive advantages.

Customer Retention

Don't innovate in ways that can be copied by the boxes. Innovate in ways that their scale can't adapt.

Another way to think of this problem is to define your *headpin* customers. This metaphor of course comes from the game of bowling, where the objective is to knock down as pins as possible with each ball. But you mustn't just aim for the headpin or you risk a "split." You have to deliver the ball into the "pocket," or that spot on either side of the headpin that causes all of the pins to topple over one another. Likewise, the guerrilla retailer will aim their marketing message to either side of their target demographic to get the greatest numerical impact from their marketing.

Try this exercise with your development team to get your strategic juices flowing.

➤ Step 1:

Brainstorm to come up with a list of unrecognized customer niches. To stimulate your thinking, look at a cable TV listing or at a magazine rack to see how the media has broken out market groups.

Examples of under-served, unrecognized or unwanted niches:

- Health conscious Baby boomers

- Football game tailgaters

- Gourmet cooking enthusiasts

- Senior citizen pet lovers

- Time-pressured business people

- Vacationers with children

- Hispanic or Asian communities

- English as a second (or third) language

➤ Step 2:

Break out your list of customer groups based on your company's ability to serve them successfully. Develop your action plan. Can you:

- Kick Butt: Nobody does this better than us

- Benchmark Well: We're among the best at these, or

- Willing to Lose: realize you can't be all things to all people. Better to serve one or two groups really well, than to try to serve them all.

➤ Age

A long time ago it became clear that McDonald's target market was children, (or more specifically, children with mothers in tow.) From the first Happy Meal to the most modern PlayPlaces, Ray Kroc's direction was clear. McDonald's doesn't mind if kids bring their parents (after all, they usually bring the money) but for better or worse, all kids love to go there.

And then a funny thing happens to those kids. They suddenly expanded their horizons, outgrew the PlayPlace and start going to Subway, Burger King, Schlotzky's Deli or, heaven forbid, Noodles & Company.

Baby Boomers

Customers born between 1946 and 1964 have different buying habits than the Generation Xers who followed them. The Generation Y buyers will be a larger cohort than even the Boomers and will have access to more disposable money than any previous generation.

The post-war Baby Boomers are beginning to enjoy the extra space and freedom of the empty nest and they don't have to pay tuition, take family vacations or be scout leaders. Free of the economic demands of raising children, now they're able to spend time and money on hobbies, passions and themselves. When they move out of the family home, it's often into a larger, more luxurious house.

They're torn between saving for retirement and blowing a wad on some great new toys. They're gaget geeks, plowing millions into lightweight hiking poles and hand-held GPS receivers, even if they're only planning to walk around the local three-mile loop. As boomers begin to retire, their lifestyles will change to focus on travel, entertainment, grandchildren and in staying young, fit and vital. Savvy retailers will remind them that since most continue to work well into retirement, they might as well spend some of that hard-earned money now.

Generation Y

By 2010 there will be over 35 million members of Generation Y, also referred to as the *Echo Boomers*. Born after 1978, these "about to be's" spend about $187 billion a year on clothing, entertainment and food. They shun brand names like Levis in favor of smaller, more trendy names like Soap and Vans.

Teens today differ from their rebellious progenitors in that all they've ever known is the new economy. They expect unflagging customer service, speed-of-light e-commerce, just-in-time delivery, generous return policies—oh and deep discounts. Simply put, they're the toughest, most demanding and most fickle customers in the world. They read few newspapers but have marathon sessions watching MTV.

You'll have to be creative to reach them and gain their attention. They don't frequent malls, but love things that are new, trendy and different.

Generation X

The term Generation X came from a book by the same name written by Douglas Coupland in 1991. It is a fictional book about three strangers who decide to distance themselves from society to get a better sense of who they are. He describes the characters as "underemployed, overeducated, intensely private and unpredictable."

More cynical than their younger counterparts, this group of 46 million young adults has a combined spending power of $125 billion a year. Born between 1965 and 1980, they were the first group to grow up with television.

Sometimes called "slackers," in fact they find themselves working harder than others because they're often faced with downsizing and corporate layoffs.

Generation Xers are not afraid to challenge authority. Unlike Baby Boomers who stuck it out at work even if they were unhappy, Gen Xers are very willing to pick up and leave a job that does not satisfy them.

Similarly, you'll have to work hard to gain their loyalty. Once you capture their attention, though, they'll wear your t-shirt, refer their friends and come back over and over.

Seniors

They're not confined to nursing homes and rocking chairs anymore. Today's "seniors" are on the go and in the groove. They've decided they're going to live forever. Their grown children are managing on their own just fine, so they're not concerned about building a larger estate for them.

Because of savings habits they developed after the Depression, many seniors have money to spend on travel, their grandchildren and their hobbies. It's not unusual to see them in groups, on tour buses, at museums and in stores.

They're the most loyal customers and your job will be to pry them away from the retailers they've traded with for years. They're looking for guerrilla service and are willing to pay more to get it.

How do the generations compare?	18 - 34 yr olds	35 - 53 yr olds	55 and older
Smoke more than a half a pack of cigarettes a day	17%	21%	14%
Have a chronic disease or condition requiring regular care	8%	20%	49%
Use vitamins or supplements or try to eat mostly organic foods	42%	51%	60%
Almost always read labels to find out about content of food	59%	63%	64%
Have a stressful job or frequently feel a great deal of stress	47%	57%	20%
Restrict the amount of red meat they eat	36%	49%	51%
Have checked their blood pressure or cholesterol in the past year	71%	78%	94%
Could easily run or jog a mile	70%	46%	22%
Have a family doctor	78%	78%	91%
Drink three or more cups of coffee a day	15%	32%	30%
Regularly do yoga meditation or other stress reducing exercises	24%	25%	20%
Drink an alcoholic beverage almost every day	9%	11%	14%

Table 3.1

➤ Gender

It doesn't take a brain surgeon to tell that there are big differences between men and women. As John Gray says, "Men are from Mars and Women are from Venus." Women shop at Victoria's Secret and men shop at the Victoria's Secret HBO fashion show.

The battle between Lowe's and its rival Home Depot is a great example of gender-based retailing. Melissa Birdsong, director of trend forecasting for Lowe's, says "Women have different shopping habits. Women want large aisles with lots of personal space so they don't get bumped by another shopper's cart." Birdsong explains that women "like to peruse, they like to digest." They want neat displays and bright lighting. The cleaner, brighter environment at Lowe's is clearly more appealing to women shoppers.

On the other hand, women find Home Depot intimidating, while men prefer their "let's get this built" atmosphere. Home Depot's focus on the skilled professional contractor is legendary. They apprciate the knowledgeable staff and well-stocked shelves. It's loud and messy and the aisles are crowded with merchandise, specials, tools, machinery, end caps, carts and ladders. Signage is obscure, but men feel like they're in a REAL home-improvement center and not in a do-it-yourself department store.

Home Depot executive John Smiley has said that competitor Lowe's is "too pretty for the pro." Women may hold up half of the sky, but when they're shopping for skylights they're more likely to feel comfortable at Lowe's.

➤ Income

Everyone wants value. Some can afford more and others can afford less, but all customers want to feel like they've gotten the biggest bang for their buck.

As a small retailer, you're going to have a tough time making your offerings appeal to the masses. You're more likely to be successful by matching your merchandise to a specific target customer's income.

Sure, we'd all like to live in a big house on the 15th green of a nice golf course, but lots of developers have been successful building for lower-income, first time home buyers or middle income families.

Successful guerrillas have matched their products' prices to their customers' income. They don't intimidate their best prospects by making them feel uncomfortable in their stores, but they also try to maximize the return on their investments by getting the highest prices possible.

Dollar General is a family of small neighborhood stores delivering convenience and value on the basics. They believe that saving time and money helps their customers have a better life. From the first Dollar General store in 1955 to the more than 6,000 stores they operate today, their strategy remains customer-driven, and their mission, *Serving Others,* keeps them focused.

Family Dollar is one of the fastest growing discount store chains in the United States. With more than 4,800 stores in 43 states from Maine to Arizona, and 43 years of experience, their success has always been based on helping value-conscious families meet their basic shopping needs.

At the same time, specialty stores that provide exceptional service on high-end products are growing rapidly. Allen & Petersen Kitchen and Appliance in Anchorage, Alaska, has fueled their business growth with a mix of specialty cooking products, kitchen accessories and cooking classes. A wide range of cooking classes including "Cooking from Costco," (their most popular) "Breads for all Seasons," and "20-minute Meals" have become important guerrilla weapons for the Allen & Petersen team. They conduct more than 20 weekly cooking classes so that their customers can learn to use the products sold in the store, while at the same time developing a "need" to buy that merchandise.

➤ Geography

The oldest marketing adage around is "location, location, location." An emerging trend in the 21st Century is *time poverty.* Everybody's just crazy-busy-nuts. Just ask them, "How 'ya been?"

"Oh busy!"

"Yeah?"

"Crazy-busy. Just *nuts!* Crazy-busy-nuts." They're actually bragging about it! You can't count on these time-starved customers to patiently drive around town looking for your store.

Today's lunch-hour shopper doesn't even have time to drive clear across town to get to your location. Guerrillas understand that it's their job to be near their customers, not the customer's job to find them.

You may not be able to afford the rent in the most fashionable mall around, but you need to be as close to your customers as possible.

Can you locate around the corner or across the street from the mall instead?

Can you find a location near other venues shoppers might frequent for other activities? For instance, if you target young mothers, is there a location between the soccer field their kids use for practice and the subdivision where they live? Better yet, can you set up a temporary display on Saturday mornings during practice?

Can you offer to come to them at their convenience if your best customers can't get to you?

➤ Education

More educated customers are likely to be more mobile, have more access to the Internet and may be more *value*-conscious than others. They shop warehouse clubs to take advantage of large quantity discounts, but they also frequent upscale boutiques for pricey brand name products. They want good value, and more often than not, that means top quality. Plus they're willing to pay more for the prestige of a brand name, unless it doesn't really matter. Even the ones who drive a Lexus may buy their toilet tissue by the case at Costco.

Those less educated shop closer to home and are more prone to choose familiar or store brands. The relationship they have with the store staff plays an important role in their shopping habits. While education is often a predictor of relative income, less educated shoppers may generally be more *price*-conscious, looking for sale items and bargains.

➤ Interests and Hobbies

People naturally congregate with others like themselves. The Handlebar Restaurant has built a steady clientele of bicycle enthusiasts who come in for a burger and a beer after a long ride. They feel right at home with the Lance Armstrong posters and bike frames hanging from the ceiling.

Chapter 4

Location, Location, Location

Decisions about where to locate your store should depend to a great extent on the customer you are trying to reach. An expensive Continental restaurant with an extensive wine list may not do as well as a basic beer and pizza joint next door to a community college campus.

The market you are targeting will determine your décor, your merchandising and even the music you play in your store.

You can't count on the right customers finding *you*. You've got to find *them*.

➤ Where to Locate

The most important decision you'll make after deciding what you will sell and who you will sell it to, is where to locate your business.

Although the first rule of traditional marketing is location, location, location, guerrillas understand that there is a balance between the cost of occupancy and the cost of attracting customers.

Whether in a mall, a strip center or a kiosk, the most important factor is that the store be convenient for your customers. If your target customers are young families with children, newly built suburbs may be the best locations. If you're targeting baby-boomers, though, you may do better in an urban setting, or in an area being re-developed with luxury town homes and condominiums.

Another way to locate your store may be in an area that is well traveled by shoppers going to other stores. Power centers with several big-box and superstores pull in tremendous traffic. Locating near the area may make shopping at your store an easy stop for your customers or, it may lead to impulse stops for those driving by.

Although some communities have had success in redeveloping downtown shopping districts, most have been unable to attract shoppers. Since downtown areas are rarely open on nights and weekends, prime shopping time, it's hard to get customers to make the trip. Parking and security are also important detriments.

Some redevelopment areas have become magnets for galleries, boutiques and gift stores catering to collectors and tourists.

Malls

Malls, for instance, can charge high rents and even compute rent as a percentage of sales because the venue itself draws customers. People who come to malls as an excursion, say, to go to the movies or to make other purchases, may also stop in your store. In some cases, mall vendors can be extremely successful with little or no advertising or marketing expense. The disadvantage is that your rent will subsidize the costs of parking, food courts, theatres and common areas that may not directly benefit your business.

Strip Center

As more and more customers look to save time, they will likely seek stores with easy access.

For instance, when you shop at a center like University Hills Plaza in Denver, it's incredibly easy to get in and out of several stores and run all of your errands quickly.

Stop at Michael's to pick up a new picture frame, dash into ABC Books for the latest best seller, and then into Performance Bicycles for a new tire. From Performance, it's a quick hop to the North Face Store to buy a birthday gift for a teenage niece, and then on to A la Card for a mailing box and birthday card. Run into Plaza Deli to order a sandwich, and it will be ready by the time you get back from the Gigantic Cleaners next door.

Grab the dry cleaning, go back for the corned beef on rye. Drive across the center to the convenient U.S. Postal Service kiosk in the parking lot to mail the gift and card. Fifteen minutes later, you'll be across the street at Office Depot or finishing your grocery shopping at King Soopers.

No mall traffic, no endless walking, mission accomplished.

A word of caution, beware of below-market rents. Strip centers that are not well-managed or well-maintained will tend to have low occupancies. In time, they start to look run down and blighted. A full strip center creates synergy for all the stores, but even a single empty unit signals customers to stay away.

Retailers Embrace the Great Outdoors

Lately, we're seeing a major shift in the way Americans shop. After more than 50 years of building big, boxy, enclosed malls in suburbs across the country, developers are turning back the clock (and filling in the spaces) with open-air shopping centers designed to look and feel like small-town downtowns.

In real estate jargon the new open-air malls are "lifestyle centers" or "town centers," but the idea behind them is simple; take the tenants of the average regional mall and move them inside a center made to look like a small-town downtown. Such centers are better landscaped than the sometimes tatty strip malls that crouch beside well-traveled thoroughfares and bigger than the power centers built around "big-box" retailers such as Home Depot or Barnes & Noble found in the middle of most suburbs.

In these smaller, outdoor malls, customers stroll along a brick-lined sidewalk past freshly cut grass where hidden speakers play music and storefronts are built shoulder to shoulder.

Shoppers find that they can get in and out with their purchases more quickly instead of having to pass ten stores in the mall that they don't care about. Plus there is just something about being outdoors. These open-air shopping centers possess that rare quality in retail, "walkability." A regional mall often requires a ten-minute walk from one department store to the next. Open-air centers generally contain less than half the one million square feet of a typical regional mall.

Developers decorate the open-air centers with water fountains, brick facades and manicured gardens. There is some parking directly in front of the stores, and with few exceptions, no intimidating parking garages. Store-lined streets are narrow to create an urban ambience. To give the centers a homey feel, planners include local touches. At Bowie Town Center, in Bowie, Maryland, Simon Properties Group designed the food court after the old Bowie train station.

The first mall-rat generation is flocking to these new urban-style outdoor shopping centers to recapture something that their parents and grandparents took for granted, a more intimate shopping experience. The International Council of Shopping Centers found that they produce better sales per square foot of total area than other types of centers.

Guerrilla retailers have also thronged to these centers, which typically charge lower rents than enclosed malls whose fees include the costs of common areas, food courts, security and HVAC.

Besides, in all but a few fast-growing communities, there is no room for another million-square-foot regional mall. Mall development reached a peak in the late 1980s, a decade when developers built out 16,000 of them nationwide. But construction has fallen sharply ever since.

Like enclosed malls, open-air centers target middle-class shoppers. Tenants include mall standbys such as the Gap, Limited and Wet Seal upscale specialty stores such as Talbots, Chico's and Williams-Sonoma. Box stores are generally frowned upon. The centers typically are built in growing suburban communities with median household incomes of at least $80,000.

In a 2003 survey of 1,500 shoppers, the International Council of Shopping Centers found that two-thirds preferred the upscale open-air shopping centers. Shoppers spent an average of $84 an hour there, compared with $58 at a regional mall, thanks in part to the outdoor venue's efficient layout.

Outlet Malls

Regional outlet malls draw bargain hunters willing to drive across town for a discount. They are also destinations for a family outing or group shopping adventure.

Although studies have shown that products are frequently sold at outlets for the same prices available in department stores, customers tend to get the illusion of making off-price purchases.

Rents in outlet malls can be steep, often as high as in new major city malls, but traffic is steady, and customers can shop an endless number of product categories.

Since outlet mall customers are always looking for a deal, stores offering closeout merchandise, factory seconds, returned and refurbished goods and imported faux imitations will do better than those trying to sell new full price products.

Neighborhood

Some neighborhoods still have small retail shopping areas. These quaint shopping streets are usually anchored by local restaurants, and can frequently be the perfect place for specialty stores and boutiques that don't depend on high traffic volume.

Denver's Old South Gaylord Street is a great neighborhood shopping area. The area is so popular that residents in the area often have trouble parking in front of their own homes. People from all over Colorado come to shop at Tandem Cycle Works, while locals frequent the bar at Reiver's. Trout's American Sportswear is the favorite outfitter for the area's upwardly mobile preppy crowd. Iris Fields is a great place to find that unique but perfect little black dress. The Paper Lady sells custom-printed stationery, wedding invitations, announcements and a host of interesting and different stationery.

The Memorial Day Old South Gaylord Street Fair is an annual classic that draws neighbors together and gives the merchants a chance to show off to the community.

Freestanding Stores

For some retailers, the best option may be to build or rent a free-standing building. Some may need a unique feature such as garage space for installation or repairs. Merchants who sell large bulky items or who buy in large quantities may need more warehousing or storage space than would be practical in mall stores. Stores that need very large showrooms for products like furniture are well suited to free standing buildings.

Although it may be easier to find suitable space, remember what you save in rent will have to be invested in marketing and advertising to draw customers. The trade-off in having the synergy of others to help create a market may be in finding a space that is just right for your particular products.

Store in a Store

Consider leasing space in a successful retailer's store as an alternative location. Starbucks is the king of co-locating, with stores in Barnes & Noble, The Great Indoors and in many grocery stores.

If you are a photographer, why not locate in a bridal shop or in a Babies 'R Us?

Why not open a home theater specialty store inside a high-end furniture store? How about locating a travel agency in a luggage store?

Temporary Venues

Not all retail stores are permanent. Smart retailers put kiosks in places where their customers might congregate.

Gear on the Go, a company that sells ski racks, bike racks and car top luggage carriers, often locates kiosks at ski areas, bicycle rides and travel shows.

Street vendors working from a stainless-steel cart are famous for some of the best hot dogs and gyros in the world.

Malls have lately learned that interesting vendors in kiosks add value to their customers' shopping experience. Many of them have programs that actively recruit these micro-store retailers to set up in high-traffic common areas.

Tuesday Morning takes advantage of seasonal short-term rental opportunities to open stores that sell closeout and off-price merchandise.

There are all sorts of opportunities for temporary retail venues. Some that you might want to consider include:

- Blanket on the sidewalk
- Tabletop
- Cart on the street
- Tent with tables
- Farmers markets
- Flea market
- Kiosk with wire racks
- Home Shows
- Rodeos
- State and County Fairs
- Concerts
- Sports events
- Roadside pole barn

- Anywhere that people congregate is an opportunity to sell to them. Consider airports, office buildings, hotels, subway tunnels and other places where people who need or want things may turn up. When it rains in mid-town Manhattan a small army of umbrella-peddling guerrillas appears magically on nearly every street corner.

➤ Factors to Consider

- ❑ Easy access
- ❑ Adequate parking
- ❑ Other similar retailers nearby
- ❑ Customer base mirrors target customers
- ❑ Proximity to suppliers
- ❑ Proximity to warehousing
- ❑ Length of lease
- ❑ Cost of rent vs. cost of acquiring customers
- ❑ Security
- ❑ Lighting
- ❑ Interior finish
- ❑ Fire mitigation
- ❑ Safety
- ❑ Sign restrictions
- ❑ Zoning

Chapter 5

Merchandising Strategy

Guerrillas understand that merchandising is one of their most important weapons.

Your target customer to a great degree determines your merchandise strategy. You obviously want to sell products with the features, benefits and price points that will fly off of your shelves and produce the kind of bottom-line profits you want.

➤ Selection

People love choices. Some shoppers continue to look at merchandise even after they have found products that will meet their needs or solve their problems.

Having the right mix is a delicate balance. With too many choices, customers can become confused, inventory can age and turns can be slow. Too little selection and consumers may go somewhere else to see what else is out there. Just like Goldilocks and the three bears, it's got to be just right.

In studies, customers cite selection as the third most important reason they buy from a particular retailer. Guerrilla retailers capitalize on this psychology by offering a *good-better-best* lineup of options within a category.

Narrow and targeted strategies will appeal to a small but loyal market segment. Customers for these products are less likely to cross-shop than shoppers as a whole. Stores with a more narrow focus will usually carry fewer lines, and some lines may be sheltered by their vendors from excessive local competition. Targeted strategies usually lead to tighter inventory control and faster inventory turns. Niche products might include:

- Luxury products and exclusive brands like St. John, Burberry, Coach, Hartman Luggage, Bang and Olufsen, and Chanel.

- Off price goods may be close-outs or seconds and are frequently sold in stores like Tuesday Morning and T J Maxx

- Generic or store brand products include merchandise such as Kirkland from Costco and 365 from Whole Foods.

- Not-so-current merchandise is often sold in outlet malls and discount stores like Big Lots.

- Wide and mass strategies appeal to the broadest base of customers, but also attract the largest number of competitors since vendors may be less selective in their distribution.

- Brand names are the foundation of mass distribution. Levi's, for example, are sold in department stores, discount stores and specialty western stores.

- Private label companies like Victoria's Secret, Talbots, J. Crew and Land's End. These are just a few examples of companies that control their entire product chain from design to manufacturing to distribution through their own stores, Internet sites and catalogues.

➤ Quality

No retailer can afford to lose a customer because of inferior product quality. The costs of returns, refunds and exchanges are significant. The cost of lost customers is even greater. Quality is the second most important reason why people are motivated to make purchases.

The Maytag repairman has come to represent quality and dependability. Generations of appliance buyers continue to buy Maytag products because their grandmother's washer lasted for twenty-five years.

The importance of quality is stressed in the Ford Motor Company motto, "Quality is Job #1."

➤ Guarantee

The most important factor in choosing products is the guarantee behind it. People want peace of mind. They want to know that if something doesn't work, the product will be repaired or replaced and that their investment will be protected.

A guarantee is critical even when choosing an overnight package delivery service. Federal Express started an entire industry with its motto, "When it absolutely, positively, has to be there overnight."

The store's guarantee can be even more important than the product's guarantee. At the very least, it adds to the value of it.

Where applicable, don't forget the importance of offering to extend the product's warranty. The larger the purchase and the more complex the product, the more likely customers will buy additional warranties. People want to know that if something doesn't work, they won't have to pay anything additional to repair it for some extended period of time.

➤ Price

A study reported in Advertising Age Magazine, asked 10,000 shoppers as they exited retail stores "What factors influenced your purchase?" In 1990, price ranked ninth; in 2000, it ranked fifth. Even so, only sixteen percent ranked price as the most important factor, while 84% said other things were more important, including selection, quality, location, service and confidence.

In the U.S. there isn't a single product category that is led by the lowest-price brand. Did you notice what happened to the black & white generic products aisles in supermarkets?

Even though box stores continue to chant the low-price mantra, most customers are interested in a *fair value*. The value proposition includes not only the price of the product, but also the level of service attached to it.

Guerrillas understand the need to have a broad good-better-best merchandise selection. They also know the value of creating a low-price perception in order to bring customers to their stores, so they offer the widest difference price points. At the low end is, "If all you need is . . ." and explain the lowest-price option. Position the high-end by saying, "If money is no object. . . " Then explain the full range of features and advantages of the most expensive, justifying the value of the higher price. Forty percent of your customers will close for the item at this point. They're those *value shopping* Baby Boomers we talked about earlier. If the customer doesn't up-sell to the high price point, then point out that, "The best *value* is the (mid-range option) because it has (list features of the more expensive alternative) and is ($XXX) less."

Discerning customers, however, will seek out full-feature products if they can be convinced that the price is justified by the additional benefits and service offered.

Guerrilla retailers understand that sure, a lot of buyers will buy low-price merchandise, but they also understand that today's consumer readily pays nearly $5 for a cup of coffee and more than $50,000 for a BMW.

➤ Merchandising Tactics

Front Face Products Daily

This simply means making sure that you move products to the front of the shelves or the front of the fixture system at all times. If you display items on peg hooks and a customer purchases the first item on the hook, move the remaining items on that peg hook to the front.

Front facing gives your customer a sense of fullness in your store, even when you may be running low on certain items. When customers look at your shelves, they should see products on every hook or shelf with no gaps or empty slots. This technique will also help you keep track of which items are selling well and which ones are not.

Spread to Fill

This tactic helps you create the impression that your store is always "full." Simply take your extra product off the shelf or hook or face-outs, and spread them out to fill in all the empty spaces created by being sold out of certain items. Pull pegged items to the front. Do not let your jobber or supplier talk you into leaving your shelf empty until the next order arrives. Make sure every fixture looks like it is chock-full of merchandise.

Color Block Your Merchandise

Take advantage of your products packaging and color. Consider motor oil for example. There are many brands and grades available.

Most retailers arrange motor oil containers horizontally on a shelf by grade and weight, from 30 weight to 10w40, up to the expensive synthetics. This means they'll display one brand on one shelf, another on the shelf below and so on.

Instead of arranging the containers horizontally, guerrillas will arrange the display in *vertical* columns, by color of package and grade. First a column of 30 weight, then next to it a column of 10w40, and so on, so the customer can now look across the top shelf and read from left to right, find the appropriate can and move on to the next purchase.

Walk into any Bed Bath & and Beyond store and you'll find great examples of color blocking. All the red towels are stacked from floor to ceiling with the pink ones stacked right next to them.

Practice the Two-Finger Rule

This means that your shelves are spaced so that the gap between the top of the product and the shelf above it is no more than two fingers wide.

Avoid Tragedy

The Disney Stores, one of the unequivocal masters of merchandising, take care to place fragile items, like the ceramic figurines of

Cinderella, Mickey and Minnie, on high shelves, beyond the reach of small, curious hands. Everything waist-level and below is unbreakable plush or plastic. This simple tactic all but eliminates enforcement of a "You-Break-it-You-Buy-it" rule, and encourages kids to pick up and handle these items without being shushed or scolded by anxious parents.

➤ CHOOSING THE RIGHT SUPPLIERS

Choosing suppliers is one of the most important keys to retail success. Guerrillas choose vendors wisely because they are fiercely loyal to the ones who can offer them the added value and exceptional service needed to compete.

- Does this vendor's pricing provide enough margin to cover all of my costs and leave me with a healthy profit? Guerrillas know that profit is the only legitimate measure of success.

- Does this vendor get my order right the first time, or am I always on the phone trying to work out differences between the order that I place and the order I was shipped?

- Does this vendor bill regularly and accurately, or do bills show up at random times with errors?

- Does this vendor ship back-orders automatically, or do I have to remember to reorder?

- Does this vendor ship back-ordered items after the season for the item is past?

- Does this vendor offer discounted terms and does my volume match the minimum to qualify for them?

- Does this vendor offer seasonal dating terms on applicable merchandise?

- Does this vendor offer regular, timely delivery as a part of the basic price, or at additional cost?

- Does this vendor have liberal return programs so I can match their competitors' "no hassle" return policy?

- Does this vendor offer value added services, such as pre-pricing, overnight shipping, or year-end order summaries?

- Does this vendor offer help with merchandising, POP signage, dumps, tonnage bins, sales training, advertising co-op promotions or store layout?

- Does this vendor offer co-op advertising support?

- Is this vendor large enough to support my goals for growth and expansion?

- Is this vendor local enough to understand my market?[1]

---

[1] Don Taylor and Jeanne Smalling Archer, *Up Against the Wal-Marts — How Your Business Can Prosper in the Shadow of the Retail Giants,* New York, N.Y., AMACOM. 1994.

ch**a**pter

Store Design and Display

Guerrillas know that their store image attracts customers, but the store environment convinces customers to make a purchase.

Guerrilla store design and ambience appeals to all of the senses. Although the majority of design focuses on sight, savvy retailers have found ways to capture the customer's attention by engineering sounds and smells into their merchandising strategy.

■ AMBIENCE

➤ Music

Retailers have used music in their stores for years. The right music can create an environment consistent with your category. Even though research has shown that classical music encourages customers to shop longer and buy more expensive items, (like jewelry) retailer Hot Topic blares Marilyn Manson, perfectly targeted to its hip young "Goth" clientele. Stores that sell trendier clothing may choose classic rock or jazz, but the genre should mirror the character of your merchandise and your customers.

➤ Scent

Movie theatres have been pumping the exhaust from the popcorn machine into the HVAC ducts for decades. Williams-Sonoma puts out hot cider and cookies at the holidays. Lately, home appliance centers discovered that nothing sells better than the aroma of freshly-baked bread or cookies. Victoria's Secret puts potpourri bowls in their stores, while The Knot Shop uses paper-pulp tiles impregnated with cigar and leather scents so that women shopping for gifts there will feel that it's the kind of store where their husbands or boyfriends would shop.

■ STORE LAYOUT

➤ Traffic Flow

The more merchandise customers can see displayed in an attractive and orderly manner, the more they will buy. Careful planning will help move customers through the store so that they can see and touch the widest selection of your products. While there are many excellent, talented store designers out there for hire, guerrilla retailers can learn the basics of store design by visiting a variety of retailers and incorporating the best ideas from all of them in their own stores.

Rupp's Drums, in Lakewood, Colorado, is a guerrilla retailer that defies the rules of music-store merchandising. Rupp's is a kind of elephant graveyard for drum sets of every shape, size and vintage.

They mix new and used instruments throughout the store. A discriminating percussionist or a punk rocker can find anything from a classic 1930s Gretsch jazz kit to the most modern heavy-weight hardware from Drum Workshop.

Need a cheap used starter kit for a high-school kid in a garage band? They've got just the thing. Need a practice kit to park in the rehearsal studio, so you're not schlepping your good stage kit around, you'll find something here that will work. Looking for just the right, bright, wet sound in a small splash cymbal, there are 50 of them stacked on the floor. If you need to replace an obscure part, you're welcome to rummage through bins of bolts, lugs and mounts and use the tool bench in back to your heart's content. Bob

Rupp, (also a successful professional drummer) started selling snare drums out of the trunk of his car 20 years ago. Today, he has three stores.

➤ Security

Security needs to be built into the store design, not added as an afterthought.

Monitored security alarms keep intruders out when you're closed. If the products you sell are high value, it's well worth the monthly fee for equipment rental and monitoring.

It's still possible for a burglar to run a truck through a front window and make off with a pile of expensive merchandise before the police arrive. Decorative concrete bollards in front of the store can block vehicle access.

Warehouse areas and storerooms are particularly vulnerable. Be sure they're locked and issue as few keys as possible. Security cameras will help keep honest staff members honest. Limit the number of doors to just one entrance if possible. If you do have a separate employee entrance, make certain that it's monitored at all times. Use push-bar activated alarms on all emergency exits that will warn of a possible security breach.

Some retailers, like Abt Electronics, have installed metal detectors like those used for airport security, at their employee entrances. Abt also offers a reward of up to $5,000 to whistleblowers.

According to shrinkage control consulting firm Hayes International, in Fruitland Park, Florida, retailers lose billions to shoplifting and employee theft. As soon as merchants figure out the latest scams, thieves create new ones.

Shoplifters are spending more time in stores these days, stealing more merchandise and taking higher-priced goods. Thieves frequently work in pairs with one "shopper" distracting store personnel while the other stashes stolen goods in strollers, shopping bags and false bottomed gift boxes.

Security systems are inexpensive and easy to install. Even if the system isn't continually monitored, visible cameras and signs warn shoppers and deter theft.

Vigilance is the best deterrent, and it goes hand-in-hand with good customer service. The sales staff should constantly observe the customer and be quick to offer assistance.

Position your cash wrap station near the front of the store or the department. Long before detector tab systems became available, Jerry Gart, one of the original owners of Gart Brothers Sporting Goods, posted a manager at the front door of the Sportscastle store to help direct customers and more importantly, to check receipts as customers leave. During the busiest times, managers were also stationed at the entrance to each department.

➤ Maximize the Merchandise

Good store design maximizes the space allotted to merchandise, while at the same time, giving the customer enough personal space to feel comfortable.

Department stores are notorious for crowding in as many racks as possible so that customers often feel like they're doing hand-to-hand combat just to get from one rack to another. Customers who feel cramped and claustrophobic often leave empty handed.

The more time a customer spends in the store, the more money they'll spend. To encourage impulse buying, plan your traffic flow so that customers can see as many items as possible.

Retailers usually choose from some form of three basic traffic patterns.

The grid layout is where merchandise is displayed in several parallel aisles similar to the way grocery stores are merchandised. The hope is that customers wind their way around each aisle in turn.

Often, though, customers walk right to the aisle that they know has the merchandise they came to buy without walking through the rest of the store. Customers often become mission oriented and make fewer impulse purchases.

A better choice would be the loop or racetrack layout. The loop provides a single major customer aisle that starts at the store entrance and loops through the entire store returning the customer to the front door. Depending on the size or shape of your space, your loop can be square or circular.

Customers can see merchandise on the left and on the right as they wind through the store. They can easily peel off the loop and into a display area or store department at any time.

The spine or snake layout combines elements of the grid and loop layouts with other free form display areas. In this kind of environment, there is usually one main wide walkway that visually pulls the customer through the store.

The main displays, which could be single free form display areas or smaller aisled areas, are on the left and right of the snake so that the customer is again exposed to lots and lots of well-displayed products.

Whichever layout you choose, remember to make aisles wide and keep them clear. If customers have to move around stacks of store specials, boxes or displays piled in their space, they'll be watching where they are going instead of looking at your products.

The best way to make sure that the aisles don't get taken over by merchandise is to design them to look different than the display areas. You can use different color tile for walkways or different flooring material. You might use tile or hardwood for the aisles and carpet where products are displayed. To separate merchandise areas inexpensively, tape off the aisle boundaries with heavy plastic tape in a contrasting color.

➤ Sight Lines

Customers should be able to see the entire floor from the front door, and any department from the main aisles, so that your selling space looks as big as possible.

Avoid using racks or fixtures that customers can't see over. Merchandise tall or bulky items like refrigerators against the walls.

Blockbuster Video stores have terrific sight lines. You can easily spot the new releases on the back wall or find your way quickly to comedies, children's movies or dramas. Impulse items like candy and popcorn are on low displays near the checkout areas.

Guerrillas think carefully about how they display merchandise along their aisles. Although retailers often put racks perpendicular to the aisles, customers walking down the aisles can only see at about a 45-degree angle from the way they are walking. Think about it. Unless you're a giraffe, you probably can't crane your neck a full ninety degrees to the side. Placing fixtures at a 45-degree angle will expose more of your merchandise to the shopper.

■ FIXTURES

There are as many kinds of store fixtures as there are products to display. Guerrillas use fixtures to highlight and enhance the merchandise. But you needn't spend a fortune outfitting your store.

➤ Coat rack

During inclement weather, your customers will need a place to secure they winter overcoats. We can't count how many times we've been inconvenienced for want of this simplest of all store fixtures. Larger stores (and some smart auto dealers) provide coat-check for customers during their visit. This is especially important in restaurants, where coats, hats and umbrellas take up precious seating and tabletop space.

At the famous Aspen Mountain ski area in Aspen, Colorado, the food-service manager of the midway-lodge solved this dilemma by installing new chairs with a shelf under the seat, perfect for stashing gloves, scarves or helmets. Concessions sales increased by 40% overnight, because more open table space meant they could accommodate more customers at a time, particularly during the peak lunch rush.

Checking coats, purses and bags may be more than just a courtesy. It substantially reduces shoplifting.

➤ Crate & Barrel

In 1962, a husband and wife team named Gordon and Carole Segal had just returned from their honeymoon in Europe where they saw and bought all kinds of unique, functional, and here's the catch, *affordable*, designs for their home. They looked around and realized that no one in Chicago was selling great design without charging the equivalent of a mortgage. Not being able to afford much of a mortgage themselves, the Segals decided to lease an abandoned elevator factory on a funky street in Chicago and opened a store to showcase the items they were finding all over the world.

With their money tied up in inventory and no budget for fixtures, they asked, "Why not use the crates and barrels?" Crumbling old brick warehouse walls? Let's just say the words "exposed brick" had not yet come into vogue. No budget for drywall? Nail up crate lumber. Display shelves? Stack the shipping crates and fill the barrels. And so out of necessity was born what immediately became the unique, down to earth Crate and Barrel style. And it made an offbeat, albeit memorable store name.

The entrepreneurs were so excited about their venture that only moments before opening did they realize they had forgotten something every store should have like a cash register. "No problem, hand me that box. No, the one with a lid."

Chicago came in waves, and raves. The humble yet contemporary store became a tourist destination of sorts. By 1971 there were several Chicago area Crate & Barrel stores including a first suburban mall store. Today there are more than 115 stores. Taking a trip to a Crate & Barrel will show you some of the most innovative ideas in lighting, display, color, store fixtures and traffic flow.

The list of fixtures available to retailers is almost endless. Gondolas are long fixtures with a large base and a wall (that can be two-sided) as high as eight feet. They are used almost universally because of their versatility. Gondolas can be fitted with a variety of shelves, pegboards, baskets, bins and other hardware. You see gondolas used in hardware stores, sporting goods stores, computer stores and in clothing stores to display accessories or items that are folded on shelves.

Before deciding what kind of fixtures to use in your store, visit a retail fixture store or go online at www.storefixtures.com to see what the possibilities are. They include:

- Gondolas
- Tables
- Dump bins
- Shelving—
  - Glass
  - Wood
  - Carpeted
  - Laminated
- Wall standards
- Pegboard and hooks (different lengths)
- Slat wall and cubes —glass, wire, laminated
- Glass showcases
- Pedestals
- Acrylic fixtures
- Hanging fixtures
- Rounders
- Spiral racks
- 2-way
- 4-way

- Hat racks
- Hangars
- Mannequins

When choosing fixtures consider the following carefully:

➤ Function

Will the fixture create more buying opportunities and impulse sales? Is it the right one for the product?

➤ Flexibility

Fixtures are significant investments. Will you be able to use the fixture for other items?

➤ Adjustability

Do the fixtures have the ability to adjust in height, length, width or depth?

➤ Size

Is the fixture scaled both to the products and to the store? For example, you need smaller fixtures to display children's clothing than garments for adults.

➤ Quantity

How many fixtures do you need to display all of your products so that they promote sales?

➤ Style

Does the fixture complement or clash with the overall ambience of the store? You may not, for instance, want to buy heavy wooden fixtures for a bright, contemporary store.

➤ Color and Finish

Does the fixture stand out more than the products displayed on it? The more neutral the finish, the less likely that the fixture will be the attraction.

Since retail stores remodel frequently, guerrillas often find good quality used, but not abused, fixtures at places like Alpha Store Fixtures, Inc., www.storefixtures2000.com, or The Recycler's Exchange, www.recycle.net/commercial/store.

■ LIGHTING

Lighting is one of the most powerful weapons in the guerrilla retailers' arsenal. Lighting creates a range of identity and mood. The bright mercury-argon ambient lighting in a big-box store says, "Discount," while the low-level lighting and crisp accents of a specialty boutique draws in the customer into a comfortable lair. Creative manipulation of interior materials, color and light can tailor your store's atmosphere to attract a certain market or demographic group.

When combined with lighting-related cooling load, lighting, is the largest user of energy in the store, so you should always be environmentally sensitive. You can use carefully placed halogen tourchier lamps to wash the common spaces with ambient light, or better still, use skylights and windows to harness daylight. Now, more than ever, environmental sustainability or "green design" can easily be part of the image for stores with a socially or environmentally conscious identity. Use only incandescent or halogen track or spots to highlight merchandise.

First, determine how the quantity of light affects your store's image. Does it provide for the needs of the customers and staff. Customers need bright, diffuse and natural-colored light when shopping for clothes or home furnishings. Staff may need special task lighting on their desktops or at the register. If high brightness levels or natural light are desirable, strongly consider the many benefits of daylighting, including:

- Increased sales potential; in controlled studies, shoppers bought more in natural daylight.

- Employee awareness of changing sun and weather conditions results in reduced stress and fatigue.

- Reduce your energy consumption by combining daylight with automatic fluorescent dimming, even when the additional heat from skylights is considered.

- Use efficient sources where they function best, in indirect and ambient lighting, as well as in special track and accent applications.

- Use less efficient incandescent and low voltage light sources for maximum effect, but use them sparingly. Use more efficient halogen lamps for additional savings.

- Use accent lighting on merchandise, but keep ambient levels low to increase the impact of the accents. Even in relatively dark, ambient environments, the accents should be much brighter than the common areas or aisles. Measure them in foot candles or lumens with an inexpensive photometer and you can optimize the relative brightness levels throughout your store.

- Design for changing day/evening cycles by reducing ambient light in the evening, particularly near store entrances. Customers will find it more comfortable for their eyes to adjust gradually when entering and leaving the store.

- For most energy-efficient operation, use programmable lighting control panels to adjust your lighting throughout the day. This includes turning off accent and decorative spots when the store is closed.

Good lighting can help draw customers into your store and move them along the aisles by highlighting featured areas and spotlighting new offerings.

Different retail environments require different kinds of lighting. There was a time when the old F40T12CW, the forty-watt, four-foot florescent cool-whites were the stalwarts of every store. But today, many guerrilla retailers are finding success in making their stores look less institutional and more like their customers' homes. They either escape the industrial mercury-halogen-washed warehouse look, or they embrace and exaggerate it.

Lighting design requires much more than just understanding relative brightness levels, but there are some guerrilla principles.

Bright light works well in toy stores or in children's clothing stores to assure security, or in stores that sell housewares and kitchen accessories. But women want slightly lower lighting levels when buying their clothes. There are thousands of light fixtures and lamps to choose from that can change the color or texture of the merchandise they light up. Generally speaking, you want the merchandise to be approximately ten times as bright as the traffic and common areas. Done properly, this strategy creates a cozy tunnel-effect that draws shoppers along, while they scan offerings on either side of the aisle.

Lighting also affects staff productivity. A study conducted by the Canadian Center for Occupational Health and Safety found that poor lighting can make people sleepy and cause headaches, neck pain, eye fatigue and poor productivity. Improperly placed lights, lights that cause glare, dim lights and overly bright lights can all lead team members to complain of eyestrain, eye irritation or blurred vision.

Workers receive nearly 85% of information through their eyes, so when lighting is poor, there is a higher risk of errors. Provide bright, even light over cutting tables, counter tops and particularly around the cash register, approximately the same brightness as the surrounding merchandise.

➤ Track

Track lighting is more expensive to install, but far more flexible. Gimbal-ring fixtures are low-cost and accept a range of lamp sizes and voltages. If you have a low ceiling, you'll need to control glare, so invest in the more expensive, can-shaped recessed fixtures. These typically include a black louvered collar that shields the bright lamp from customers' eyes.

➤ Floods vs. Spots

Reflector lamps are available in a wide range of wattages. Subtle changes in the shape of their reflectors makes them suitable for different applications. You'll most likely use "par" lamps (for parabolic reflector) in your track. Use a mix of floods and spots.

Flood lamps typically cast beams 40 degrees wide, providing a soft wash of light. The same voltage lamp in a spot configuration casts a beam only nine degrees wide. This concentrates the light in a tight, focused beam.

Brightness is inversely proportional to distance, so the closer the fixture is to the merchandise, the brighter the accent will be. This allows you to use lower-output lamps that conserve energy.

➤ Incandescent vs. Halogen

Incandescent filament lamps are inefficient, turning more than 85% of the electricity they consume into heat. They also have the disadvantage of producing light that is very red-shifted. They can be great for creating a warm atmosphere. More modern halogen bulbs use far less energy, produce a fraction of the heat and are color-shifted toward the green, creating a hip, cool atmosphere. Halogen lamps are more expensive to buy, but they save money two ways: reduced energy consumption, reduced HVAC consumption and they last a lot longer.

➤ Exterior

A good merchandising strategy includes exterior lighting that feels inviting and secure. Night lighting should say that you're "closed" and not "out of business." Certainly your exterior signs should remain lit at night. The best-lit parking lots are next to the most frequently-shopped stores, particularly if the customers are women and/or children.

The Wizard's Chest is a game, toy, costume and magic store in Denver. The exterior façade is done up to look like a castle and even late at night, it's lit up to look like Cinderella's pad at Disneyland.

➤ Floor Covering

Guerrillas use a variety of materials in floor covering. Carpet can be relatively inexpensive to purchase and install and comes in a wide range of colors. High traffic areas may soon look worn or dirty. Carpet wears best if glued to a good, level concrete or wood substrate. Quickly cleaning spills, spots and stains will extend the life of the carpet.

Laminate impregnated floors such as Pergo are good alternatives to more traditional ceramic tile, vinyl or hardwood. Rubber flooring is durable, resilient and low-maintenance. In addition, it's much quieter than other hard-surface products.

Combinations that include carpet, wood and tile help visually separate departments and define the differing kinds of products sold in different areas of the store. Guerrillas are beginning to use bamboo, cork and even leather in areas that need to be highlighted and set off from other high-impact and high-traffic areas.

Whatever flooring material you choose, be sure to keep it clean and dry. Use mud rugs or walk-off mats (rented from a linen service) in entry ways so that snow, sleet and rain won't be tracked throughout the store. In bad weather, mop up wet areas quickly so that customers and staff don't slip.

➤ Color

Color should enhance, not detract from, the products that you sell. Colors are trendy. We often refer to stores who haven't kept up with the times as "orange shag carpet stores" referring to the color and textures found in the '60s. Paint provides a less expensive alternative to wallpaper and laminate so that you can afford to keep in step with the changes.

Monochromatic color schemes use different shades, tints or tones of a single color and create a harmonizing effect, bringing areas of the store together. Complementary colors are two different values on opposite sides of the color wheel like yellow and blue. When placed side-by-side, these colors seem to shimmer and vibrate with energy.

Softer colors impart a more contemporary, relaxed feeling. If you prefer a more formal traditional palette, select jewel tone colors with gold and silver accents.

Differing colors can also separate departments. You might consider using bright blue, red and yellows for kids' areas, while darker burgundies, browns and blues might highlight products for men.

Red expresses excitement, high energy, warmth and vibrancy. It is the strongest of all colors. It is a very stimulating and active color.

Green represents nature, growth and relaxation. It is a soothing color and may remind us of rebirth. Green goes well with almost any color and in its darker and more neutralized shades, it can be used as a neutral. Green is also the color of money and lends a rich air.

Pink hints at trustworthiness, happiness, youth and sweetness. Pink is a very complementary color to skin tones.

Blue reflects a calm, restful and relaxing environment. Blue is one of the most popular colors, and using various tints of blue will make a room appear more spacious.

Yellow represents happiness and optimism, however vivid and light tints can appear even brighter and more glaring than white.

Yellow is an excellent color to use in a room or in a dark area that does not receive any natural daylight.

Brown conveys contentment and comfort. It is a subtle and masculine color.

Purple is a regal color, which can denote nobility, dignity and luxury. Deep purple or plum is a wonderful color to make your customers feel like they are getting the "royal treatment."

Orange symbolizes spirit, warmth, comfort and action. Orange would be a good accent color in a trendy, high traffic area, but an extremely vivid shade of orange can be tiring when painted over a large surface.

Taupe communicates conservative thinking and is considered a very sophisticated color. Taupe changes quickly as different accessories and accent pieces are used with it.

White implies virtue, purity, cleanliness, spaciousness and innocence. White rooms tend to be very dramatic and create a feeling of quiet luxury.

Gray depicts a sedate, neutral and composed environment.

➤ POP

A very high proportion of buying decisions are made at the point-of-purchase. Always merchandise like items together. For example, when displaying bedding, shelve together matched sets of coordinated sheets, dusters, pillow slips and comforters. Likewise, a bicycle shop should display helmets, locks and air pumps near the register area for easy add-on sales.

➤ Impulse

Putting the candy next to the cash register isn't just a tactic reserved for the mega-grocery outlets. McGuckin Hardware puts upscale chocolate bars right under your nose at checkout. There ought to be a law.

➤ Accessories

Any retailer can increase their sales by an average of ten percent and increase their profits by an even wider margin, by selling accessories *as if they were not optional*. A men's store should never sell a suit or sport coat without suggesting a matching shirt and tie. In fact, I can't remember ever buying a suit *without* the shirt and tie. The same holds true for women. Always suggest the matching shoes and a purse. These small add-on sales can mean big profits for guerrilla retailers. Some salespeople may feel that they're being pushy by accessorizing, so a good rule of thumb is to keep showing the customer more choices until they say, "no."

Orvel Ray was shopping for a suit for his son, Aaron, to wear to a family wedding. They found just the thing at The Men's Warehouse store in suburban Chicago, a lovely navy wool with a subtle pinstripe. In addition to the white shirt we asked for, the sales clerk promptly picked out three additional colored shirts, and tucked a coordinated tie under each color. "This way," she said, "you'll have several different outfits." They bought the suit, and two of the shirts, *and* a pair of shoes.

Up-Sell sheets

Our friend Roger C. Parker tells us about a computer store in Seattle, where every product on display is accompanied by a printed up-sell sheet, that describes the product's attributes in one or two sentences and includes both "list" and "sale" prices. More importantly, it includes a table listing every conceivable accessory that the buyer of the product might need, along with a check-box, a make and model number, a benefit description and a price.

For example, the up-sell sheet for a laser printer would include descriptions of six-foot cables, twelve-foot cables, network cards, expanded memory, fonts and books written about laser printing.

Customers would up-sell themselves while waiting for a sales person to take their order!

Cut the Cord

Sometimes you can sell the accessory right up front. The star salesman in a retail electronics store starts every stereo demo by asking the customer, "When you set this system up in your living room, how far will it be from the receiver or amp to the speakers?"

"Oh, maybe ten feet."

He goes to the counter, reels off 25 feet of speaker wire, cuts it, ties it in a bundle and hands it to the customer. "OK, let's listen to some loudspeakers first, because that's really the heart of the system. It's the part that actually makes the music." The customer sits through the rest of the demo, having *already taken delivery* on the first component of their new stereo system, the speaker wire.

■ INSIDE SIGNS

Inside signs are a vital part of the guerrilla retailers merchandising strategy, because 74% of purchase decisions are made at the point of sale. Good signage makes the features and the price clear. Signs can set off impulse reactions, and you can use them to sell and cross-sell accessories.

■ NEATNESS

➤ Premises

Disney has turned cleanliness into a marketing weapon. In an era of carnivals and state fairs, Walt Disney envisioned a place where families could bring their kids, without everyone getting filthy.

Clean your store daily, or even more often. Staff should arrive an hour before opening and use this time to front-face, spread-to-fill, unpack, stack and straighten, all merchandise, vacuum, dust, wipe, polish and buff all floors, fixtures, countertops, cabinets, displays, doors and windows. Guerrillas create a pre-opening checklist and inspect everything before opening their doors to the public.

➤ Practices

Your store's operational practices should be just as neat. If the door says you're open from ten to six, then don't disappoint customers by opening late, or closing early.

➤ Products

Always keep merchandise neatly stacked, hung, folded, and pegboarded. Sloppy merchandising undermines the quality image you've worked so hard to create.

➤ People

Elly bought a mattress, a very expensive mattress. The delivery guys showed up in a Budget rented truck, dressed in sneakers and jeans. And even though they set up the bed quickly and were knowledgeable and polite, their appearance was not professional.

Be clear with your employees from the start, that personal hygiene and grooming are part of the job description. And don't hesitate to send a staff member home who is not appropriately dressed and groomed. Use your own good judgment.

Getting Lots of Customers Into Your Store

■ GUERRILLA MARKETING FOR RETAILERS

You've spent weeks decorating and merchandising your store, and filled the shelves with better mousetraps. Now you're ready for the world to beat a path to your door. If only it were that simple. Now we have to master the art of Guerrilla Marketing.

Marketing is a process, not an event. Whether your entire marketing budget measures in the low three figures or your Internet budget alone is equal to the GNP of a Scandinavian nation, marketing is every single contact any part of your business has with any segment of the public.

If you're a guerrilla, you view marketing as a circle that begins with your ideas for generating revenue and continues with the goal of attracting a large number of repeat and referral customers. The three keys words in that sentence are "every," "repeat" and "referral." If your marketing is not a circle, it's a straight line that leads directly to Chapters 7, 11 or 13 in the bankruptcy courts.

Guerrillas carve out unique market positions in many ways that include:

- Lower pricing
- Exclusive offerings
- Exceptional product expertise
- Proximity to an underserved group
- Service-while-you-wait

- In-home demonstrations
- Pioneering new products
- Lightening fast service
- Drive-through
- Customer-focused individual sales presentations
- Inviting store ambience
- Attentive sales associates
- After-sale service
- Service and repair
- Creating community among customers
- Personal relationships with their customers
- Precise delivery or installation appointments
- Inviting special orders
- Preferred customer events
- Loyalty programs
- Understanding the value of time
- Providing customers transportation to and from the store
- Targeting diverse ethnic groups
- Family friendly
- Community involvement

Author Sam Geist says it best in the title of his book, *Why Should Someone Do Business With You...Rather Than Someone Else?* Guerrillas never stop asking that question. If you can't answer that one question, you may not have given your customers a compelling reason to buy from you. If they don't have that compelling reason to buy, they simply will not.

Competitive Advantages

Make a list of all the competitive advantages you can offer. Is there something you can do that adds value for your customers? A family-operated dry cleaners in Petaluma, California borrowed an idea from fast-food restaurants and installed a drive-through window. They give each customer a canvas laundry bag printed with a personal customer code. All you have to do is drive up and hand the bag to the clerk, who then retrieves your clean clothes from the racks, and automatically charges your credit card.

What's your "WOW Factor"?

Our friend Tom Peters writes about this in his book, *In Pursuit of WOW!* Your WOW factor is something about your business that you probably take for granted, but if you explained it to your customers, they would likely say, "WOW!"

For example, Orvel Ray holds the highest level of certification recognized world-wide by the speaking industry: the Certified Speaking Professional. He has the initials CSP right after his name, right there on the cover of this book. You probably didn't even notice, but for professional speakers, this is a very big deal. There are more brain surgeons in Los Angeles than there are CSPs in all the world. Wow!

Brainstorm your WOW factor with your staff and make it part of all of your marketing.

What is your "Purple Cow?"

Our fellow guerrilla, Seth Goden, coined this term to refer to a business that is so different, so outstanding, that it shocks us into paying attention. Black & white cows? Ho-hum. But a *purple* cow, now that would be something!

It is better to be different than to be better

Print that phrase on a poster and put it up in your store. What can you offer that is different, that provides more value, that is in scarce supply, that makes you unique?

Guerrillas have learned to carve out unique positions for themselves in the crowded retail landscape. Without millions of dollars to go head to head trying to steal market share from another veteran in the marketplace, they have discovered how to fly under the radar of their bigger competitors by offering their customers something different.

Lots of people talk about niches, but few have really managed to carve one out. On the other hand, All About Fitness, a locally-owned company in the Denver area, goes up against the giants like Sportmart by selling only those products used specifically to improve fitness. Their customers don't have to fight their way through a maze of skis, golf clubs and backpacks to find the weights, treadmills and fit balls. The All About Fitness staff works with personal trainers in the area to become more knowledgeable about the needs of their fitness-conscious customers.

Murder by the Book, a mystery bookstore, successfully competes against Amazon.com, Barnes and Noble and Borders by selling just those books to those who read Sue Grafton, Stephen King and Faye Kellerman. They carry the bestsellers and the backlist books, new, used and collectables. They also scatter comfy chairs with good light throughout the store, inviting browsers to linger.

One way to determine your niche is to ask your existing customers. If many of them shop your store for the same reason, there's your answer.

Define your niche in thirteen words or less. If you can't, how can you expect your customers to?

The name of your business contributes to your position in the marketplace. Pick a name that will have some meaning to your customers, thereby making your marketing job a little easier. Compare "John Gross and Co." to the name "Accurate Information Research."

Although the Papyrus chain may be effectively communicating their product focus, those who go to The Paper Lady know exactly what she sells.

Once you've decided how to express your position in words, get the word out. Put it on your advertisements, brochures, business cards, checks, coupons, direct mail envelopes, direct mail letters, gift certificates, invoices, letterhead, newsletter masthead, promotional gifts, proposals, signs and thank-you notes.

One way to find an unfilled niche is to visually map out how your competitors do business in a number of pertinent variables and try to find voids that you can fill.

Your competitor's map might look like:

Price	Low ___X_____		High
Service	Low ___X_____		High
Customer Age	Young _____X_____		Old
Customer Gender	Male _____X_____		Female
Customer Profile	Single _____X_____		Married
Merchandising Strategy	Narrow _____X____		Wide
Target Market	Urban _____X___		Suburban

Figure 7-1

If all of your competitors mapped similarly, you might do well to target your store to younger single men living in the city who might appreciate a narrow product assortment geared to their particular lifestyle that is combined with a high level of service.

Putting a Premium on Being Cheap

During a period of economic slowdown, discount retailers are all the rage. As consumers are forced to become more frugal, stores like Big Lots are attracting more business. Big Lots is known as a closeout retailer. They purchase discontinued or repackaged products and sell them for up to 70% off the suggested retail price. The range of products is wide, including furniture, clothing, health products and even household appliances such as vacuum cleaners. Because Big Lots is experiencing such success, it has become a darling on the New York Stock Exchange.

Big Lots doesn't want to compete with retailers like Wal-Mart. Big Lots is staying true to its roots by offering products that may be slightly less current or lower in quality for the best pricing. This has been a great niche for reaching bargain conscious consumers during tough times.

Big Lots' goal is to continue growth by focusing on internal procedures and not acquisitions or new store grand openings. Initially, low prices were the only lure that Big Lots used to draw consumers into the stores, but now those stores are focused on being cleaner, better lit and more organized, which were not some of their strengths in the past. These store makeovers cost about $80,000 per store, but investors are hoping the investment will pay off.

Let's look at how Big Lots is unique in their niche. Even though Big Lots and Wal-Mart are both discount retailers, they are not in the same retail category. Wal-Mart is in the *superstore* category, offering a wide variety of products, while Big Lots offers a narrow selection within each category, at even lower prices, and is known as a *closeout* retailer. There are also big differences in the service levels. Wal-Mart is focused on customer service, imposing the famous "10 Foot Rule," (employees are required to offer assistance to any customer that approaches within ten feet) while Big Lots is focused on offering lowest price and has not made service a focus.

Not all consumers buy on low price. Some class conscious consumers do not view themselves as discount retail shoppers and only shop at brand name stores. Some consumers will not set foot in a K-Mart or Wal-Mart. Others may want and be willing to pay for convenience or better customer service.

Jupiter Strikes Back

Jupiter Lanes, an independent, family-owned bowling center in Dallas, out-sells the competition two-to-one. With five other bowling centers within a five-mile radius, Jupiter is smack in the middle of the most competitive market for bowling in America. With only 24 lanes, Jupiter is also the smallest in its market.

Yet in the key performance area of Revenue-per-Lane-per-Day, Jupiter is clobbering much larger chain centers owned by AMF and Don Carter. For a typical bowling center, sales of $50 per lane/day is considered good; $75 per lane/day would be excellent. Last year, Jupiter's average daily receipts were $143 per lane.

Bowling Alley vs.	**Bowling Center**
Dark, dirty, dingy	Bright, clean, friendly
Dull earth tones	Hot pastel colors
Manual scoring	Automatic scoring
Dented wooden lanes	Perfect synthetic lanes
Pool halls	Billiard rooms
Smoke-filled bars	Smoke-free private clubs
Gutter balls	Bumper bowling
Pinball machines	State-of-the-art video arcade
Snack bar	Cafeteria-style restaurant

How does a small business with limited funds and a small staff go up against the big guns without getting creamed? By using guerrilla tactics. And Jupiter Lanes is a classic study of what it takes to survive and succeed in a viciously competitive market.

Redefine the Battlefield

The number of regular bowlers has dwindled from twelve percent of the population a decade ago to less than two percent today, so the industry has to find new players to introduce to the game, and that means going after *families*. Phil Kinzer, Jupiter Lanes' owner, doesn't consider other bowling alleys his competition. "We compete with miniature golf and movie theaters and McDonalds," he says. "Our competition is *anywhere* else a family might go for an evening's entertainment."

Realizing that, he set about to literally *redefine* the business he was in. "A 'bowling *alley*' is a dark, dirty, dingy place with pool tables and a smoke-filled bar. Our 'bowling *center*' is a bright, clean, colorful fun place with a five-star restaurant and a playroom."

Remove Barriers

The most common objection to bowling for young families is that it is a very difficult game for small children. After a few gutterballs, they get frustrated and bored. Back in 1982, Jupiter Lanes installed metal rails that could fold out over the gutters for the length of the lane, changing the game forever. A rank beginner could experience the thrill of victory their very first time out. Phil eventually sold the patents to AMF and today "bumper bowling" is available in better bowling centers nationwide.

A Clear Mission

Phil strives to be *the* leader in the bowling industry and encourages innovation at every turn. He sets the standards personally by paying *full retail* for everything he eats or drinks at the center, while employees get generous discounts. He has invested heavily in equipment, installing a video surveillance system for the parking lot and *another* for the playroom. Posted conspicuously near the door, a sign greets every customer, "Our Mission: To Make Our Community Proud of Us."

Create Smart Customers

Parents sometimes complain that bowling is expensive. "At $2.50 a line, it can add up quickly," Phil says. "One game for a family of four and you've dropped ten bucks." To combat this perception, the Jupiter staff conducts tours of the back end, explaining the machinery that makes it all work. "Each pin setting machine has more than 5,000 pieces and more than 2,000 *moving* parts, so they require constant adjustment and maintenance. Each pinsetter cycles a set of 21 pins, which cost about $11 each and have a life span of about 10 months. Each machine uses about seventy-five cents worth of electricity for each line of play. Add the costs of labor, insurance, housekeeping, maintenance and repairs and you can see how it all adds up." Through education, customers develop an appreciation for value once they see where their money goes. They begin to see that $2.50 a line is really a bargain, particularly when compared to the price of a movie ticket or a couple rounds of miniature golf.

Good Housekeeping

Jupiter Lanes is also a far cry from dark and dingy. Staff services the restrooms every half-hour, carpets are vacuumed *twice* daily, tables and counters are wiped constantly. Even the back-end where all the machinery operates is neat, clean and well organized; no dust, no grease and not a tool out of place.

An elaborate Total Quality Management system tracks every machine failure that might affect a customer's game. From a "180 stop," to "no ball return," to "dead wood on the deck," the mechanics know *exactly* how each machine is performing, by the day, by the week and by the month. The mechanics keep an extensive inventory of belts, bolts and spares on hand, all tracked by computer, so Jupiter *never* has a dead lane. Consequently, they respond to *half* as many service calls as the competitors, and customers have fewer delays and aggravations, which improves profitability.

➤ Lifetime Value of a Customer

Your average league bowler will spend about $350 over the course of league play for lineage and entry fees, but could potentially spend *that much again* on food & beverage, arcade games, pro shop services and other items.

Jupiter's commitment to the long-term customer relationship with growing families is a winning game.

➤ Scarcity

People will pay more for anything that is in short supply. The Washington Monument, in Washington D.C. is actually capped with aluminum, because at the time, it was more scarce and more expensive than gold. Of course today, modern manufacturing methods have made aluminum so cheap that we waste it.

➤ People Pay More for an Original

At the Musée du Louvre in Paris, you can stand in line for half an hour to gaze upon what is perhaps the most famous work or art in the world, Leonardo Da Vinci's *Mona Lisa*. In the giftshop, you can buy a postcard of the *Mona Lisa* for forty francs, and a full-size poster is only twenty Euros, while the original is considered priceless.

■ WHEN TO MARKET

➤ Seasons & Holidays

For a great website listing holiday promotions and ideas, see: http://www.holidaysmart.com/holidaylist.htm

➤ Special-Purchase Events

These events are opportunities for you to purchase some special product from your supplier. You might be offered the end of a manufacturing run or a special price on last year's models. In the fashion industry, you might be offered an opportunity for your customers to preview next season's products at a trunk show.

➤ Fashion Show

In Phoenix Arizona, an alluring young woman saunters through the hotel restaurant during the lunch rush, modeling dresses and handing out tiny scrolls tied with a bit of colored ribbon, coupons for a 20% discount. "My store is just across the street," she says, "and this jump suit I'm wearing is only $79." Lovely. Ten minutes later she's back modeling a different frock. The customers love it. So does the restaurant, whose sales are up as a result of the fashion shows.

■ HOW DO YOU REACH THEM?

Well before you open the doors of your store, there are some important preparations you must make to launch your guerrilla marketing attack.

➤ Marketing Plan

The first step is to write a Guerrilla Marketing Plan. Your marketing plan will be your road map. It shows your destination and the route you must travel to reach it. While most corporate marketing plans are carefully crafted and would fill a ring binder, they're are put on a shelf and never looked at again. A Guerrilla marketing plan has only seven sentences. It should be brief because you'll be forced to focus on your objectives and tactics and because brief marketing plans should be easy to read. It may even fit on a single page. You can show it to your employees, your boss or your banker. You might even frame it and hang it on the wall where everyone in your operation can see it every day.

- **The first sentence states the purpose of your marketing**. That's pretty easy. Is your purpose to get people to visit your store? Motivate them to browse your website? Send for your free video? Call your toll-free number? Whatever action you want people to take, the first sentence of your marketing plan is the place to say it.

- **The second sentence emphasizes the main benefit you offer** to motivate people to take action. Ideally, that benefit is also a competitive advantage that you offer.

- **The third sentence describes your target audience or audiences.** You may have more than one target. Don't limit yourself. With several targets, you have a better chance of hitting a bull's-eye.

- **The fourth sentence lists the marketing weapons you'll deploy.** It's the only long sentence in your plan, the longer the better.

- **The fifth sentence identifies your niche, what you stand for.** Is it quality? Economy? Selection? You must know your own niche and have it come shining through in all of your marketing materials.

- **The sixth sentence defines your identity.** It does not describe your image. Image implies something that's counterfeit or fake: Ronald McDonald is an image and if you have a wheelbarrow full of money to spend on advertising, building an image can work. Guerrillas instead strive to communicate their identity, who they really are. And your identity will automatically be more credible because it's genuine.

- **The seventh sentence defines your marketing budget, usually stated as a percentage of your projected gross sales.** The average retailer re-invests three to four percent of sales back into marketing. And they consider it an investment. Initially you may want to double that ratio to establish your brand.

Sample Guerrilla Marketing Plan — Page One Bookstore

1. The purpose of your marketing.

"The purpose of Page One Bookstore marketing is to build an increasing base of repeat customers."

2. How this purpose will be achieved, focusing upon the benefits of your offering.

"This will be achieved by stressing the selection of book and non-book items within the store."

3. Your target audience.

"Our target audience is book-buying adult females within a one-mile radius of Page One Bookstore."

4. Proposed Marketing Weapons

"Marketing vehicles to be employed will include newspaper ads run weekly, numerous signs inside that merchandise and cross-merchandise, a yellow pages ad, quarterly autograph parties, quarterly author lectures, quarterly in-store seminars, FM radio advertising, postcard mailings every two months, brochures, a catalog, a one-time magazine ad, tie-ins with all local conferences, accessing co-op funds, and use of our marketing theme on bags, bookmarks, invoices, gift certificates and gifts."

5. Your niche in the market.

"Page One's niche will be a careful selection tailored for the community."

6. Your identity

"Our identity will be portrayed as warm, honest, knowledgeable, up-to-date and ultra-friendly, as evidenced by our greeting people by name, taking phone orders, setting up charge accounts, shipping anywhere in the world and doing free gift wrapping."

7. Your marketing budget expressed as a percentage of your gross sales.

"10% of gross sales will be re-invested in marketing."

➤ Marketing Calendar

You'll have more than a hundred ways to market your business and most of them are free, so it's important to know just when you'll be doing that marketing. There are several important reasons to write a marketing calendar:

- So you can plan ahead and be ready to fire
- So you don't overlook opportunities
- So you can get suppliers to participate
- So your team knows what will be happening and when
- So that you can schedule enough staff for peak times
- So you can kick off holiday promotions
- So you can promote an anniversary sale
- So you can take advantage of special events
- So you can participate in manufacturer promotions
- So you can schedule warehouse or truckload sales
- So you can qualify for additional co-op and promotional funds

A Guerrilla Marketing Calendar is the essence of simplicity. You can set one up in Excel in a matter of minutes. It has four columns and either twelve rows (one for each month) or 52 rows (one for each week of the year). Depending on your business, a monthly marketing plan may be adequate, but if you sell seasonal items like clothing, lawnmowers or air-conditioning, you should plan at least week-to-week. Grocers plan different marketing initiatives three times a week, Monday, Wednesday and Weekend.

The first column is called "Week" and lists the week number.

The second column is titled "Thrust," and identifies the thrust of your marketing that week. Is it a sale, a new product, or a seasonal theme? This is where you list it.

The third column, "Media," lists the media you'll be using that month.

The fourth column is where you transform yourself into a college professor and give a letter grade to that week, depending on profits. Did it learn an A, or did it get a measly D?

At the end of the year, review your marketing calendar before making a new one and eliminate the things you did that earned anything other than an A or a B. It takes about three years to develop a perfect marketing calendar, one that's loaded with A's. Once you have it, keep it under lock and key, because it will be one of your most precious business assets.

Armed with a marketing plan and a marketing calendar, you're almost ready to move forward into taking action. You know what you must do, what you want your plan to accomplish for you and when you must do it. That means you're primed to attack, succeed and profit. So far this has cost you no money, only your time and imagination.

Guerrilla Marketing Calendar for Retail Florist

Month	Thrust	Media	Results
January	Store Anniversary Sale	Window signs, newspaper	A
February	Valentines Day	Roses and gifts promotion	A
March	Garden and bedding plants	Val-Pak coupons	B
April	Easter	Egg hunt party	A
May	Mother's day	Newspaper ad	A
June	Father's day, Graduation, Weddings	Campus newspaper Bridal shop	B
July	Independence Day	Store dressing	C
August	Back-to-school, gift baskets	Flyers under dorm doors, campus "Welcome" packet	B
September	Football themed arrangement	Coupon dist. at football game	B
October	Halloween	Costumed employee with sign	A
November	Thanksgiving	Turkey Shoot drawing	A
December	Christmas ornaments, New Year party decorating	Store dressing extended hours	A

➤ Name

The right name can give your retail business a competitive advantage from the get-go (as in Git & Go, a convenience store in Phoenix, Arizona). At the same time, a bad name can hobble your business success, stymie your potential for growth and even land you in court.

There are few things more frustrating than having to change the name of your business once it's up and running. So the idea is to start with the right name in the first place. Guerrillas realize that there are only two kinds of names, bad names and good names. Bad names are hard to pronounce, exaggerative, common, suggestive of other companies or difficult to spell (Gougenstein's Pianos). Good names say what you do, (Jiffy Lube), imply a benefit (Best Buy) and are easy to remember (Car Toys).

Names can be confusing. A company named Dreamscapes suggests mattresses or bedroom furniture. Actually it's a landscape center. You can name your retail store after yourself (Paulino Gardens) or the brand you carry (Techline, The Maytag Store). It's better still if you use a descriptive name (Business Interiors, need we say more?) or a name that suggests the product (The Spoke, a bicycle shop).

Don't let your name paint you into a corner. A company that specialized in making copies named itself the Copy Factory. A few years later, when it discovered that its prime source of profits was actually offset printing, it had to rename itself the Print and Copy Factory. A showroom with a wide selection of beds called itself Santa Rosa Bedding. But the business sold so much furniture that it had to go through the process of changing its name to Santa Rosa Bedding and Furniture. Boston Chicken, after becoming known for its high-quality, home-style meals, had to re-flag some 650 stores to become Boston Market. It was very costly.

Don't let your name prohibit your growth, expansion or diversification. Tailor it to how you'll use it. If people will be looking for you in the Yellow Pages, it might be a good idea to start your name with two A's (Aaron's Office Furniture). Being first on any list is always a good idea (AAA anything). Let your name carry a sales message rather than be meaningless (Fireplace Superstore instead of Energy Experts, Inc.). There are lots of huge companies out there with nondescript names such as Lord & Taylor, Neiman Marcus and J.C. Penny. But they invested fortunes in helping people get to know the companies behind those names. You'll be investing time, energy and imagination instead of massive marketing money.

Avoid cutesy names like Lawnmowers R Us. It's been done, and you might even get a nice letter from someone's law firm.

Size does matter. Remember that the shorter your name, the larger you can make it in your marketing materials. And don't dive into marketing your name until you've checked that it's available, legal and protectable. You can hire a trademark and patent attorney, or you can do your own on-line search through the Office of the Secretary of State for the states where you wish to do business.

Also consider the availability of Internet domain names when selecting the name for your business and reserve it with the Internet Corporation for Assigned Names and Numbers http://www.icann.org. ICANN is the worldwide institution responsible for allocating domain names on the Internet. Reserve as many variations as you can (we reserved the word guerrilla, of course, but also guerilla (one r), guerrila (one l) and guerila (only one of each). While you're at it, reserve the .com, .net, .org and .biz extensions for your domain name, if for no other reason than to protect them from imitators. Expect to pay about $100 each per year to reserve these names. As in the great gold rush of a century ago, grabbing territory on the Web is a good investment that will pay a mother lode of dividends in the future.

➤ Identity

Your marketing should tell people who you are. Your identity is not the same as image. Identity is who you really are and what you really stand for.

Establish your identity by building a list of adjectives that describe you, your people and your business. Start with the obvious ones, like "convenient" and "friendly." You can add "knowledgeable," "passionate" or "fanatical." Better still, invite a group of your customers to participate in a focus group and ask them to describe their experience when doing business with you. Come up with a list of twenty-five key words that you then work into the copy for all your marketing materials.

➤ Logo

An effective logo is simple, reproduces well in black-and-white and serves as a meme[5] for your business. It should be compatible with your name, your identity and your future plans. McDonald's Golden Arches certainly qualify on both counts. Design for the next twenty years, or better still, the next 100, so that you won't ever have to change it.

Design it so that it is clearly discernible whether it's a yard wide on a sign or one inch square on a business card.

In this day and age of proliferating marketing from all sides, you need a meme to stand out in the clutter. You should use that meme in all of your marketing, on your website, on your stationery, on your business card, wherever and whenever you can. It is no longer enough to have a logo, which represents a company but stops too short. A meme represents both a company and an idea, usually the main benefit offered by that company. The Maytag Repairman is a meme for quality and reliability. The Green Giant is a meme. So are the Michelin Man and the Marlboro Cowboy. The Nike "swish" is a great logo, but it falls short as a meme. Your job is to develop a meme for your business. Do it now and use it for the life of your business. Get your own Pillsbury Doughboy or Energizer Bunny and let them spearhead your marketing. Just visualize your main benefit, then distill it, compress it, simplify it and focus on it and you're off to a good start.

➤ Theme Line

It doesn't cost a cent to develop a winning, lasting and memorable theme line. A theme line is a set of words that describes the sprit of your company, ("Fly the Friendly Skies of United," or "You're In Good Hands with Allstate"). You'll easily complete these theme lines: "Coke adds _____." "Finger lickin' _____." "We try _____."

You should never, ever change your theme. This is one of the most frequent and most costly mistakes made in marketing. In 1931, The Campbell Soup Company introduced their classic, "M'm! M'm! Good!" jingle to radio listeners, and repeated it until it became part of American pop culture. Then in the mid nineties, when Americans were buying more than 70 cans of Campbell's soup every *second*, the good folks in Camden, New Jersey decided to change their theme line. Without skipping ahead to the next page, can you recall what they changed it to?

Like your meme, you should use your theme line whenever you can, in your advertising, on your website, in your e-mail signature, on your business cards and stationery, even in your tattoo if you have one. The theme line grows from your identity and makes people think of you whenever they see it or hear it. Combined with your meme, your theme gives you double-barreled memorability. Federal Express made its theme line the centerpiece of all their marketing: "When it Absolutely, Positively, Has to be There Over-night." It not only explained the product, but also made a powerful promise that differentiated it from the competition. That means you should create your theme with the future in mind. Once you create it, hold it up to the test of uniqueness. If it reminds you of any other company's theme, abandon it and get something you can truly call your own.

The best theme lines say something good about a company, but never use superlatives, "Diamonds are Forever," "Just Do It," "Breakfast of Champions." No bragging in any of those. Your theme line must be as believable as all of your other marketing. If it boasts or exaggerates, it will undermine your credibility every time you use it.

By the way, the new Campbell's theme line was, "Soup is Good Food."

➤ Days of Operation

For centuries, businesses were operated at the convenience of the owner, who might open their shop on a particular day, or not, depending on their mood. It wasn't until the late 1940's that businesses started to cater to the needs of their customers. These days, retailers are not only open every day of the week, but some are open 24 hours a day. Saturday is still the best day of the week for retail, producing as much as 40% of the week's sales revenue, with Sunday coming in a close second.

➤ Hours of Operation

The Southland Corporation created a new retail category by putting the "convenience" in convenience stores. Remember when they really were open from 7 AM to 11 PM?

➤ Stationery

How important is stationery for a retailer? Not very. I've never seen a letter from a company that was so beautifully engraved, on such extravagant paper stock, that impressed me so much that I called them right away to place an order. Likewise, I've never seen a letterhead that was so ugly that I called immediately to cancel my order, resolving never to buy from them again.

Even so, your stationery sends an important message about your business. Invest in professional design and quality paper. Letterheads should include your name and theme, as well as carry your address and contact information. Buy extra reams of matching blank paper for second sheets. While you're at it, order matching printed #10 and 9x12 envelopes.

➤ Business Cards

Your business card is a powerful marketing weapon. Sometimes it's the first piece of marketing that your customer sees. Often, it's the last thing they have to remember you by. Guerrillas turn them into mini-brochures, including lots of information: your name, your address, your office, home and mobile phone numbers, your e-mail address, your fax number and your hours of operation, your theme and more. Consider printing on both sides, or making a fold-over panel to provide more space. Can you fit a thumbnail map to your store? Also consider an odd size or shape. Best Buy die-cuts their business cards to be shaped like their yellow "price tag" logo. Can your business card also double as a bookmark, a coupon or a refrigerator magnet? Print on quality card stock because it sends a message about your identity. Color is always worth the extra expense.

One of the most effective items to include on your business card is also the one most frequently omitted, your picture. Guerrillas include their picture on their business cards because the part of your brain that remembers faces is ten times larger than the part of your brain that remembers names. That's why everyone at that conference you attended was wearing a nametag. Our friend and fellow

guerrilla, Patricia Fripp says, "Dharling, there's no use going anywhere they didn't remember you were there."

Printing business cards is cheap, fast and easy, yet most retail employees don't have them. Test this for yourself. Next time you're
out shopping, just ask the salesperson for a card. On several occasions I've asked an exceptionally helpful store clerk for their card
so that I could commend them to their boss, only to be told that the
company is "too cheap" to provide them.

A young salesman working on commission in an audio-video store
spent two hours demonstrating an expensive stereo system to a
prospect. The prospect left the store to run an errand, but returned
while the salesman was out to lunch. Another clerk got the credit
and the commission, for simply writing up the order and rolling the
boxes out to the car. This young guerrilla soon discovered that the
price of 1,000 business cards was less than his lost commission, so
he paid to have them printed himself. The following month and for
many months thereafter, he was this store's top producer.

Providing business cards can have a dramatic impact on the attitude of your people. One of our clients, Marriott Hotels, decided to
provide business cards for all of their housekeepers. That's right,
the housekeepers. They kept their box of business cards right on
top of their housekeeping carts and were instructed to leave one on
the night table every time they cleaned a room. What the management didn't expect was that turnover of their housekeeping staff,
which is chronically high in any hotel, dropped by almost half.
These anonymous workers, who toil unseen behind the scenes,
now had a name and a title. It made them feel important, special
and appreciated, and their tips increased as well.

➤ Circulars

A circular is usually a single sheet printed on one side. They're
simple, inexpensive and they have immediate impact. You can use

a whole sheet of 8½ by 11 paper, or save money by printing three-up on a page (8½ by 3⅝) and cut them to create a #9 mailer. These fit neatly in a #10 envelope or under the windshield wiper of a car. Or you can print them four-up on a sheet, (cut to 4¼ by 5½) printed on two sides.

➤ Brochures

A brochure is typically a multi-page document. It can fit on two sides of a single sheet, or it can be a multi-page, staple bound booklet. The advantage is that it can convey all the details about your business. Phillip Rosen, founder of Spiral Language Systems, explains his unique, intuitive method for teaching foreign languages in a simple, double-sided brochure that folds to a #9. He used a computer and the brochure templates in Microsoft Publisher, then printed them in small quantities on an ink-jet printer. That way, he can include his schedule of upcoming introductory classes, and update it every week.

Having a brochure also enables you to do the "guerrilla marketing two-step." You save money and save space in your print advertising by including the taglines, "Call for our free brochure" or "Visit our website."

Smart guerrillas turn their brochure into a reference piece that the customer will keep and use for another purpose. The brochure for a line of weed-control products includes a table for calculating the correct dilution of their products.

➤ Flexibility

This is one area where a small business can out-do big business every time. Guerrillas are not stuck in a policy and procedures manual vice lock, but rather, go out of their way to accommodate every customer.

In chain stores, for instance, most returns and exchanges have to be approved by management or by someone in the dreaded customer service department. Guerrilla retailers empower their front line team members to *do whatever it takes* to satisfy each and every customer.

➤ Outside Signs

Two centuries ago, the majority of the population could neither read nor write, so shopkeepers used simple picture signs to convey what goods they sold; a loaf for the baker, a boot for the cobbler, a hog for the butcher's shop. In today's fast-moving market, it pays to tell your story visibly. Your customers often can't read your sign, not because they're illiterate, but because they're in a hurry, hurtling down the street in busy traffic.

On a country road outside Richmond, Illinois, a professionally lettered steel sign with neat black letters on a white background promises "Farm Fresh Eggs Next Left." Just a few yards further, another hand-painted sign promises "Farm Fresh Eggs Next Right," but this one features a colorful drawing of a fat red hen and a wire basket full of eggs. The illustrated sign sells three times more eggs than it's neighbor across the road.

Keep in mind that a car driving 25 miles per hour will take less than two seconds to pass your store, so keep sign copy super-short, a maximum of six words.

Look for imaginative locations for your signs. Can you put them on the roof, or perhaps in the middle of the highway median. Remember your delivery truck can be a billboard. Fantasy Orchids in Louisville, Colorado started as a greenhouse addition to a single-story ranch style home. The greenhouse business grew until the owner moved out and a commercial strip center sprang up in the adjacent field. Now they do a thriving business, but residential zoning prohibits them from having anything more than a small sign over the front door. The owner bought a ten-foot box van and had it painted with the company name over a beautiful bright pink cattleya, eight by ten feet square, on both sides. The van is certainly handy for making the occasional wholesale delivery, but it spends most of the time parked in the lot right out front, right next to the busy street.

Check routinely to make sure that your store signs are working correctly and lit completely. Your sign is your identity, indeed, your good name. Never let it be seen half-lit. Change burnt-out floodlights, backlights or neon tubes at once.

Use a series of signs if you can. Consecutive signs command attention longer than any single sign. Of course, the classic example was the Burma-Shave Jingles, short lines written on five or six signs with the last sign usually reading "Burma-Shave." By having the rhymes build suspense until the fourth or fifth sign, Burma-Shave forced travelers to read the full series. For example:

THE BEARDED LADY
TRIED A JAR
SHE'S NOW
A FAMOUS MOVIE STAR
BURMA-SHAVE

or

WE'VE MADE GRANDPA
LOOK SO TRIM
THE LOCAL DRAFT BOARD'S
AFTER HIM
BURMA-SHAVE[6]

Goats on the Roof

For thirty years, The Coombs Old Country Market, in Coombs, British Columbia, has delighted locals and tourists alike with an unusual combination of merchandise, service, food and fun. Goats on the roof mark the site so blatantly that no one driving by could possibly miss it.

This place is a must-see destination. The Market is famous for its "goats on the roof." As you walk into the doorway of the market the sweet aroma of fresh baked breads gently caresses your senses and draws you in. The breads are fabulous and the cookies are nothing to shake a cheese stick at either.

The Old Country Market tries to provide products that give an international feeling to their business. The deli is a great example. With exquisite cheeses, smoked wild salmon and deli meats from Canada, Denmark, England, France and many other parts of Europe they can certainly please any palette.

The store also boasts a produce department with the freshest, unsprayed, fungicide free fruits and vegetables picked fresh each day by Vancouver Island's best growers to ensure the highest quality.

A restaurant featuring a wide selection of mouth-watering wraps and sandwiches will round off the "Coombs Experience". Burgers dripping with cheese and mushrooms, sandwiches filled so high with fresh ingredients that you have to use three hands to eat them, soups so tasty you would think that there was a hole in your bowl.

The owner, Larry Geekie, has a flair for finding interesting and exotic gifts from around the world. He has brought back antique furniture from China, terra cotta fireplaces and margarita glasses that have been hand-blown by Mexican families who have perfected the craft. Products from India range from lanterns to bangles. In addition, there are baskets in every size and shape from all corners of the world.

And if all of that wasn't enough, the big attraction is the herd of goats that are airlifted to the store's sod roof each April. Millions of tourists have bribed the goats with ice cream cones or cookies just to get their pictures taken with them.

➤ Word-of-mouth

It's often called the most valuable advertising you can get, and even though you can't buy it, you *can* encourage it. Guerrillas accomplish this by creating a *new customer brochure*. This is a simple, one-page summary of your company and your story, who you are and what you do. Give it to all your new customers with their first purchase, so they are encouraged to tell your story. If you put the right words in the right mouths at the right time, your store will soon be the talk of the town.

Joe Romano is a very successful restaurateur in Boulder, Colorado. He was opening a new restaurant, the Brasserie Ten Ten. His Mediterranean Restaurant, which is right next door to our office, was already one of the most popular in town, voted "Best Of" by the local newspaper several years running. Before opening his new restaurant, Joe visited every hair salon in town and gave every stylist an engraved invitation good for dinner for two, no conditions, no limit, wine and drinks included. Of course they talked up the Brasserie to every client in their chairs for the next week and for the first month after it opened, there were people lined up down the block waiting to get in.

➤ Testimonials

If you do a good job, customers will volunteer nice things about you or your staff. When this happens, ask them, "Would you be willing to summarize that comment on your letterhead and direct it to my boss' attention?" That's the guerrilla twist. Most customers will comply gladly.

When the letter arrives, call to thank them and ask, "May we please have your permission to include your comments in our marketing?" Of course they'll agree. Now you can quote them in your brochure, your newsletter, your web site and your print ads. Then, frame the original letter and create a "Gallery of Fame" in the break area or warehouse area, somewhere where every employee every day can be reminded of the great job they're doing serving customers.

➤ Referral Program

The best source of new customers are your existing customers, so guerrilla retailers are always looking for ways to *reward* referrals.

Of course, the first step is to *track* referrals. Especially in the early days after you open, ask every new customer, "How did you hear about us?"

Encourage referrals by asking customers, "Who else do you know…" who is remodeling their kitchen, looking for a new car, or interested in RC modeling. Offer to send their friend a gift certificate, *on your customers' behalf*, in exchange for the contact information.

Double-Dipping

One of the most effective tactics is the Double-Dip coupon. When a customer makes a purchase, give them a coupon with their name on the back, for them to pass on to a friend. When the friend redeems the coupon, you send a discount coupon or gift certificate (along with another Double-Dip coupon) that they can redeem the next time they visit. The viral effect of this type of campaign can be amazing, as each customer recruits more and more friends.

Always *acknowledge and reward referrals* when they come your way. Send a thank you note, at the very least, to the customer who sent the referral, whether their friend buys or not. If the referred purchase is substantial (a house full of furniture, say, or a new kitchen) then a gift is in order. We recommend a gift certificate redeemable in your own store, or if that's not practical ("I just completely *redid* my kitchen,") then dinner for two at a local restaurant is a good alternative. You may even be able to negotiate a deep discount from the restaurant on the gift certificate.

➤ Loyalty Programs

Frequent flyer miles are likely the most familiar form of loyalty program, where customers receive benefits based on the size and frequency of their purchases. These programs are structured to keep good customers coming back. Unlike contests or sweepstakes, these programs directly reward additional purchases.

Major grocery stores quickly followed the airlines' lead with their discount card programs. Cardholders get special pricing on unadvertised specials including Buy-One-Get-One offers and significant discounts in all departments. Customers using their cards see their total savings tallied on their receipts. There's nothing like saving money to make customers come back.

Women's fashion chain Chico's has built a base of committed customers with their Chico's Passport program. After their first $500 in purchases, Passport holders get a lifetime five percent discount, free shipping, special catalogues that include coupons for $20 to $50 off, and discount coupons on their birthdays.

Punch Cards

Our neighborhood coffee house gives customers a "Buy 10, Get 1 Free" punch card. Of course, over the course of 10 refills you're going to buy a lot of Danish and the occasional breakfast burrito.

The hosiery department in most major department stores offers a punch card for a free pair of nylons after the purchase of a dozen.

Aveda stores offer a punch card for $40 in free merchandise with every $400 spent there. That's a hefty 10% discount for their frequent buyers. Aveda goes one step further by keeping the cards on file for their customers in their stores.

Preferred Customer sales and special events are another great way to reward customer loyalty. An Early-Bird postcard grants early admission to the store, so preferred customers can get the best deals before the doors open to the public. Guitar Center stores attract mobs of potential customers with invitation-only, in-store concerts and talent competitions.

Private sales remain the most successful promotions of all. Customers appreciate the opportunity for the first chance to buy at sale prices.

The Boulevard, in St. George, Utah, runs three private sales each year just prior to their major themed events, including Safari Days, Beach Bonanza and Fiesta Days. One is held in January, one the weekend before Mother's Day and one just prior to the holiday selling season at the end of October.

The store is closed until noon before the private sale so that all products in the store can be re-tagged with a special price for the promotion. Each tag has a perforated portion on the bottom showing the special savings available only on the first day of the sale to customers who received an invitation in the mail.

Customers need tickets to gain admission and receive free gifts, food, drinks and chances to win prizes that include merchandise and dream vacations.

Before opening the next day, sales associates tear off all of perforated tabs on the sale tags and customers during the rest of the sale pay higher prices.

Retailers who run preferred customer sales often say that they generate the equivalent of a month's revenue in one eight hour evening.

➤ Yourself and Your People

Sell yourself and your people at every opportunity. The strongest differentiator you have is the knowledge and experience of your staff. Display any certifications or special qualifications proudly.

How do you develop a team you can brag about? Always be looking for good people. Every once in a while, perhaps in a restaurant or a department, just when you least expect it, someone really special will serve you. When someone treats you really special, recruit them on the spot.

When Jerry Gart, of Gart Brothers Sporting Goods, meets a waiter or waitress with exceptional customer service skills, he leaves his business card behind on the table with his tip and a note, "If you'd like to explore a new opportunity, call me."

➤ Free Shipping and Delivery

If you're selling large items like appliances or furniture, of course you have to deliver the product to your customer. Even so, even small retail specialty shops can increase sales by offering shipping. Your customer may be visiting from out of town, or they may not own a car. Offering to pack and ship their purchase home for them will trigger impulse purchases.

The San Francisco Sourdough Bread Company store and restaurant in Fisherman's Wharf offers to send your bread home for you, much preferred to trying to stuff it into your suitcase.

➤ Removal

Likewise, your customer will need assistance disposing of an obsolete appliance or mattress. Guerrillas offer this as a service, and charge additional fees. This service can make your free delivery run actually pay.

➤ Community Involvement

Guerrilla retailers get involved, and are always looking for ways to put together promotions with the local school, fire department or service clubs. These can range from offering goods or services for fund-raising, to building a float for a parade.

Select carefully where you'll get the most bang for the buck. Young people are amazingly energetic and can energize your promotions.

Your personal favorite may not be the best group to support, at least from a marketing point of view.

Done right you'll get a lot of free media. Invite the press to cover your car wash, raffle or beauty contest for seniors.

A simple, no-cost tactic that draws traffic is to host events in your store, from a story circle for kids (at a bookstore) to a meeting of the mountain club (at Neptune Mountaineering).

➤ Sharing

Guerrillas become known as leaders in their community by sharing their time and expertise. You can participate in table-top shows and Business-to-business expos organized by your local Chamber of Commerce. Share your experiences and your expertise with others and it will open doors of opportunity for you.

➤ Professional Associations

Attend the conferences and conventions of the associations that serve your categories, starting with The National Federation of retailers, and any one or more of the hundreds of sub-groups. These are great places to meet peers, prospects and your competitors. These meetings are the best place to keep up with industry trends and to pick up new ideas. If you can't afford to fly to the convention, at least order the seminar tapes.

➤ Clubs

Can you make your store the local headquarters for a quilting club, model airplane club, or orchid society? Hold special sales events just for club members. Sponsor competitions and contests that attract new customers while giving your existing customers a reason to buy from you.

➤ Speaking to Service Clubs

Rotary, Kiwanis, Jaycees, Chambers, all are constantly on the outlook for guest speakers. They can't pay you, but they can give you a wonderful platform to promote your business.

Talk about your experience, and share lessons of value to other businesspeople. You can spell out your benefits, service and expertise, but be very careful not to over commercialize your presentation. Tell, don't sell.

You can offer a door prize, and circulate a small basket to collect business cards for the drawing. Winner gets the prize, and you get to add the cards to your mailing list.

➤ Courses & Seminars

One very effective way to attract customers *and* add value, is to conduct "how to" seminars for your products. Camera stores routinely offer workshops ranging from "How to Use Your Digital Camera" to more advanced photographic techniques like lighting and portraiture.

For a You-Paint-It ceramics shop, their courses are their *entire* marketing plan.

Allen & Petersen had been the only appliance store in Anchorage, Alaska for years. Then they were suddenly losing business to Sears, Lowes, Home Depot and even Costco, who were selling the same appliances, often at lower prices.

We helped the GM, Leon Barbachano, to realize that he could sell *more* than just appliances; he could sell the *total cooking experience*.

Instead of just lining up rows of ranges and refrigerators, Leon built elegant working kitchens, using free design services and coop money from his suppliers. Then he invited guest chefs from the best restaurants in Anchorage to come in and demonstrate their skills and teach prospective customers the joys of cooking. Now customers could test-drive commercial-style ranges before purchasing.

They soon added a full display of high-margin dishes, cookware and kitchen gadgets. These daily classes have become a profit center in their own right and are sold out weeks in advance.

Sales *tripled* and margins are through the roof. Most important, Allen & Petersen developed a unique retailing model that they'll soon be rolling out in the lower forty-eight.

If you don't have a fully-equipped teaching venue, contact your local universities and community colleges. Professors are always looking for guest speakers to lecture to their business school, (or pr art school or music school. . .).

Many also offer Continuing Education courses that guerrillas can teach. Tuition is usually quite modest, (and the instructors' honoraria even smaller). But the big payoff comes when you pick a class title that will attract people who are likely to buy from you. If you can teach the classes in your own store, so much the better.

➤ Audiences

Guerrillas know that they're operating in a global economy, even if they only have a single location. In multi-cultural markets like Los Angeles, San Francisco or even Dearborn Michigan, you may need to prepare your marketing materials, in Spanish, Farsi and Japanese, as well as English.

The marketing you use to target college students is very different than the copy you would write to reach seniors.

Jason Busch owns Body Balance, a mid-sized downtown health club that competes with a 24 Hour Fitness and a Gold's Gym, as well as two other aerobics centers, a rock gym and the Y.

In order to differentiate he wanted to attract single working women, because they often complain about the meat-market atmosphere in health clubs. They also tended to be the most profitable members, because they are much more likely to sign up for classes than male members. Women report that they join health clubs primarily for *social* reasons, rather than just an interest in sports or body building. "Besides," he reasoned, "if we can get the women, the men will come."

We started by emphasizing the exceptional cleanliness of the club and backing up that promise by switching to a better (and more expensive) cleaning service. Then he expanded the schedule of yoga and Pilates classes and partnered with a judo studio to offer kick-boxing and self-defense classes on site. He even re-evaluated the mix of magazines available in the rack by the cardio machines, replacing *Muscle & Fitness* with *Shape* and *Self.* The new pre-natal and post-partum fitness classes are promoted through every OB/GYN in town.

➤ Gift Certificates

This weapon is a no-brainer. All you need to do is tell your customers that they're available. Simply put a framed sign near the cash register that says, "Ask about our gift certificates."

You can also send them to your customers, as a way to say "we're sorry, we made a mistake" as well as "thank you for the referral." The perfect way to get good customers to come back.

➤ Coupons

Most coupons offer a discount. Others give advantages such as a BOGO (buy-one-get-one-free) or a freebie if your purchase is large enough. Some Americans toss away all coupons. According to the Direct Mail Marketing Association, about 15% of Americans save them and swear by them. Whenever the economy falters, coupons have more marketing power as more people become coupon clippers. Almost any business, not just retailers, can benefit from the extra sales power of coupons.

Coupons are much more effective if they have a face value, rather that a percentage. We don't understand it, but customers are more likely to redeem a coupon good for $10 off of a $100 purchase than they are to redeem a coupon good for 20% off a purchase of $100 or more. Go figure.

Extra Lettuce

In Ft. Collins, Colorado, a sub sandwich shop owner tucks a crisp, new $20 bill wrapped in Saran into every one hundredth sub they make. They've built a loyal base of university students who are hoping to hit the jackpot, and at lunch, people jockey for position in line, hoping to be the next lucky customer.

➤ Opportunities to Upgrade

A great guerrilla tactic is to give the customer the opportunity to trade in a "weenie" for a "ham". Many Bernina sewing machine stores will let you bring your new sewing machine back and trade up within six months. Or let your customer upgrade their 27" TV to a plasma HDTV. Dell Computers recently started offering computers that you can upgrade for the next two years.

➤ Contests & Sweepstakes

Why do companies sponsor these silly contests where you have to describe, in 25 Words or Less, why you prefer a particular brand or product? Simple. If someone is going to commit 25 words about your store to paper, it reinforces their brand loyalty. These contests are low cost, easy to organize, and can be repeated over and over again.

Your contest can be as simple as having customers drop a business card in a fishbowl. This is a great way to get names for your mailing list. Or you can involve clubs, schools, or other community groups.

Many appliance dealers organize a drawing during the holiday shopping season for a giant Christmas stocking, 8 feet tall, full of toys (available from NARDA). From Thanksgiving on, they hang this giant stocking from the ceiling, and each customer can fill out a slip for a drawing a few days before Christmas.

Another low-cost but high perceived value alternative is to give Lottery tickets with a qualifying purchase. Imagine the press you'll get if your customer wins the jackpot.

➤ Cause-Related Marketing

Eighty-three percent of consumers said they would pay extra to patronize a business that was environmentally responsible, while 63% said they would pay more to help the US economy. Can you tie your products to an environmental, social, or political cause?

➤ Toll-free Number

People are eight times as likely to call if the number is toll-free, so if your customers are spread across the country or around the globe, this can be an effective weapon. However, guerrillas never advertise their toll-free number in their local market, because shoppers want to know where to find you if they have a problem.

Don't try to spell a word with your toll-free number. The good ones, like 1-800-FLOWERS or 1-800-SOFTWARE are already taken. Customers who hear your toll-free number in an ad will *think* that they'll remember it, but they won't. Better to have a number that they *have* to write down, like ours: 800-247-9145.

➤ Fusion Marketing

Big companies use this guerrilla tactic all the time. You're watching a TV commercial for McDonalds, and then morphs into an ad for Coca Cola, and ends by promoting the latest Disney movie. That's fusion marketing, and guerrilla retailers use it to great advantage.

During the month before Mother's day, A-1 Appliance, in Harvey, Louisiana, gives customers a $15 gift certificate to a local florist with any purchase over $399. They pay very little for the gift certificates, because they're driving traffic to the florist. A-1 does a similar promotion leading up to Father's day, with a gift certificate for the local fish and tackle shop. Of course, everyone upgrades.

They also co-market with a local Cajun restaurant, offering a certificate for a free entrée for two, Monday thru Thursday. The restaurant is happy to sell A-1 these certificates at a substantial discount, because the promotion brings in customers they normally wouldn't have, who also buy appetizers, drinks and desserts.

➤ Success Stories

Confidence is the #1 buying motive, so make your success stories a regular part of your marketing. If the copy feels like you're bragging, preface it with, "Our customers tell us... ." as in, "Our customers tell us that we have the most extensive selection of fabrics in town."

➤ Catalogs

As customers become more and more time impoverished, they are turning to alternatives to getting in the car and driving to a store. Last year, 93% of Americans bought something out of a catalog. You can strengthen your relationship with your customers by putting together a catalog of your most popular items. This catalog does not have to be slick and expensive, but it does have to contain lots of information about your products. If you mail catalogs to past customers, knock yourself out on the cover and the envelope. Catalogs are especially effective for seasonal promotions, and new product introductions.

➤ Customer Mailing List

This is one of the simplest and least expensive marketing weapons available, yet the majority of small retailers don't take advantage of it. Every time a customer writes a check, you have an opportunity to capture them for your mailing list. Simply photocopy the checks before you deposit them, then have a staff member type the information into a computer.

Better still, set up a database that includes information about what they bought and when. This will allow you to target future promotions with the precision of a laser-guided smart bomb.

George Walther, in his book, *Upside Down Marketing,* points out that the majority of businesses market primarily to attract new customers, which is the *least* efficient and the *most* expensive. Then perhaps they get around to marketing to their current customers. And they don't even bother to market to lost customers.

Guerrillas turn this priority list upside-down, marketing first to lost customers. Some of them die, some move away, but the majority of lost customers just drift off. Perhaps they were seduced by the promise of a bargain at a big box, or maybe they had (heaven forbid) a bad experience in your store. Guerrilla retailers will track them down, call them and ask, "What happened? We missed you! What can we do to win your business back?"

Then the guerrilla turns their marketing attention to up-selling, cross-selling and re-selling *existing* customers, because that's where the profits are. Every time a customer returns to your store, you are leveraging the initial investment it took to capture them in the first place. You are collecting dividends on those early investments.

Only then do they pursue new customers. It costs five times as much to create a new customer as it does to sell the same dollar volume to an existing customer.

➤ Prospect Mailing Lists

"Yes, but I'm just getting started. Where do I find potential customers?"

Look in the phone book or on the Internet for List Brokers. These companies compile information on millions of households and businesses. You can buy names, addresses, and even telephone numbers by the thousands, and the price you pay will depend on how you use them. For a single-use set of mailing labels, expect to pay about ten cents a name.

But before you delve into the world of direct mail or teleselling, carefully profile the customers that you already have, by gender, geography, age, interests, and as many other parameters as possible. Give this profile to your list broker and ask them to run a match up. They can then tell you how many names in their database match your customer profile. Market *only* to this subset, and resist the temptation to promote to everyone.

➤ Direct-mail Letters

Direct mail letters are still an effective promotional medium. While 76% of Americans said that they find junk mail annoying, it is a very effective form of marketing communications if it is very precisely targeted. The United States Post Office agrees, ranking direct mail third just behind TV and newspapers in marketing effectiveness. Direct mail generates five percent of U.S. company revenues. Of all sales revenue devoted to marketing, 22% is invested in direct marketing. However the key word is *targeted*, so guerrillas avoid the stock form letter and the mass-mailing list.

Along with its all-important accountability, consider some of the other advantages of direct mail over other advertising media:

- You can more accurately measure results.
- You can be as expansive or concise as you wish.
- You can zero in on almost any target audience.
- You can personalize your marketing like crazy.
- You can expect the highest of all response rates.
- You can use unlimited opportunities for testing.
- You can enjoy repeat sales to proven customers.
- You can compete with, even beat, the giants.

The best list to use is your list of current customers. They will be familiar with your name when they receive your letter and are much more likely to open something from someone they know.

You can easily personalize every letter by using your own computer to insert imbedded variables from the database, like their first name (Dear <<FName>>,) or where they live (. . . this is a special offer for families in <<City>>.)

The most effective sales letters are short and to the point. Limit yours to three paragraphs. Put your *second* most important idea in the first paragraph, your *least* important idea in the second paragraph and your *most* important idea in the third paragraph.

Whether you send a postcard or letter, be sure you work backwards. That means preparing the response device or writing the call to action before you write the actual copy. This way, the copy will be more on target.

Before you write your copy, do a couple hours of research. Ask a handful of your customers to tell you in their own words what they like most about doing business with you. Ask them that way. What they will tell you will be the most important benefits they perceive. Use those benefits to start your letter.

Come up with a really dynamite reason for someone to respond to the letter. Make an extraordinary offer. Find a new and appealing way to bundle together a number of your products or services. Or offer special payment terms. Or an unusual guarantee.

When you start writing, use short words and short sentences. People can't, won't, and don't read long, complicated stuff. Not if they don't have to.

They won't read your letter unless it's EASY to read.

Never start a sentence with a first-person pronoun (I, We, Our). Instead focus on the *benefits* for your customer. You will see greater sales and greater profits when you practice this simple rule. Count the number of you's and your's in the letter. Your letter should have at least *twice* as many you's and your's as I's, we's, me's, our's and your company's name. A ratio of 4 to 1 is even better.

When they read your letter, your customers like it when you talk about their dreams, their problems, and the solutions you can provide.

Stress your main points with underlining or a yellow highlighter.

Whatever you do, *don't* mail it out immediately after you write it. No matter how good a writer you are! Let it sit a day or two. Then, rewrite your letter to make it simpler, clearer and more compelling. After that, read it out loud. Then, show your letter to some customers. If their reaction is that it is interesting or well written, you may have a loser on your hands. A sales letter isn't an essay. It's a sales piece, first and foremost. So, if after reading your letter, your customers say, "How can I get one of those?" then you've got yourself a guerrilla letter.

Check to see if it's clear what you're offering and how a reader can take you up on the offer. One great way to test this is to have a child read your letter. Children often see the obvious that adults, caught up in the more abstract problems and distractions of life, miss.

Include a deadline for action that motivates the recipient to stop in, call, write, fax, or e-mail back to you by a given date. Schedule the action deadline within two weeks of when they will *receive* the letter.

When hard-core guerrillas send a direct mail letter, they invest in first-class postage, but not in a first-class stamp. Instead, they use 11 stamps, a six-center, two four-centers, two three-centers, and six two-centers. That's because hardly anyone has ever received a letter with 11 stamps. They'll notice it. They'll open it. And it will be the first letter they'll open.

Remember that they will also read the envelope. We recently received a big, 9x12 white envelope with big red letters on the outside that said, "This is not a bill." Inside the letter explained, "That was the envelope. *This* is the bill." So we paid it.

Your prospects and customers are bombarded with a blizzard of direct mail. Guerrillas find ways to get through the storm. Now you do, too.

➤ Direct-mail Postcards

One of the most effective, inexpensive, proven and reliable methods of marketing is direct-mail postcards. Every piece of direct mail itself has three goals:

1. To be opened

2. To be read

3. To get the customer to respond

Direct-mail postcards achieve these first two goals automatically. Everyone reads postcards, even the mail carrier. They are amazingly easy to produce and capable of generating a heartwarming response, especially when mailed to your own customer list. Postcards enable you to make a strong offer and be confident it will generate profits.

Your postcard should stand out in some way, with an outstanding design, creative use of colors or with a huge, compelling headline. Be sure it tells recipients exactly how they'll benefit, along with what they are to do: visit your store, look for a particular display, mail something back, or call a toll-free number.

Be brief, but if your offer is enticing, readers will want enough information to buy, so don't be skimpy with the facts. Use your postcard to show something if you can. A dazzling color photo is a superb attention-getting device, especially if it closely relates to your offering.

Want a key thought to remember? Here's one: Don't think in terms of a postcard mailing; think in terms of a *series* of postcard mailings. Still, one-shot mailings do work for retailers.

Open your mind to oversize and full-color postcards. Color increases retention by 57% and inclination to purchase by 41%.

You can also get fancy and have a built-in response device with your postcard, often a smart idea. The costs for double-panel postcards are not prohibitive. Try to use the front of any postcard you mail to entice your readers to read the back. On the back, put your main offer into a headline.

Because of the low cost, simplicity and ease of production, elimination of an envelope, savings on postage, and the opportunity to make an offer instantly, we are very high on postcards. We've seen clients double response rates while cutting mailing costs in half.

You can use color destination postcards next time you're on vacation. Linda and Don Evans were in Orlando taking a break from the kitchen-gadget shop they own in Portland, Oregon. When heavy rain washed out Don's golf game and cooled Linda's plans to lay by the pool and read, they went to the gift shop and picked out a handful of Disney postcards, then sat in their room and addressed them to many of their best customers. "Don't Mickey Mouse around with your next anniversary gift." "You'd be Goofy to shop anywhere else." Years later, customers still remember getting those postcards.

A simple alternative is to print a Four-Up postcard, so named because you fit four of them on one side of an 8 ½ x 11 sheet of card stock. Cut them into individual postcards, apply an address label and a stamp to the blank side and they're ready to mail.

Don't send out all your letters or postcards at once. Do a test mailing and measure the results. Just send out a few dozen, or a few hundred, then do the math and calculate your profits.

➤ Lumpy Packages

Include an item that makes the package "lumpy." No one can resist opening a package that promises a prize inside. Depending on the size and shape of your enclosure, you can send it in bubble pack envelopes, boxes, mailing tubes or regular #10 envelopes. The key is to appeal to your prospect's curiosity and make the package enticing. You can include a variety of items that tie into your theme and your copy. For example:

- A packet of aspirin. "Eliminate your home-improvement headaches with the helpful staff at ABC Hardware."

- A pack of Forget-Me-Not seeds. "Don't forget to change your furnace filter for the winter season."

- A bag of peanuts. "You'll save more than peanuts at our Labor Day Weekend Sale."

- A dog biscuit to announce the grand opening of a pet store; "We'd also like to treat *you* to free hot dogs and ice cream."

- Refrigerator magnets. "Place this magnet on the back of your new (washer, drier, refrigerator, range) and you'll have our number handy if you ever need service."

- A box of matches. "Come by and see all the hot deals we have this weekend."

All of these items are inexpensive and memorable. It is best if you include an item that has your name and phone number imprinted on it.

Never include a food item such as a packet of ketchup that can spoil or leak if the envelope is damaged.

Fellow guerrilla Kyle Poulson, who sells printing, includes an enclosure with his direct mail letters when introducing his firm to new prospects.

"Each enclosure has a theme and each theme is designed to play to the strength of the service I provide. For example, I'll enclose a Nestles *Crunch* chocolate bar, along with a letter encouraging the prospect to call me next time they're in a crunch with a printing project.

"I bought a bunch of eleven-inch Gumby dolls for $1.99 each and enclosed them with a letter around the theme of flexibility and how we are flexible in meeting customers' special printing needs.

"I sent a letter to marketing directors explaining how my services can help them be creative with their printing and enclosed a Mr. Potato Head kit to stimulate their creativity.

"I also have a prospect letter about the advantages of color printing and include a coloring book and a box of Crayola® Crayons. This works especially well with female buyers. Some prospects have called and asked me to come and meet with them, even before I can follow-up by phone to introduce myself.

"The objective is to differentiate myself from other print salespeople who just send out a mass mail letter or just call people on the phone. Typically, the recipient has a good laugh and recognizes my name when I call. A common response is, 'Oh, Kyle, how are you doing?' as if we're already old friends. This warms up the cold call and I get many more appointments. I also get complemented on my ingenuity. I have often heard the response; 'I would not have seen you had it not been for the letter you sent with the gimmick.'"

These tactics are lethally effective.

Kyle continues, "Just today, one of my colleagues set up an appointment with a buyer who had refused to meet with her on at least two previous occasions. She sent out the Crunch candy bar letter and when she called to follow up, the prospect was laughing and ready to meet."

P.S.

While the postscript is the last sentence on the page, it will be the first sentence they read. Guerrillas use it to motivate people to read the rest of the letter.

➤ Birthday Cards

If you take a credit application, you can capture your customers' date of birth and send them a card at the appropriate time. You can save time and money by sending them out in a batch at the first of each month.

If you don't know the correct date, send a birthday card anyway. Everyone will be impressed that you sent it and most will call to say, "Hey, thanks, but my birthday's not until . . ." Then you can add this valuable information to your database and next time, send the card at the right time.

Another variant is to send a birthday on the anniversary of the purchase. "Congratulations! You new TV is a year old. Does it need a new DVD player for its birthday?"

A very successful businessman we know sends a dozen cards a month to clients, customers and suppliers. The card simply says, "Congratulations," over his signature. When asked, he explained that the typical response was, "How did you know?"

"People are always having things happen in their life," he says. "Their son graduates from high school, or they buy a new house, or they get a promotion at work. And everyone craves acknowledgement. It's just that most people don't take the time to do it."

➤ Holiday Cards

It's common for businesses to send greeting cards at Christmas time, and consequently their message gets lost in the shuffle with dozens of other cards. Guerrillas maximize their impact by sending cards for Valentines Day (second largest holiday spend after Christmas) or Halloween (the next largest holiday spend after Valentines Day) or even Groundhogs Day. Retailers depend on holiday spending for up to 50% of their profits each year.

For even greater impact, tie your holiday card mailing into your regular seasonal promotions.

20 Steps to Boost Direct Mail Profits

1. Decide exactly to whom you will be mailing. This is the first step and the most important step. Do this one wrong and nothing else will go right.

2. Decide which specific action you want your reader to take.

3. Create an outer envelope or other packaging for your mailing. Its primary goal is to get people to open it and study the contents.

4. Come up with an offer that your prospects can't possibly ignore.

5. Write a headline and P.S. that compel your prospect to read your letter.

6. Describe your offer in the most enticing terms possible.

7. Explain the results your offer will deliver, the main benefit it provides.

8. Explain why your offer makes so much sense to your prospect.

9. Give your prospect other key benefits of your offer.

10. Show that you know who your prospect is.

11. Describe the key features of what you are offering.

12. Make it irresistible to take action right now.

13. Tell your prospect the exact steps to take.

14. Set measurable goals.

15. Make a plan for your follow-up, either mailing or phoning.

16. Track your results.

17. Improve results by increasing what's working, eliminating what's not.

18. Consider bolstering your direct mail with e-mail, fax, or FedEx.

19. Identify new markets you can tap.

20. Increase your sales and profits with better copywriting throughout.

➤ Newsletters

Why should retailers advertise with newsletters?

Among the reasons are increased sales from current customers, maintaining contact with current customers, adding value to your services, locking down your niche, educating prospects, establishing expertise, saving selling time, spurring word-of-mouth referrals, networking through news, and staying in contact with the press. Two more guerrilla reasons: it's easier and it's less expensive than ever before.

Your newsletter should be 75% giving and 25% selling. By that we mean three-quarters of your copy should be news items about topics of interest to your customers. But a quarter of it should re-sell your store, your service, your reputation, your brand-name lines and your upcoming sale. Customers want to know the news, but they also want to know what's new in your store that they can come buy.

Hausermann's Orchids in Chicago mails out a simple, one page newsletter that includes blurbs from the local orchid societies, when and where they're meeting, and a story about the upcoming guest speakers and programs. They also feature the newest, most exotic plants that just happen to be blooming in the store.

Some retailers actually charge a subscription fee for their newsletter, so they can be a profit center of their own.

The most important benefit of publishing a newsletter is that it establishes you as an authority on your category in your community.

➤ Public Relations

If you pick up your local newspaper, stories about natural disasters, sports scores, weather maps and the stock tables are all legitimate. The rest is planted there by a publicist or PR firm. Guerrillas find multiple ways to take advantage of this extraordinary source of marketing firepower.

Publicity Contacts

Cultivate relationships with the reporters who cover the local beat in your community, particularly the major dailies and the local business newspapers.

Public Service Announcements

Most radio and TV stations reserve a certain amount of airtime for PSA's, but you usually have to be a non-profit to qualify. If you're doing a fund-raiser for the fire department or the local Scout troupe, tell your story here.

Community calendar of events

Similarly, every newspaper publishes a calendar of local events. Include a listing of your classes or workshops. They're free.

Press releases

Send out a press release whenever you have a bit of news to share, even if it's short, to keep your store's name in the news. Remodeling? Adding a new line? Celebrating ten years in business? Announce it.

All-talk radio

There are more than 300 all-talk radio stations in the U.S., broadcasting more than 900 different programs. Collectively, they have tens of thousands of minutes of air-time to fill and they're constantly looking for guests to interview. Call the Executive Producer, or the Host of the shows that your customers might listen to and offer yourself as a guest. You don't even have to go to the radio station; you can do these right over the phone.

Article for Publication

Do you have specialized expertise in a field like gardening, sewing, cooking or setting up stereo equipment? Write a full-length feature article and submit it to your local or regional newspapers or magazines. Your cover letter should offer the publisher "first rights," meaning that they can be the first publication to run your article. But include "All other rights reserved" in the copyright notice. That way, you can print reprints, or run the article elsewhere. Once it has been published, you can send a tear sheet to other publications and offer "reprint rights."

While publications seldom pay for unsolicited material, you *can* negotiate for them to include your photo in the by-line and the phrase, "For more information call…" Include your toll-free number and web-site address in the by-line as well.

Frame an original tear sheet of the article to hang in your store.

Then, print 10,000 reprints, that can be used as an in-store handout, a direct-mail enclosure, or as back matter when submitting new articles.

Column

Once you've established a relationship with the local press corps, suggest a column. Read the targeted publication carefully to make sure that your writing style fits the format and slant of the publication. Then write the first installment and include with it an outline for twelve more installments.

Columns typically run in cycles of thirteen weeks and editors are always looking for fresh ideas. Those deadlines have a way of catching up with you. Doing a weekly column is a big commitment, that pays big dividends.

➤ On-line Websites

There are currently approximately 30 million registered domain names on the Internet. Of those, 35% are public (like Amazon.com) , 29% are private (like the employee-information portal for IBM) and 35% are provisional, either aliases of other domain names, or placeholders for sites not yet built.

According to the Online Computer Library Center (OCLC.org) that works out to 8,712,000 unique web sites. Neilsen.net tells us that there are 580 million Internet users worldwide and of those, 170 million are in the U.S. That works out to about 20 pairs of English-speaking eyeballs per website, or only 67 worldwide.

On-line spending accounts for only three percent of retail sales, but it is growing at a rate of more than 30% each year, as shoppers become more and more comfortable buying on-line.

When asked why they chose to buy in the Internet, on-line shoppers cited *convenience* (65%), availability of vendor *information* (60%), *no pressure* from salespeople (55%) and *saving time* (53%).

➤ On-line E-mail

Of those Americans who have access to the Internet (about half) 85% use the Net daily, and 86% of those use it primarily for e-mail. Considering that you can send tens of thousands of e mails for practically nothing, that makes e-mail one of the most attractive of all marketing weapons.

So many marketers have adopted it that today the Internet is virtually groaning under the load of commercial e-mail, not-so-affectionately referred to as SPAM. According to the London-based consulting firm Black Spider, more than half of all e-mail today is SPAM. Compounding the problem, one in every 128 e-mails contains a virus!

New restrictions enacted by Congress restrict unsolicited e-mail unless you have a pre-existing commercial relationship with the addresses, that is, they are already a customer.

Even still, the LAST thing a guerrilla retailer should do is put together a fancy color HTML page with all their specials and then e-mail it to a list of names. This will not only offend potential customers, but it could get you blacklisted with your ISP.

Don't Trigger the Spam Filter

Software for filtering SPAM is getting more and more sophisticated, so you have to be careful, or your marketing e-mail will be blocked before your customer even sees it.

Here is a list of some 250 words and phrases from two spam filter lists. It is not complete because the porn trigger words have been left out. Most spam filters work on a point system, so that the occurrence of just one "spam phrase" probably won't trigger rejection, except some which the filter considers notorious.

SpamAssassin (a filtering program), for example, assigns default points for these top offenders, as follows:

- Reverses aging   3.37
- 'Hidden' assets   3.28
- stop snoring   3.26
- Free investment   3.19
- Dig up dirt on friends 3.12
- Stock disclaimer statement 3.04
- Multilevel marketing   3.01
- Compare rates   2.83
- Cable converter   2.75
- Removes wrinkles   2.69
- Compete for your business 2.57
- free installation   2.51
- Free grant money   2.50
- Auto email removal   2.36
- Collect child support   2.33
- Free leads   2.29
- Amazing stuff   2.26
- Tells you it's an ad   2.21
- Cash bonus   2.20
- Promise you ...   2.15

- Claims to comply with spam law   2.11
- Search engine listings   2.09
- free preview   2.07
- Credit bureaus   2.03
- No investment   2.01
- Serious cash   2.00

But even if you don't use these notorious phrases, other spam words can add up. Be aware of these in your e-mail newsletters, and ads contained in your newsletters:

Accept credit cards, Act now! Don't hesitate!, Additional income, Addresses on CD, All natural, Amazing, Apply Online, As seen on, Billing address, Auto email removal, Avoid bankruptcy, Be amazed, Be your own boss, Being a member, Big bucks, Billion dollars, Brand new pager, Bulk email, Buy direct, Buying judgments, Cable converter, Call free, Call now, Calling creditors, Cannot be combined with any other offer, Cancel at any time, Can't live without, Cash bonus, Casino, Cell phone, Cents on the dollar, Check or money order, Claims not to be selling anything, Claims to be in accordance with some spam law, Claims to be legal, Claims you are a winner, Click below, Click to remove, Compare rates, Compete for your business, Confidentially on all orders, Congratulations, Consolidate debt and credit, Stop snoring, Special promotion, Copy DVDs, Credit bureaus, Credit card offers, Cures baldness, Dig up dirt on friends, Direct e-mail, Direct marketing, Do it today, Don't delete, Drastically reduced, Earn per week, Eliminate bad credit, E-mail marketing, Expect to earn, Fantastic deal, Fast Viagra delivery, Financial freedom, For instant access, Free access, Free consultation, Free DVD, Free grant money, Free hosting, Free preview, Free quote, Full refund, Get paid, Get started now, Gift certificate, Great offer, Have you been turned down?, Hidden assets, Home employment, Human growth hormone, In accordance with laws, Increase sales, Increase traffic, Join millions of Americans, Laser printer, Limited time only, Long distance phone offer, Lose weight, Lower interest rates, Lower monthly payment, Luxury car, Mass e-mail, Meet singles, Money back, Money making, Month trial offer, More Internet traffic, Mortgage rates, Multi level marketing, MLM, Name brand, New customers only, New domain extensions, Nigerian, No age restrictions, No catch, No claim forms, No cost, No credit check, No fees, No obligation, No purchase necessary, No selling, Off shore, Offer expires, Once in lifetime, One hundred percent free, One time mailing, Online biz opportunity, Pennies a day, Potential earnings, Refinance home, Removal instructions, Removes wrinkles, Requires initial investment, Reverses aging, Risk free, Safeguard notice, Serious cash, Shopping spree, Stock alert, Stock disclaimer statement, Take action now, Talks about hidden charges, Talks about prizes, Terms and conditions, The best rates, This isn't junk, This isn't spam, University diplomas, Unsecured credit/debt, Urgent, Vacation offers, Viagra and other drugs, Wants credit card, Weekend getaway, What are you waiting for?, While supplies last, While you sleep, Why pay more?, Winner, Work at home, You have been selected.

Be aware of these words and phrases and their close variants. Avoid them in your own e-mail copy, so you don't trigger rejection.

➤ Advertising

For the guerrilla retailer, advertising is only 1% of marketing. There are at least 99 other weapons in your arsenal. Of these, advertising is the most expensive and the most misunderstood, so guerrillas always do it last. Advertising doesn't work unless you do all the other things first, and do them right.

➤ Advertising Specialties

Tchotchkes, trash and trinkets, giveaways, logo items, SWAG (stuff we all get at trade shows); the polite term for them is "advertising specialties."

The best advertising specialties for guerrilla retailers are useful items that customers are likely to keep and use. The best example is the Domino's Pizza Refrigerator Magnet. Think about it. Mom comes home after a long day, opens the fridge, nothing to make, closes door, sees magnet, calls Domino's. End of story and everyone lives happily ever after.

We've always wondered about banks. They just don't get it. You're standing at the counter endorsing a check for several thousand dollars, which you are about to entrust to them, and they put their cheap pathetic plastic pen on a chain. Go figure.

If they thought like guerrillas, they'd keep box of imprinted pens under the counter, put them out a dozen at a time, and encourage every customer to take one. Take *two*! You'll think of this bank a *hundred times* before you lose it, break it, or give it to someone else. Pens are useful, but you certainly don't want your name imprinted on a cheap one that doesn't write. Make sure yours reflects the high quality of your store.

Or hotel hangers; don't you HATE it when you check into a hotel room and you're paying $300 a night and they give you those worthless hangers that don't even have a hook. You have to slide them into the stupid little slot in the hanger holder. These hotels are so pre-occupied trying to prevent guests from stealing the hangers that they're missing a marketing opportunity.

A smart hotel would order those nice big, molded, plastic hangers, the ones that keep the shoulders of your suit looking just so, and have them imprinted with their name, address and 800-number.

Then they would encourage every guest to take one for his suit when he packs for his *next* trip. Now when he unpacks, he's reminded what a great stay he had.

The Serrano Hotel in San Francisco puts little wooden puzzles in every guest room, and if you can solve the puzzle during your stay, they'll give you another one. Now that you know the solution, *keep* it. And they don't even bother to imprint them, because they know that you'll keep that puzzle on your desk for the next ten years and think of their unique hotel every time you look at it.

And now hear this! A few weeks after our stay, they mailed us a bottle of private-label Serrano chili sauce. Now we remember that unique hotel with the quirky puzzles every time we open the refrigerator!

Any item that helps your customer do their job makes a great ad specialty. A landscape nursery in Florida provides their contractor customers with a wheel-shaped slide rule that will quickly calculate the correct dilution ratios for all the common pesticides that they use.

Once you know where to start, create an offer that is so irresistible, so compelling and so desirable, that your prospect would be motivated to *do* something to get it. But make your customer *earns* the incentive. She'll have to come to your store to collect it.

There are many items that are worthwhile ad specialties, but the rule of thumb is that it can't appear *too much* like a bribe. Many companies won't allow executives to accept gifts beyond a token value of about $50. So your job is to figure out how to make a token gift have great value.

Autographed merchandise makes a great incentive because of its high perceived value. Offer a baseball, basketball or football signed by a major-league star from your hometown team. Or give them an autographed piece of artwork, a poster, or sculpture, or an autographed book by a favorite author. Autographed works have a high perceived value and are actually fairly easy to get. For sports figures and authors, contact an entertainment agent in your town, tell them what you want and they will get it for you, for a fee. For autographed books, contact the publisher for the author's address and send the author a letter explaining what you want. In return offer to send an honorarium to the author's favorite charity.

In fact, if you order any book or tape from our office, we will autograph it for free. Just call us at 800-247-9145 and ask.

When you give your customers a gift, make it personal. Better yet, have it monogrammed. Guerrillas refuse to give run-of-the mill advertising specialties like coffee mugs as a gift. If it has your company imprint on it, it's a tchotchke, not a present.

People are suckers for kids, especially their *own* kids. Send your customer an age-appropriate gift for their kid and they'll remember you for years. Send them a coffee mug with a *picture* of their kid on it and they'll remember you forever. You can find a vendor at the local mall who will do it in 15 minutes.

> Classified Ads

One of the advantages of classified ads is that they are already or-ganized into categories, and the larger the newspaper, the more categories. This means that your ad is actually *more* likely to be seen by your prospective customer, not less. When shoppers go to the classifieds, they are already pre-qualifying themselves.

Our good friend Bob Rupp (who's store is profiled on page 64) started selling drums out of the trunk of his car more than 20 years ago. His secret weapon was a classified ad. Category: Musical In-struments for Sale – Drums and Percussion. Copy: Rupps Drums. Lowest Prices. Coolest Guys. Holly at Evans. 303-555-1212. Ten words, 10¢ a word, that's $365 a year in advertising. And he has run it every day for 20 years. Today he owns one of the largest professional drum shops in the country.

The same can be said for classified ads in national magazines. Sixty-one percent of readers say they read magazines back-to-front.

The Two Step

Classifieds are actually a great place for the *guerrilla marketing two-step*. This is not a dance like the tango or the foxtrot. In the guerrilla marketing two-step, you run a simple, inexpensive ad and include the tag line, "Call for our free brochure." Interested prospects take the initiative and self-qualify before you send them your expensive collateral.

Our all-time favorite classified, imagine this twenty-four point Helvetica bold headline: **POOP VAN SCOOP**. Eighteen-point sub-head: We Pick Up Where Your Dog Left Off. Twelve-point body copy: #1 in the number two business. Phone number.

This company, started in the early eighties by two starving students at Colorado State University, was so successful, that they have since expanded it into a national franchise.

➤ Yellow Pages Ads

Only advertise in the yellow pages if your customers are likely to look for you there. And if you're going to make that commitment, then also commit to being the biggest ad on the page, even if you're not the biggest store in the category.

Twenty years ago, Robb Candler opened his music store in a closet-sized space in Boulder, with guitars hanging on one wall, and just enough room for a barstool and a cash register. But Rob took our advice and bought a half-page ad under "Music Stores." Today, Robb's Music, at 7,000 square feet, is the biggest music store in Boulder, and he still runs the same half-page ad.

When designing your yellow pages ad, don't waste valuable space. It's not a work of art. People go to the yellow pages for information, so cram as much pertinent information into your ad as possible. Communicate graphically with a map of your location, logos of the brands you carry and icons for the credit cards you accept.

Then, never tell anyone you're in there. If you run a radio campaign that says, "Look for us in the yellow pages," they may find you there all right, along with all of your competitors.

➤ Newspaper Display Ads

These only work if you're in there regularly, at least weekly, so don't blow your budget on a full page spread. Smaller ads that appear consistently will produce better results. The best location for your ad is in the main news section, on the right-hand page, near the margin and above the fold. Most papers will charge a small extra fee for specified placement, but it's worth the investment in improved response.

And this is *very* important: never let the newspaper design your ad. If you do, then your ad will look just like everyone else's ad in the paper.

➤ Newspaper Inserts

Using newspaper inserts, even the smallest retailer looks just as big as the superstores. The high cost of newspaper display ads forces locally owned companies to take out small ads, which may be buried wherever the paper has a few inches to spare. Without prime placement, small black and white ads just don't get noticed.

Color inserts and circulars stand out from the rest of the paper and get noticed quickly. They are thick and beefy, have room for large pictures and product descriptions and can be designed to look unique and distinctive.

Guerrillas often partner with other similar retailers, like those in their buying cooperatives, to split the cost of design and printing their inserts. The real savings comes from printing in large quantities.

Unlike display ads that run in all newspapers that are printed, guerrilla retailers can target the insertion of their inserts so that they are only delivered to those areas of the city closest to their stores.

➤ Magazine Ads

Guerrillas use magazine advertising to enhance their credibility and professionalism. Most national magazines print local editions that reduce the cost.

Magazines are particularly good at enhancing the perceived value of luxury products. Clear colors and glossy paper make pictures look almost life-like. Magazines are good vehicles to place your products in lifestyle vignettes.

After running the ads, mount reprints of them on posters throughout the store noting, "As seen in….." You can also feature these ads in circulars and POP displays.

➤ Radio Commercials

Radio is the most intimate of the mass media, because you're really speaking to an audience of one, usually sitting in the car in drive-time traffic. They won't pull over to write down your phone number or the model number on sale this week. Radio is relatively low-impact advertising. All you want to do is to create an urge to see the products you sell and to come to your store. Keep this in mind when planning your ad, and speak to your customer as if you're sitting right there in the passenger seat. The best radio spots are ones that create pictures in the customer's mind.

Avoid humor in your radio spots, because the joke is only funny the first time you hear it, which disables your most important advertising weapon: repetition.

Radio is an effective medium to target specific demographic groups. Guerrillas choose radio stations carefully based on the audience they are trying to draw into their stores.

It's best to split your radio advertising budget between a couple of radio stations, but the key to its effectiveness is *frequency*. The more often customers hear your name, the more likely they are to remember it. Run your spots a bare minimum of five times a day, four days a week, for at least three consecutive weeks each month.

Producing radio ads is very inexpensive. Guerrillas negotiate to include the cost of production with the cost of their spots.

Radio advertising is fluid and flexible. The best part of radio advertising is the speed at which it can be produced. If you see a competitor's ad in this morning's newspaper, you can beat their offer by noon. Get a new product delivered today and you can advertise it tomorrow.

➤ TV Commercials

TV is the WWF heavyweight of advertising media. Even so, the cost of air time has come down dramatically because of the number of cable and satellite choices now available. Although network television still draws a tremendous number of viewers, cable advertising can be targeted to specific groups, making it much more attractive for the guerrilla retailer.

Although television production costs have come down considerably with new technologies, it's still more expensive than creating a newspaper ad or a radio spot.

Many cable companies sell packages that might include spots on ESPN and CNN, as well as on The Food Network or other popular programming. But don't be lulled into buying a whole lot of cheap overnight spots on channels that no one is going to see.

Like radio, TV advertising is usually priced based on the total number of viewers likely to see the ads. Spots with few viewers are relatively inexpensive compared to prime time ads. In general, you get what you pay for with TV advertising.

The biggest advantage of television is the opportunity to create a multi-dimensional message with great visuals, graphics, movement, music and color. Even in thirty seconds, you can tell a complete story that gets customers drooling to buy your products.

Remember, though, you're competing with Madison Avenue in capturing the TV viewer's attention. It takes a creative, imaginative spot to differentiate yourself on the small screen.

➤ Infomercials

Remember Ron Popiel, the pitchman who sold us useless contraptions like the *Vegematic* and the *Pocket Fisherman*? His contemporary counterpart would be the *George Foreman Lean Mean Grilling Machine.* Entire industries have blossomed from the use of infomercials. With cable companies vying to attract viewers and fill schedules, guerrilla retailers use infomercials more now than ever before.

Fully 55 percent of all Americans report having watched infomercials at some time, and that's only counting the ones who are willing to admit it. Although the number of regular viewers might be smaller, those who do watch infomercials are great consumers. They love the lure of a great sales pitch and are frequently early adopters of new products.

Unlike other media that have some limit to the amount of product or company information that can appear, a ten or fifteen-minute infomercial can be very descriptive. There's plenty of time to talk about all the advantages of buying from you, while fully describing the benefits of your products.

To add credibility to your infomercial, use a well-known local celebrity or newscaster to co-host your program. Interviews and demonstrations are highly effective ways to get your message across to your audience. Your local cable-access studio can save you a bundle on production.

➤ Movie Theaters

In the ten or fifteen minutes before the show starts, guerrillas can have a captive audience at the movies. With their popcorn and Cokes in hand, they sit in the dim light in wild anticipation of the feature presentation, watching the slides or short subjects used to fill the time before the trailers.

Guerrilla retailers can target their message by geography, by selecting theatres nearby, or to specific groups depending on what kind of film is playing. You get a different demographic at an animated Disney feature than you would from the latest Jean-Claude Van Damme action flick. You can target free-spending teens, or families and young children, and find the perfect audiences for electronic gadgets, baby furniture or family restaurants.

Action movies that appeal to young men might be good places to advertise mobile audio products and video games while romantic comedies would be good venues to advertise women's clothing.

Some theaters show still slides, while more and more are running full 30-second spots creating additional opportunities to air commercials that may have originally been produced for TV.

➤ Billboards

They're not for everyone, and usually not for guerrillas. The one exception is if you can apply the "Next Exit" Rule. That is, if the billboard is situated in a location where you can say, "Next Exit" and direct them to your store, then you've got a winner. A liquor store in West Virginia waited for three years for the billboard off the nearby interstate to become available. It cost nearly as much as the lease on their storefront, but it tripled sales overnight.

An "adult toy store" named Secrets leases the billboard right on their own roof to remind customers that they've just found that very special store.

Good billboard messages rely on pictures rather than words for their impact, because you only have about three seconds to tell your story to drivers speeding by. Limit text to fewer than six words to communicate effectively in this medium.

➤ Special Events

In today's "everything's on sale" world, it's difficult for consumers to distinguish one retailer from another. Special events help guerrilla retailers bond with their customers and differentiate their businesses.

Saturn dealers routinely sponsor parking lot barbeques for their new car customers. These outdoor parties are enormously popular, often drawing hundreds of proud Saturn owners.

Jerry Gart was one of the pioneers in event promotion with Gart Brothers' famous Sniagrab® ski sale (that's "bargains" spelled backwards). In the early 1970s, National Geographic magazine featured a picture of the crowd lined up around the block on the Saturday before Labor Day waiting for the sale to open.

Special events can be planned in your store, on the parking lot or offsite. Tent sales produce a circus-like atmosphere, while warehouse sales promote a low-priced discount feeling.

Filene's Basement, in Boston, is famous for its annual bridal dress sale. Hoards of brides practically come to blows for the chance to buy a designer wedding dress for pennies on the dollar. It's not unusual to see a 170 pound girl beaming with her newly-acquired size 6 Priscilla original.

The most important part of event promotions is to follow the theme completely through. For a safari event, dress your sales associates in khaki shorts and pith helmets, and dress the store with rented foliage and life-size plush animals. Make sure your advertising, point of purchase materials and prize giveaways all match the event theme.

➤ POP Aids

If 74% of purchase decisions are made at the point of sale, then using Point of Purchase sales aids are an important part of any guerrillas merchandising mix. These can be as simple as a comparison chart, a graph, or cardboard callouts that explain a product's features. Callouts are especially important on large products like boats or kitchen cabinets. Pages slid into plastic sleeves bound in a ring binder can add structure to a presentation, and help a new sales associate sound like an expert. Comprehension increases 68% if people see and hear your message, so guerrillas combine photographs, computer text, computer graphics, or even video multi-media to tell and sell.

➤ Posters

A picture is worth more than 1,000 words, especially when you blow it up poster size, so say little and show as much as possible. Large format ink-jet printers make creating your own posters simple and relatively inexpensive. Consider B&W or just one color to control costs.

➤ Reputation

Far too many merchants leave this very important task to chance. Guerrilla retailers decide in advance what they want to be known for, then build that reputation into their identity, and feature it in all their marketing. They market consistently, and eliminate unhappy customers, at all costs. More on this in Chapter 19.

➤ Credibility

You only get one chance to make a first impression, so go first class on your stationery, your business cards, your signs, hang tags and collateral. Use professional art and computer typesetting. Any hint of amateurism in your marketing will destroy your credibility.

Develop fusion relationships with respected manufacturers and well known members of your community.

Build celebrity value as well as credibility by publishing a newspaper column, or appearing as an expert on TV and radio.

Take a leadership role in your local Chamber or Downtown Merchants Association. You will always get back more than you put in.

➤ Brand-name Awareness

Brand name awareness is an important business asset. Just ask Coca Cola or Domino's or FedEx. Guerrilla retailers build brand-name awareness in their community three ways: repetition, repetition, and (at the risk of repeating ourselves) repetition.

Repeat your name, your theme line, your location, your holiday specials, and your contests in all your marketing.

Take advantage of the brand-awareness of the manufacturers you sell, from Maytag to Mitsubishi.

➤ Designated Guerrilla

Face it. You didn't decide to open your own store so that you could sit at a desk all day and do marketing, But every business needs someone to ride herd over all the weapons that you use. Make it a key results area for one of your employees, hold them accountable for results and reward them for success, and watch your profits soar.

➤ Competitiveness

Even though there are more than 100 Guerrilla Marketing weapons, most retailers rely on only three or four. Even sophisticated marketers are using perhaps ten or fifteen. Guerrillas use 40 or 50. Half the weapons in this book are free, and the more of them you deploy, the more they reinforce each other and multiply your marketing firepower.

➤ Satisfied Customers

This is the most important marketing tactic in the book. Every satisfied customer is one more weapon in your arsenal. Never let a customer leave your store unhappy.

➤ How to Evaluate the Effectiveness of Your Marketing

John Wanamaker once said, "Half the money I spend on advertising is wasted; the trouble is I don't know which half."

Advertising effectiveness cannot be measured simply by the results in profitable sales. It also must be measured by how effectively it communicates with the consumer and how well it achieves the objectives of the campaign.

Evaluation by sales:

It is appropriate to evaluate an ad campaign by the sales generated, especially for a promotional advertising campaign. This can be done by tracking sales before and after the advertisement and by conducting simple exit interviews (a method which also allows the retailer to gauge the media effectiveness).

Evaluation by image impact:

Image or store brand advertising doesn't have an immediate impact on sales. Instead it seeks to influence consumer attitudes and build a favorable image for the store. One way a retailer can evaluate the effectiveness of this type of advertising is to conduct customer surveys before the campaign begins and then again after it has been in place for a period of time, for example, six months.

It is important for retailers to know whether the advertising they pay precious dollars for is having the desired impact. Stores must clearly define the goal of each advertising campaign and then measure how well the ads achieve that goal.

■ RANKING THE WEAPONS

Your next assignment on your way to becoming a guerrilla retailer is to review this list of marketing tactics and give each of them a letter grade, as follows.

A: I'm using this weapon now, and I'm using it correctly.

B: I'm using this weapon now, but could be improved.

C: I'm not using this weapon now, and I should.

D: This weapon is not appropriate.

When you've finished, go back and add all the As, Bs, and Cs, to question 4 of your Guerrilla Marketing Plan.

Chapter

The Telephone as a Marketing Weapon

■ OLD CUSTOMERS, NEW BUSINESS

Pat is a guerrilla who brokers sailboats in San Diego. He keeps a deck of 3x5 index cards in his pocket. With each customer he serves he explains, "I'm just going to make some notes here so next time we talk, I can offer you this boat at the same price or better, okay?" He writes down the model, the price, serial numbers, and any other pertinent information. He also records the prospect's full name, address, phone number and e-mail.

He maintains a file box of everyone he talks to, and another for every boat he's offered. Then, when an owner drops the asking price, he calls every prospect who has looked at that boat or a similar model, and invites them back to the marina for a second look. Eight out of ten are at the, "Still just looking" stage, but the second look, or the lower price, is often just enough to close the deal.

This broker knows the guerrilla marketing principle that one of the best sources of new customers is your current customers. When he has an especially beautiful boat to sell, he contacts every customer he's sold smaller boats to over the past seven years. Pat knows that sailors will often trade up if they're offered something unique or special.

When the yacht brokerage picked up a new line of small sailboats, Pat rummaged through the shop files, pulling the file-copy invoice for every customer, going back thirteen years. "You will not believe your ears!" he said on the phone as he described the virtues of the new ten-foot Sabot. Many of these customers upgraded their older dinghies to better-quality, safer equipment. The result: he sold more than 100 of them, $150,000 in sales, in three months.

He also routinely follows up on power boat buyers, reminding them when they need to change oil and replace filters. This service-oriented approach makes him memorable and results in considerable referral business.

It's frustrating for the other salespeople in the marina who stand around half the morning waiting for their next up, only to have three or four customers in a row walk in and ask for Pat by name. Of the scores of boat dealers in San Diego selling the same brands, this guerrilla outsells them all. He single handedly produces as much dollar volume as any ten other salespeople combined.

■ PHONE DEMEANOR

Have you ever called a business only to have a harried voice answer abruptly, "Hello, XYZ Company. What the hell do *you* want?" (Well, they don't actually *say* it that way, but that's certainly the way it makes you feel.) The message is clear, they have more important things to do.

Train everyone in your store to answer the telephone correctly. Midas Muffler was experiencing a very high rate of no-shows. Customers would call to make an appointment to bring in their car for service, yet 50% of the appointments never showed up. The problem turned out to be how the phone was being answered. Consider the mechanic, up to his elbows in grease and grime, dropping his wrench, snatching a rag, and then racing to answer the phone on the fifth or sixth ring. No wonder his phone demeanor was less than friendly, enthusiastic, or helpful.

Midas instituted a company-wide training program on telephone courtesy. Employees were not allowed to answer the phone until they had completed the course. The result, their no-show rate fell to just under 17%.

You'll find a raft of constructive suggestions for training your team in the book, *Guerrilla TeleSelling – Unconventional Weapons and Tactics to Sell When You Can't Be There in Person*, by Jay Conrad Levinson, Mark S.A. Smith and Orvel Ray Wilson.

Limit use of HOLD

Retail stores are often busy, demanding environments, so you may frequently have to put the customer on hold while you check availability, pricing, or other information. You should limit the time the customer is left on hold to 20 seconds or less. After that, they start getting impatient and are likely to let their fingers do the walking to the next competitor on the page. Instead, ask for a number where you can call them back in a few minutes. This allows the sales clerk to find the desired information, complete the current transaction and respond to the call in a relaxed friendly way.

Ask Permission

Always ask *permission* before putting a caller on hold. And *wait* until they have a chance to respond. You don't want to treat them to, "Hold please! (Click!!)" Tell them *how long* they can expect to hold. The biggest lie on the phone is, "Would you hold for just a second?" These things *always* take longer than "a second."

People will normally wait about 20 seconds on hold before becoming impatient, *unless* you tell them that "it will be a minute or two," in which case, they will wait up to two minutes.

If they're going to be holding for more than a couple of minutes, offer to call them back instead. "This may take several minutes. Would you like to hold, or is there a convenient number where I can call you right back?"

Company and Name

One evening recently, after traveling to speak at a conference, we were standing at the front desk of the hotel waiting to check in and listened in as the front-desk clerk answered the phone in clipped, heavily accented English, "Itsa cropduster day ud win um hardens odel this is on hold speed king out weigh my hell poo?"

After listening to this greeting three or four times, (and taking a clue from the promo card on the countertop) we finally worked out a translation. The clerk was saying, "It's a Blockbuster day (refer- ring to the free-video-rental-with-room-stay promotion) at Wind- ham Gardens (the name of the hotel). This is Ronald speaking (from his nametag). How may I help you?" Whoever wrote that copy didn't realize what a tongue-twister it was. Just try, just try to say it three times fast, and heaven help the poor customer who didn't have the slightest clue.

Our advice is keep it simple. Let your caller know where they've called and with whom they're speaking. This is the classic, "Furni- ture Fair, this is Debbie."

Never Say it the Same Way Twice

Staff will repeat the same scripted greetings until they become rushed and robotic. Encourage your staff to change the script around from call to call.

"Good morning, Furniture Fair, this is Debbie."

"Hi, this is Debbie at Furniture Fair."

"This is Furniture Fair. My name is Debbie. How may I be of service?"

"Good afternoon. You've reached the central switchboard at Furniture Fair. I'm Debbie. How may I direct your call?"

By changing up the time of day, company name, receptionist's name and the offer to serve, you keep the greeting fresh and natural-sounding, projecting a friendlier, more professional atmosphere for the call.

Tone and Attitude

The tone and attitude projected should be, above all else, friendly and helpful. Put a smile in your voice. It's easier for a prospect to hang up and call the next number in the Rolodex or yellow pages than to put up with a surly service provider.

If this is a concern for you, call your own office and tape-record the conversation, then sit down with the offending individual and play the tape, giving them the benefit of a customer's perspective.

Handling Handoffs

One of the things that drive customers *nuts* is being handed off from one person to another. This is especially true if they've just told their whole story and then have to start all over again with someone else.

In an ideal world, the same person who answers the phone would handle the call all the way through. But things are seldom ideal.

When you do have to hand off a customer, ask permission to put them on hold, get the person you need on the line and bring them up to speed, saving the customer the frustration of telling their story again and again.

International Callers

When speaking with international callers, you may need to really focus your attention. They may speak with an unfamiliar accent, or use words that you don't understand and they could respond differently than you expect. The key is to speak slowly and pronounce your words clearly. Give them time to understand what you're saying. A common mistake is raising your voice, as if shouting would somehow make the message more intelligible. Instead, slow down, rephrase and simplify the sentence. And don't make jokes. Humor seldom translates as intended.

➤ Message on Hold

Consider a custom-recorded on-hold message. You can script it yourself and record it in a professional studio for only a few dollars. Callers given nothing to listen to will hang up after only 22 seconds. If you take this opportunity to tell your story, 85% of on hold callers will listen for two minutes or more. Use this opportunity to answer common questions, like your days and hours of operations, directions to your store or a summary of the lines you sell. You can change your on-hold message periodically to highlight new products or services that you're offering.

➤ Twenty Things that Drive Callers Nuts

If you fervently wish to annoy, alienate and aggravate your customers when they call, here's how:

Just say "No" at the beginning of the sentence.

"Does your store carry Sony?"

"No. We carry Toshiba."

Instead, respond with something, anything, positive. "We carry Toshiba instead, because we've found that it's a better value. The Toshiba products typically offer more features at a lower price."

An obviously canned pitch. Today, people view themselves as being unique and want the products that they buy to reflect that uniqueness. An obviously canned and scripted pitch turns away savvy buyers. Instead, guerrillas ask lots of questions and tell their story only after determining the caller's concerns.

People who don't know the products. Prospects are underwhelmed when they're looking for answers and all they get is, "I don't know." Service Intelligence, a research firm based in Suwanee, Georgia, assigned fifteen mystery shoppers to call six major software companies. Once they got through, they asked a question taken from the FAQs list on the company's web site. In one out of every four calls, the technician gave the wrong answer, or declared the problem unsolvable. Guerrillas know that regular product training creates a competitive edge. Make certain your staff is trained on every department and every product in the store, or can refer the customer to the right person for more details.

"We can't do that." The customer called because they wanted to find out what you *can* do. Sometimes salespeople make matters worse by explaining, at length, *why* they can't do what the customer has asked. Guerrillas will immediately switch the conversation to what they *can* do. "Can I return this and get my money back. I don't have the receipt?" "Well, what I *can* do is give you a

store credit, or exchange the item for any other product in the store."

"You'll have to . . ." As in, "You'll have to talk to my supervisor. You'll have to go to customer service. You'll have to come back tomorrow." Hey, we're all adults and we HATE being told that we HAVE to do anything. You can't make me, you can't make me. Guerrillas avoid this trap by suggesting positive action. "The store manager is the best person to help you with this." Or explain the situation and take responsibility. "We've had a problem with our pressing machine and your dry-cleaning will not be ready until tomorrow. Where can we deliver it?"

Being interrupted. Let customers talk! Men are the worst offenders when speaking to women, frequently interrupting the conversation. Let your prospects complete what they're saying and don't try to second-guess what they'll say next. If you jump ahead, you'll miss important information, details that could mean the difference between you making a sale and your competitor getting the business. This is tough to do when you've heard the same question again and again and already know the answer. Start every conversation as though you have no idea what your customer wants.

Background noise. A friend grouses, "When I hear lots of other people speaking in the background, I know I've just been called by a telemarketing company. I ask, how many other people besides you are there making calls?" When they reply, she counters, "Then there are plenty of other people you can talk to. Good bye." Guerrillas call from a quiet place, because they know that the customer wants to feel like he's the only person in the world that you are calling.

Refusing to end the call. We have no idea why it's popular for companies to end a call with, "Well if you change your mind, call us at 1-800-. . ." And we haven't gotten anyone to admit that it increases sales. Guerrillas know that when the caller has heard enough, they'll either want to buy or want to move on. Keeping customers on the line who are not interested is a waste of your time and it leaves them feeling uncomfortable about your company.

Sloppy pronunciation. There is a psychological connection between the quality of the company and the quality of speech used by that company's representative. Guerrillas know that the deck is stacked against them when they pick up the phone, so they stack the deck in their favor with careful diction and pronunciation.

Continuous throat clearing. Some people have a habit of clearing their throat while others are speaking or just before they speak. This is very distracting and some people think it's rude. Ask your colleagues if you frequently clear your throat. Or listen for throat clearing when you speak. If you have this problem, see your doctor. Continuous throat clearing is also very hard on your voice and it can indicate other problems as well.

Discourteous behavior. "Could-you-hold-please-(click)" is one of the biggest offenders in this category. Others include, "He's out, can he you call back?" and the blunt, "I don't know." Hanging up too soon when the caller has an afterthought is also a turn off. Guerrillas always wait for the caller to hang up before disconnecting.

Guerrillas always assume that the caller can hear them, even if they're on hold. Dave called a store to inquire about a computer part, and during the conversation he had to look some information, so he muted his headset. The sales associate thought he had been put on hold and proceeded to rant to a co-worker about "this idiot on the line," complete with expletives. Dave calmly took note of the whole diatribe, returned and said, "May I speak to your boss please? I just heard what you said about me, I was on mute – not hold, and my goal is to make sure that you never refer to a customer that way again."

Multiple hand offs. Often, callers are transferred to the next department and have to re-explain the situation. When this happens several times in a single call, customers get irate. If they don't get mad, they get even. Guerrillas always *hand off* the phone conversation, preferably in a three-way call, so the customer can hear the hand off procedure.

"Mr. Levinson, I need for you to talk to Lori in the accounting department. With your permission, I'll get her on the line right now, introduce you and fill her in on what's happened. Will that be alright?"

"Sure!"

"Lori, this is Suze. I've got Mr. Levinson on the line with us."

"Hello Mr. Levinson. I'm Lori."

"Let me explain what's happened so far…"

Long, convoluted voicemail menus. One of our clients in the healthcare field found that even four menu choices caused confusion. The reason, when people are ill they can only concentrate on one or two things simultaneously. Guerrillas keep menu systems simple and easy to understand. Never use more than three different levels of menus with three choices at each level.

Being called at a bad time. No one is waiting by the phone, hoping it will ring, wishing it were a salesperson. Seventy percent of all inbound calls interrupt something more important. If you or a sales associate need to call a customer, always begin by asking, "Have I reached you at a good time?" Guerrillas remain sensitive to this and always test if it's a good time to speak before proceeding.

Not taking " no" for an answer. While it's true that on one-shot telemarketing calls, objection responses lifts sales, Guerrillas know that "no" doesn't mean "forever," just "no for now." Use the Guerrilla sales process described in this book and you'll say no before they will.

Free things that aren't really free. With the recent changes in telecommunications law, this is now treading on dangerous territory. Guerrillas never use this tactic.

Make me wrong or stupid. "You *should* have called earlier, before the warrantee expired!" or "That wasn't very *smart* of you!" or "That's *not* our policy." Guerrillas understand the customer's point of view and work to a mutually satisfactory solution. Since one in five dissatisfied customers will tell 20 people about it, make your customer right and smart for buying.

Left on hold forever. It's easier for your caller to hang up and call the next listing in the phone book. Guerrillas check every 20 seconds, because that's the limit of the caller's patience.

That awful music on hold. We called a local car dealer to check on availability of a particular model we were interested in buying. We were placed on hold and found ourselves listening to a local radio station over the phone line. While we waited, we heard an ad for a competing dealer, hung up and called them instead. Guerrillas never let a disk jockey somewhere decide what their customers will hear. Choose a suitable on-hold message, and as a last resort, choose music that reflects the identity of your business.

Automatic HOLD cues. Imagine your customer's frustration when they hear, "Your call will be answered in the order in which it was received. The current wait is . . . seven . . .minutes."

Think about the things that callers do that drive *you* crazy. Ask your staff to do the same, and you'll make sure that you don't drive your callers nuts. Being courteous, knowledgeable and polite to every caller is just the first step. Of course, if you want to drive them crazy, *and* risk a hefty fine, then call when they've asked you not to.

➤ National Do Not Call Registry

Millions of people are declaring their phone numbers off limits to sales pitches by registering their home, business and fax numbers with the national do-not-call list. On October 1, 2003, the FTC began enforcing these requirements. Telemarketers may not make unsolicited calls to numbers in the registry, and of this writing, more than 60 million numbers have been listed. There are about 166 million residential phone numbers in the United States. The numbers remain in the registry for five years.

The registry is intended to block most unwanted telemarketing calls, even though political organizations, charities, telephone surveyors or companies with which you have an existing business relationship are exempt.

What that means for Guerrilla retailers is that you must be aware of the restrictions, and be prepared to demonstrate a pre-existing business relationship through sales or credit records.

The telemarketing industry estimates the do-not-call list could cut its business in half, costing it up to $50 billion in sales each year.

This is good news for Guerrilla retailers, because that's an additional $50 million that consumers will have to spend in your stores.

Of course, your best lists are your past and current customers. You are still free to make calls for the purposes of following up with customers, surveying customer satisfaction, checking on the performance of a product, or conducting market research. If the call really is for the *sole* purpose of conducting a survey, it is not covered. Keep in mind that callers purporting to take a survey, but also offering to sell goods or services, must comply.

Even if your customer has put their number on the registry, you may still call them for up to 18 months after their last purchase or delivery from you, or their last payment to you, unless they ask you not to call again. Also, if a prospect makes an inquiry to you or submits an application, you may call them for up to three months afterwards. However, if the customer specifically asks that you not call them, even if you have an established business relationship, then you must honor their request, or you may be subject to a fine of up to $11,000.

You can read all the details at www.donotcall.gov. If you wish to scrub your call lists (saving time, expense, and not to mention, further annoyance to customers) browse to https://telemarketing.donotcall.gov and subscribe.

Low Cost, High Impact Promotions

How can a guerrilla retailer create buzz and excitement in the community without spending a fortune? By investing time, energy and imagination instead.

All of these guerrillas have won the Pinnacle of Promotion award at the NARDA Institute of Business Management. Read through these true-life examples of award-winning retail promotions, then put on your creative thinking cap and devise your own.

➤ Treasure Chest Key Innovation

Guerrilla: Nodak Supply Co., Fargo, North Dakota.

Cost: $2,952 for printing and mailing to 10,000 customers, prizes were donated by vendors.

Sales: Projected at $100,000 but actually achieved sales of $134,145.

The sudden sales slowdown after the terrorist attacks of September 11, 2001, required Nodak Supply to launch an instant promotion to kick-start sales. This merchant remembered a treasure chest promotion he'd once seen. Short on time to manufacture and mail real treasure chest keys, the dealership sent a perforated picture of a key on a postcard instead. During the four-hour promotion, customers could punch out the picture and exchange it for a real key to the treasure chest.

Vendors and representatives donated a washer, refrigerator, dryer, television and $400 worth of boots, clothing and other prizes. Every customer who made a purchase at the sale won something, from a two-liter bottle of pop to the big prizes from the treasure chest.

This guerrilla was able to produce the promotion piece in only seven days by designing the graphics for the card digitally and then e-mailing them to a printer.

➤ Don't Let Go of the Rope

Guerrilla: Cole's Appliance, Lincoln, Michigan.

Taking a cue from promotions in other industries, Brad Cole developed one reminiscent of the dance contests held in the 1930s. Participants in the "Don't Let Go of the Rope" contest had to hold onto a rope strung across the store's parking lot for as long as possible.

Contestants were chosen from callers to a radio show and received prizes from their sponsors. The store stayed open for the full 68-hour period that it took to declare a winner. Portable outdoor toilets were set up for the contestants to use during short breaks every two hours.

Friends and relatives camped out to cheer on the contestants, and local musicians provided entertainment. Some kind of entertainment or event was going on during the entire time of the contest. Doctors periodically examined participants to ensure they were healthy.

The last person with a hand on the rope won $10,000 in appliances and consumer electronics prizes.

➤ Alaskan Fiesta

Guerrilla: Allen and Petersen Kitchen and Appliance, Anchorage, Alaska.

Cost: $9,360 because $23,627 in co-op funds were offset by $32,987 spent on advertising, which included a remote radio broadcast from the store.

Sales: The first year, sales boosted 28%; the second year, sales for the first quarter rose 11% despite bitter cold temperatures of 20 to 30 degrees below zero.

For the dealership's Mexican Fiesta, store windows and the sales floor were decorated with props from south of the border including sombreros and piñatas.

The promotion included a contest to guess the number of Mexican "Jumping Beans" (which were actually ordinary pinto beans) in a washer and in a freezer. The appliances were awarded to the customer whose guess was closest to the number of beans they actually contained. The washer held 191,846 beans and the freezer 361,845.

The marketing manager who conceived and staged the promotion personally counted the beans into small groups, but only the store manager knew how many groups he put into the units. He wrote down the number and kept it in a sealed envelope in the office safe.

A dishwasher was the prize in another contest during the promotion. Entrants had to submit a form acknowledging that the sales associate had explained the dishwasher's nine major features to them. Manufacturers contributed the appliance prizes. The three winners of the appliances also qualified for a drawing for a $2,500 trip for two to Mexico contributed by a local network television affiliate on which the dealership is a major advertiser.

This promotion won the Pinnacle of Promotion trophy at the North American Retail Dealers Association (NARDA) Institute of Business Management.

➤ Free Furniture Day

Guerrilla: Battleford Furniture, Battleford, Saskatchewan.

Cost: Advertising $25,000; customer refunds $18,000.

Sales: Up 54% for the month, with a 78% increase in net profit.

"Get Your Free Furniture!" shouted television, radio and newspaper ads during this 28-day sale. The full purchase price of all merchandise bought was refunded to those customers who bought products on the day in which total sales were closest to the daily average of the month-long sale. Advertising emphasized that a 1-in-28 chance gives you far better odds than the lottery.

An accountant tallied each day's sales so that not even the owner knew the winning day. All purchases, even special orders, had to be paid for in full before the end of the month for the customer to qualify.

A policy of no refunds was established for furniture purchased during the month of the contest. The free furniture refund excluded taxes, delivery charges and protection plans.

The sales staff let customers credit their purchases to different days during the sale if they did not want to have their purchases reflected on the actual date of purchase. Many customers credited parts of multiple purchases to different days. Some came back and bought more than once during the month to increase their odds of winning.

At the promotion's end, a total of eighteen customers ended up with $18,000 worth of free furniture. The smallest refund was for $39.95 and the largest was $8,000 for four appliances.

The store estimates it was giving away three percent of gross sales with the promotion. By comparison, offering six-months-same-as-cash financing would have cost the store 3.5%.

Business the month after the promotion also ran strong. The successful event enabled Battleford Furniture to increase its sales staff from sixteen to twenty, and won the Pinnacle of Promotion award at the NARDA Institute of Business Management.

Have your attorney check to make sure this promotion complies with local laws. One requirement may be to allow consumers to submit entries to the contest without making a purchase and still participate in the winnings or a drawing for additional prizes.

➤ Race Car Celebration

Guerrilla: T&M Appliance and Electronics, Clinton, Missouri.

Cost: $4,000 with $2,000 of it from co-op advertising, plus $5,000 in prizes given by suppliers. Extra manufacturer participation added an additional $1,000 to the event.

Sales: Up 28% over the previous month.

The NASCAR Celebration raffled rides in a stationary racecar that uses video game technology to simulate operation of the vehicle.

Each hour, T&M raffled off ten rides in the simulator, as well as a washer, stereo system, racing videos, posters and jackets, footballs, baseball caps and other merchandise. Winners had to be present to collect their prizes.

Two local radio stations, one country and one rock-and-roll, broadcast six-hour remotes from the store. Other local merchants donated popcorn, sodas and hot dogs that were given away.

Store signs, radio and newspaper ads and flyers publicized the event. Customers lined up outside for their chance to drive the simulator or win a prize.

➤ Baseball Savings Cards

Guerrilla: Allen & Petersen Kitchen and Appliance, Anchorage, Alaska.

As part of their Grand Slam promotion, customers scratched off a circle on baseball diamond trading cards to reveal how much they won in additional savings off their purchases. They also held drawings for vendor-donated prizes.

The trading card, advertising and point-of-purchase materials looked so professional that customers asked if the dealership was part of a national chain. It's actually a one-store operation.

Scratch cards can be purchased from Geiger West, 10572 Acacia St., Suite 10, Rancho Cucamonga, CA 91730. 909-980-8028

This was the dealership's third win of the NARDA Pinnacle of Promotion award.

➤ Bedding Test

Guerrilla: Mutual Home Stores, Greer, South Carolina.

Cost: Postcard printing, postage, 100 $2 bills, a $100 bill and small gifts for those who return at the end of the month totaling less than $1,500. Postcards mailed to customers with a photo of a $2 bill.

Sales: Bedding sales increased four to five times for the month. Sales in other categories also increased.

Postcards offered a $2 bill to customers and a chance to win a $100 bill for coming in to one of the dealership's stores and taking the Bedding Rest Test.

The test consisted of four questions:

1. What is the size of your present bed?

2. How old is your present bedding?

3. When do you anticipate replacing your present bedding?

4. When you replace your present bedding, what size bedding will you purchase?

Then they asked each customer to lie down on any bedding group on display in the store. At the bottom of the test page, customers filled in their name, address, phone number and the date. This enabled Mutual Home Stores to build a mailing list of potential future bedding customers.

On the last line, customers listed the serial number of the $2 bill they received. They were invited to come back to the store at the end of the month to see if their $2 bill was the winner of the $100 bill.

For the promotion, the dealership obtained several hundred dollars in new $2 bills from its bank. They made a large copy of one of the bills and then shuffled that bill back into the stack.

On the Saturday after the promotion, they posted the large copy of the winning bill in the middle of the showroom. The customer who brought this $2 bill back won the $100 bill.

Of those who took the rest test, 85% returned to see if they had won the $100 bill.

➤ County Fair Exhibit

Guerrilla: Hiscox Maytag HAC, Chesterton, Indiana and Portage, Indiana.

Cost: $4,185 which included rent on a 15x40-foot show booth of $900; $1,500 for advertising; $500 for a 19-cubic-foot refrigerator given away in a drawing; $400 of overtime pay for part-time help and staff; $750 for 5,000 magnets; $925 for 6,000 balloons; $160 for helium; $400 for giveaways of fly swatters; $300 for grandstand ushers' T-shirts; 50% co-op on all costs except small giveaways and T-shirts.

Sales: 180 appliances sold over the course of the promotion

Since 1990, Hiscox Maytag has had a booth at the nine-day Porter County Fair, which is attended by 150,000 people. People who came to the Hiscox booth could register for a drawing for a refrigerator.

Setup for the fair required a full day. Approximately 60 appliances were hauled out to the fair including a small number of closeout products. Every appliance had two price tags. The lower price applied if the customer returned to take the product home at the close of the fair.

Sales were up the whole month after the fair. Even though the dealership's normal retail area is a 30-mile radius, they sold appliances to customers who live as far as 80 miles away.

➤ Half-Time Football Kicks

Guerrilla: Puyallup Valley Appliance, Puyallup, Washington.

Cost: Cash for kicking field goals

Sales: Tripled sales volume in three years

Football is big in Puyallup, so the owners of Puyallup Valley Appliance began sponsoring a half-time football kick at the three local high schools' games. Whoever kicked a 40-yard field goal won $1,000, and a matching $1,000 grant was awarded to the athletic fund of the high school where it occurred.

The half-time contest also rewarded successful amateur kickers $100 for a field goal kicked from the 3-yard line, $200 from the 10-yard line and $300 from the 20-yard line. Eventually, the booster clubs at each high school started selling tickets to participate in the kicks as school fundraisers.

■ DEMONSTRATIONS

➤ In-Store Cooking School

Guerrilla: Baron's Major Appliance and TV, Plaistow, New Hampshire.

Cost: Working appliances

As part of a campaign to reposition the dealership and upgrade its image, Baron's renovated their sales floor and expanded it to include working display models. Baron's also changed its old slogan, "The lowest price or it's free," to "The Demonstration Location," and established a monthly in-store cooking school.

Then they invited local chefs to prepare food at the store for an audience of customers. Some of the first schools were broadcast on cable television. The cooking school was a huge success and attendance for subsequent cooking schools filled up months in advance.

➤ Vendors Demonstrate

Guerrilla: Murdale True Value Hardware, and Murdale Just Ask Rentals, Carbondale, Illinois.

Cost: Less than $4,000, not counting funds from co-op advertising

Sales: More than $90,000 in a single day

For the Great American Home Improvement Sale, more than 40 vendor representatives were in the store to demonstrate their products for customers. Murdale sent letters announcing the promotion to building professionals and preferred customers. They distributed a 28-page advertising insert.

Incentives for customers included a $5 gift certificate that could be used for any item in the store and gift certificates for purchases.

For example, anyone who bought one or more of several specific appliance brands received a $10 gift certificate per appliance toward additional purchases made that day.

Customers bought hot dogs and sodas in the store, with the proceeds going to the local drug prevention program.

➤ Restaurant Wine Tie-In

Guerrilla: Baron's Major Brands, Salem, New Hampshire.

Cost: $8,000, mainly in television advertising

The Baron's stores in Salem, Concord, Plaistow and Laconia, N.H., partnered with top-notch restaurants to give cooking demonstrations for groups of 20 to 25 invited customers seated around the stores' cooking islands.

Working with a distributor and a refrigerator manufacturer, the dealer participated in a joint promotion with the New Hampshire State Liquor Commission, a wine distributor, several wineries and the "Cook's Corner" television show.

Four fully stocked wine storage units valued at $2,750 each were given away in a sweepstakes. Boxes for the sweepstakes drawing were set up in the dealership's four stores, and in the 72 stores run by the New Hampshire State Liquor Commission.

The New Hampshire state liquor stores supported the promotion, called "The Big Chill," with print and television advertising. A They also displayed a fully stocked wine chiller in each of the commission's four stores that had the highest sales of wines. The refrigerator manufacturer donated the wine chillers and the wineries, through a distributor, donated the 46 bottles of wine per cooler. The wineries and the liquor stores provided funds to print ads on cards to fit over the necks of the wine bottles.

Wineries flew executive chefs to New Hampshire to conduct demonstrations and wine tasting in stores. A well-known local restaurant provided food to accompany the wine.

"Cook's Corner" broadcast a segment on the promotion on New Hampshire's largest television station.

The 100,000 entries received from the sweepstakes were put in the Baron's database for future promotions and for appliance demonstrations that included wine and food.

The promotion was not specifically a selling event but rather built an image of quality for the dealership that increases sales year-round.

The promotion garnered attention from the distributor and the manufacturer, who produced a video on the event for other dealers.

➤ Try Out Ranges

Allen & Petersen Kitchen and Appliance, Anchorage, Alaska.

Cost: Demonstrator ranges and $4,000 for a high-capacity gas hookup to feed all the ranges evenly. Manufacturers' co-op funds paid $3,000 of the expenses.

Sales: 41 instead of seven 30-inch, professional-style ranges

Allen & Petersen bought professional-style stainless steel ranges from several different manufacturers and set them side-by-side next to the store's test kitchen. Salespeople ran tests, such as determining which one boiled water most quickly, and which one's burners held heat most evenly in a low simmer.

Then they posted the results of the tests with each range. Customers were encouraged in ads to "come in and test drive" the ranges themselves.

■ SEASONAL

➤ Christmas Tour of Stores Sale

Guerrilla: Bruxvoort's Decorating Center, Pella, Iowa.

Cost: Services or small items for free

The Monday before Thanksgiving, a Christmas tour of festively decorated stores sponsored by the Pella, Iowa, Chamber of Commerce kicked off the holiday shopping season.

Instead of marking down products, Bruxvoort's provided services or small items for free. These included free cords with the purchase of a range or free installation of an over-the-range microwave.

A manufacturer's representative came into the store and demonstrated appliances by cooking a turkey, barbecued ribs, prime rib, steaks, pies and cookies. The cooking demonstrations kept people in the store and demonstrated the capabilities of the manufacturer's products.

➤ Pumpkin Decorating Contest

Guerrilla: T&M Appliance and Electronics, Clinton, Missouri

Cost: $250 for prize money, $95 for 150 pumpkins, $75 for orange flyers and $35 for store decorations such as straw bales.

Sales: 207 units sold, up from the monthly average of 130.

T&M advertised the contest with flyers, gave away 100 pumpkins, and set a three-day period in the week before Halloween for judging by a community group and awarded cash prizes. All the friends and relatives of the entrants came into the store to vote for the award in the People's Choice category.

The town of Clinton only has a population of 1,500. Even so, a total of 500 people came into the store four times: first in early October to get a free pumpkin; they returned on October 26 or 27 with their carved Jack-O-Lantern, and to vote for fellow entries in the People's Choice award.

On October 29, during the Moonlight Madness costume contest and parade on Main Street, customers returned again to pick up their pumpkins.

Some tips are:

- Have flyers printed in September.

- When all the pumpkins are gone, tell customers they may still enter with their own pumpkins.

- Put the finished pumpkins on paper plates while on display in the store because they will leak.

- Start giving away pumpkins early in October. Every day they are in a customer's home reminds them of the store.

- Take promotional flyers to the local library, day care centers and public schools.

- Keep a list of customers who receive pumpkins and those who return them.

- Display the carved pumpkins throughout the store so customers will see all the store's merchandise.

- Coordinate the promotion with other holiday promotions in the community.

- Phone the local newspapers to print photos and stories about the promotion.

➤ St. Patrick's Day Sale

Guerrilla: Nawara Brothers Appliance, Bedding and TV, Grand Rapids, Michigan.

Cost: $500 in savings on purchases; special tickets

Employees dressed in green, Irish music played, appliances carried green price tags and customers drew Lucky 7 chances from a pot of gold.

Admission tickets had a graphic of a pot of gold on them that could be scratched off to reveal up to $500 in savings on purchases. The gold had to be scratched off by a sales associate to qualify.

➤ Women's Night Out

Guerrilla: Longenecker's Hardware Co., Manheim, Pa.

Cost: Snacks, door prizes.

After Thanksgiving, when the husbands take off to go deer hunting, Longenecker's treated the wives to a night out. The local high school football team provides valet parking and a box for contributions to the team.

Longenecker brought in a live choir for holiday entertainment and provided snacks, door prizes and special promotions all evening long. The promotion in this mixed rural and industrial community of 6,000 brought in 200 women.

➤ Free Christmas Bells

Guerrilla: Mutual Home Stores, Greer, South Carolina.

Before Thanksgiving, the dealership mailed out a card saying "Christmas Bells Are Ringing!" and offering a six-inch-tall jade porcelain collector's Christmas bell just for coming into the store. No purchase was necessary.

The front of the card featured the bell decorated with holly and a red bow. Inside, the card folded out to a four-color ad offering sale-priced furniture for the holidays.

The back of the card featured a picture of a nine-inch-tall angel music box that was free with a purchase of $199 or more.

The question, "What special gift do we have for you this Christmas?" was printed on the envelope of the cards. This teaser ensured that the envelope was opened and produced a response rate of up to 35%.

Mutual Home Stores has offered music box premiums every Christmas for so many years that many of their customers now collect them.

Because Mutual buys several thousand music boxes at a time, they cost no more than $12 each, although comparable music boxes sometimes were priced in gift stores at $79.95 retail.

When music boxes were left over after Christmas, Mutual Home kept them behind the counter and on desks where salespeople wrote contracts. Staff members gave them to good customers who expressed an interest.

Mutual Home Stores does a similar promotion every Easter, featuring a lovely Easter bell that customers received free just for coming into the store. Mutual orders the bells by the thousands so they cost substantially less than $1, yet customers perceived the value of the bells at between $5 and $10 each.

Customers who make a purchase before Easter can select an egg from an Easter egg tree in one of the dealership's five stores.

Each egg contains a piece of paper inside with a discount written on it of from ten percent to 50 percent. Their purchase was then discounted by that percentage. The lowest discount actually on the tree was 15%, so all the customers thought they were receiving more than the minimum discount.

➤ Ham or Turkey for the Needy

Guerrilla: Swick TV and Appliance Inc., Coldwater, Michigan.

Cost: Hams and turkeys

Swick TV did a switch on the old free turkey or ham giveaway at Thanksgiving. When a customer bought a new gas or electric range, the dealership donated a ham or turkey to the needy in that customer's name.

■ BUSINESS BUILDERS

➤ Discounts by Weight

Amundson Appliance, Rice Lake, Wisconsin.

Cost: Dollars for pounds

Amundson Appliance built a "Triple-saving Event" around an offer to women for discounts on appliances based on their husbands' weight.

The ad read, "Your husband is worth good money this week at Amundson's. Fix him his favorite big meal, bring him in and put him on our scales. His weight is your discount. We are paying top market price for your husband."

Among the discounts offered by the dealership were 25 cents per pound of husband off on washers, 30 cents per pound off for dishwashers and 50 cents off for refrigerators. A special of $1.25 per pound was offered on white side-by-side refrigerators with ice and water through the doors.

Amundson even arranged to have the local farm reporter broadcast the dealership's "livestock report" on how much "beef" went for the promotion. For the record, the total was 5,948 pounds. The husbands' average weight was 238 pounds. The heaviest customer was 368 pounds.

➤ Spanish Promo

Guerrilla: Welborne's Furniture, Dallas, Texas.

Cost: $100,000 with $45,000 in co-op advertising

Sales: $1.5 million, up from $1.1 million in sales for the comparable two months in the previous year, and exceeding the projected goal by $200,000.

Aimed at Hispanic customers, the eight-week "Mucho Mas Por Mucho Menos" ("A whole lot more for a whole lot less") promotion is held during October and November. Approximately 25 commercials are run weekly on each of two Hispanic television stations and one commercial every hour on four radio stations on four alternating Fridays.

Welborne's Furniture offered free doughnuts, hot dogs, popcorn, ice cream, pizza and mugs with the promotion's theme line. The slogan was echoed on store signs, employee shirts and on gifts for children, including yo-yos, school packs and whistles.

➤ Visit the Store Dog

Guerrilla: Island Appliance, Wilmington, North Carolina.

Cost: Dog food

What started as a cute tag line for a six-week TV campaign turned into a love affair with the owner's "grand dog," a Weimaraner, and spread to all the dealership's advertising. In the commercials, the canine, named Dog, wore a big red bow and was featured with all the products.

Two months after the ads stopped running, customers still came into the store parroting the campaign's tag line, "We're not shopping, we just came to visit the dog." Others insisted they bought products from the dealership because of the dog. The promotion was the dealership's best traffic-builder ever.

➤ Family Photographer

Guerrilla: T&M Appliance and Electronics, Clinton, Missouri.

Cost: Space and order-taking.

Customers love bringing their children to the store when a portrait photographer visits. T&M provides the space and an employee to take orders for photos.

Parents browse through the store while they wait their turn with the photographer, and checked out the merchandise again when they returned to review proofs and order prints.

The photographic studio comes to T&M approximately every three months and always right before the holiday shopping season.

➤ Private-Label Water

Guerrilla: Puyallup Valley Appliance, Puyallup, Washington.

Sales: Tripled sales volume in three years.

Cost: $0 Pays for itself and advertising.

After buying an existing dealership, the owners of Puyallup Valley Appliance realized that they could not afford much advertising. In addition to sponsoring half-time football kicks at the three local high schools, the dealership parked a company truck with banners inside the gates at every game, and sold its private label Daffodil Springs Water.

The high schools' booster clubs requested their own private label water named after the high schools' football teams to sell at the games: *Viking Quencher* for Puyallup High School, *Spartan Splash* for Sumner High School and *Ram Rain* for Roger High School.

The name of Puyallup Valley Appliance appears prominently on every label. Sales of the water average 20 to 30 cases per game. The booster clubs bought the water at 50¢ a bottle, but the dealership's bulk rate was 35¢ a bottle. This profit paid for advertising the dealership.

➤ Discount Program for Condo Owners

Edmonds Appliance Centre, Burnaby, British Columbia

Cost: $25,000 printing and distributing promotional materials fully reimbursed by co-op funds.

Sales: $170,000 in the first year; goal was $250,000 annually

Most condominium owners belong to the Condominium Home-owners Association (CHOA) of British Columbia through their management companies. This enabled the dealership to create an exclusive discount program for the condominium owners.

An impressive, full-color brochure presented to CHOA used a question-and-answer format. It explained that because the management company of that particular condominium belonged to CHOA, all members were entitled to the CHOA/Edmonds' bulk purchase program, which offered prices 5% to 10% lower than Edmonds' best sale pricing.

Each brochure contained an individualized membership card in the CHOA discount program that was printed on a magnetic backing to stick on each customer's refrigerator until she needed a new appliance.

The brochure explained that the card only could be used by individuals who were members of that homeowners association, not by their friends or relatives. On the back of the brochure was a map to the store, the brands carried, store hours and an invitation to Kidsville, where customers' children could amuse themselves while their parents shopped.

Mailings totaling approximately 35,000 pieces were delivered to more than 400 different condo developments.

➤ Mattress Trial

Home Appliance, Shelby, Ohio.

Cost: $1 per customer.

To alert customers that this Radio Shack dealership had added mattresses to its product mix, customers were offered money to try out the mattresses.

When a customer entered the store, a salesperson approached the customer and offered him or her a dollar coin to try one of the mattresses. As potential customers explored the display and tested for the perfect mattress, the salesperson discussed the mattress's features and benefits.

Approximately 75% of the customers took the dollar and tried out the new mattresses. They could not believe they were being given money to lie down. An estimated 60 to 70% of these customers bought mattresses.

➤ But Wait, There's More!

Obviously we could go on for pages and pages. We have so many more stories to tell, like the spa dealer who put a working hot tub, complete with bikini-clad models (actually, the store's sales team) and plastic palm trees on the back of a rented flatbed truck and entered it as a float in the Fourth-of-July parade.

Then there's the Seattle sporting goods store that sponsored a tree sitter for two years, eventually saving a swath of old-growth forest from logging and driving home their concern for the environment.

But the best examples are to be found in your own community, right there under your nose. A guerrilla retailer considers every shopping trip a reconnaissance mission (like you needed another excuse to go shopping!) And here's a guerrilla tip you can take to the bank: pay close attention to the *fun factor*. The more *fun* the promotion is, for your customers and for your sales team, the more effective it will be.

Watch for creative promotions in your own community, and look for ways to adapt these ideas, amp them up, expand them, adapt them, and partner with your suppliers and your community to make them happen.

Chapter

Attracting the Right Staff

■ PEOPLE ARE YOUR GREATEST ASSET

A great location, a great name, great merchandise, great display and great promotion can all be undone by less-than-great people. Your staff is the most expensive item in your budget, and the most important investment you'll make in your business.

The most universal complaint we hear from business owners is, "We just can't find good people." Well, let us encourage you. They're out there. Your mission is to track them down and then persuade them to defect to your team.

From their sales associates to their cashiers, bookkeepers and delivery people, guerrillas know that their team is the keystone that holds their business together. They put the same effort into recruiting a stock clerk as they do when hiring a merchandising manager. Although the specific example we'll illustrate here refers to sales guerrillas, these techniques will work to help you hire the cream of the crop for any position.

■ RECRUITING AND HIRING SALES GUERRILLAS

Because the best predictor of future sales behavior is current sales behavior, guerrillas are always on the hunt for good people. You'll find them serving you in restaurants, shops, hotels, spas, museums and cafes. Whenever someone really impresses you with their sales and customer service skills, ask for their name and number. Let them know that, while you may not have an opening right now, you're *always looking for good people,* and you'd like to have permission to call them if something opens up. This way, you'll always have a backlog of qualified candidates.

This is also a good reason to regularly shop your competitors. We know it sounds a bit mercenary, but you would be appalled at how poorly some employers treat their best people. When you hire away one of their best, you win *twice*, because you gain a skilled employee at your competitor's expense.

If you have to resort to the traditional classified ad, this guerrilla approach to screening sales applicants will give you an opportunity to *observe their sales skills* before putting them on the retail floor. By seeing how well they *sell themselves to you*, you can predict with remarkable accuracy how effective they will be at selling others.

Set Up Voice Mail

Arrange with the telephone company to set up a dedicated number for you that rings into a DDE (direct-dial extension) equipped with voice mail. You will only use this number when you need to recruit salespeople.

Run your classified ad outlining the basic qualifications for the job, but do not mention the name of the company. You do not want people dropping in or mailing you their resumes. The last sentence of the ad closes with the language, "To schedule an interview call (phone number)."

Put an outbound recording on the voice mail that says, "Due to the overwhelming response to our ad, we have had to automate our screening process. At the tone, please leave the following information: your name, your daytime and evening phone numbers, a brief summary of your qualifications and why you think you would be a good candidate for this job. If your background meets our requirements, you will be contacted for an interview." (BEEEEP).

Let the add run for a week or two and every few days, dial in to your DDE to check the voice mail. Keep in mind that the outbound recording was intended to *discourage* callers from taking the next step because of the "overwhelming response." Job-hunters who give up at this point are not good candidates for your business, so we eliminate the quitters right up front. Those who do leave a message are more likely to take initiative and follow through with your customers.

First listen to the voice. Is it warm? Friendly? Intelligent? Is this the voice of someone who you would feel comfortable representing your firm? If so, save the message. If not, delete it.

Did They Follow Directions?

Once you have narrowed the field, listen to the messages a second time with a pen and legal pad in front of you. How well did each candidate follow the specific directions they were given in the outbound recording? This will be an accurate predictor of how well he will follow your directions in the future. Did she state her name clearly? Did she spell it if the spelling would be in doubt. Did she next give you her contact phone numbers and *volunteer a best time to call*? Did he summarize his skills and experience (benefits) or just read you his resume (features)? Most important, did he close with some sort of call to action, "asking for the order."

Situational Interviewing

Call back the ones who pass this litmus test, and conduct your initial interview by phone. What you *hear* is what you'll get, so listen carefully to each candidate from the perspective of one of your customers. Open with the question, "Tell me about yourself?" Confirm that she has the requisite experience by asking questions along the lines of, "Tell me about a situation where you..." (dealt with some particular challenge or situation they are likely to encounter in your employ.) Watch for her to try to take control of the interview (any good salesperson will) and start asking *you* questions.

Ask for a Resume

By now you should be able to make a decision. Is this someone you think you would like to hire? If so, they must pass one more test, "The FAX Test."

Ask, "Could you please FAX me a copy of your resume? Yes, right *now*." You will get one of two answers. Either she will stall and apologize and make excuses ("My resume isn't really current and it's late and I don't have access to a fax machine," etc.) or she will say, "Sure. I can do that!" *That's* the response we would expect *our* salespeople to offer a customer in need. Then check the time/date stamp on the fax and calculate how long it took her to get it to you. More than a couple of hours is too long.

You can reasonably ignore the resume, *except for the references.* Call each reference and ask, "Tell me about your experience with Mr. Larsen...." If the references check out, call the applicant back and invite him in for a face-to-face interview. By now you should have already decided that you would like to hire this person, or don't bother with the interview.

Ask Them to Fill out an Application

Before you start the face-to-face interview, ask him to complete a job application form. This makes sure you get the same information from every applicant and covers you from certain EEOC liabilities. Can he follow directions? How is his penmanship? Will he be able to write price tags and thank-you notes? This is also an informal test of his reading skills.

Is the information provided on the Application the same as that listed in her resume, or did she invent a new high school? This gives you a quick test of the validity of the information.

Does the Candidate Sell You?

An interview is like a blind date. In some cases, that's as good as it gets. Too often, managers interview by just reading back the information that the applicant put on the resume. After hiring, they sit back and say, "gee, he sure is quiet." Well, no wonder! That same manager did all of the talking during the first meeting.

Ask open-ended questions like these to find out what kind of person you'll really get.

➤ Interview Agenda

What to Ask	What You'll Learn
Getting Acquainted	Appearance
	Poise
	Self-Confidence
Past Work Experience	
Favorite and least favorite	Organizational skills
supervisors? Subordinates?	Relevance of work
Favorite approach to learning?	Work ethic
Major accomplishments?	Skill and competence
How were they achieved?	Productivity
	Sense of urgency
Most difficult problems faced?	Adaptability
How did you handle it?	Motivation
Ways most effective with	Interpersonal relations
people? Ways less effective?	Leadership
Level of earnings?	Commitment
Performance relative to peers?	
What looking for in job?	Decision making skills
In career?	Problem solving ability
Education	
Subjects liked most?	Relevance of schooling
Liked least?	Tenacity
Level of grades?	Intellectual abilities
Effort required?	Versatility
Special achievements?	Depth of knowledge
Toughest problems?	Goal orientation
Role in extracurricular	Motivation
activities?	Reaction to authority

What to Ask	**What You'll Learn**
How financed education?	Leadership
Relation of education to career?	Initiative
Consider further schooling?	Teamwork
Able to set and accomplish	Time management skills
goals?	Organizational skills
	Maturity
	Management of time,
	energy, money.

Activities

Things like to do in spare time?	Diversity of interests
Extent involved in community?	Intellectual growth
Individual or group activities?	Social skills
Role played in organization?	Leadership qualities
	Basic values and goals

Strengths

What contributions to job?	Creativity
What are your assets? Talents?	Talents
What makes you good investment	Skills
for an employer?	Knowledge
	Energy
	Motivation

Areas for Improvement

What areas need improvement?	Honesty, self-awareness
What qualities wish to develop	Social effectiveness
further?	Character
What constructive criticism	Goal attainment
from others?	Realistic self-perception
What further training or experience,	Realistic career goals
might you need?	

During the face-to-face interview, your primary objective is to *listen* to the candidate. Once you've decided that you've got a winner, sell *him* the job and get him excited about the possibility of working in your store. Give them the tour. Introduce them to other key people on the team.

Finally, after meeting all the finalists, make an offer to your favorite candidate(s).

Each of these hurdles is designed to give your candidates an opportunity to *sell themselves to you* as a potential employee. It is this sales *behavior* more than any other factor that is the best predictor of their future success.

Managing Turnover

Every day, nearly 80,000 people start a new job. Although it can cost as much as $6,000 to hire and train each new team member, less than half stay more than seven years. Just when they become the most valuable, they're gone. Poof! There goes your investment in training and motivation, their skills and knowledge, and now you're back to finding the right person for the job again.

Many leave because they were never made to feel welcome in the first place. Developing an orientation program helps new staff members understand the company culture, and provides them the skills and tools they need for the job.

Training significantly reduces turnover. People 'want to learn. On-going training opportunities keep employees at the top of their game and ensure that they continue to improve their skills.

Clear-cut job descriptions that outline the duties, responsibilities and expectations of the position also help reduce turnover. Team members who know what their jobs are can do them well and be successful.

In his book, *First Break All The Rules*, Marcus Buckingham writes about the characteristics that most affect job performance and tenure. One of the most important, he discovered, was having a *best friend* at work, not just a collegial relationship, but a best buddy that team members seek out to spend time with after work.

Creating a climate that fosters that kind of friendship may be the most important thing in reducing turnover. Guerrillas provide plenty of opportunities for team members to play together.

At The Guerrilla Group, for instance, most of our team members play some sort of musical instrument. It's not uncommon for us to stage an unplanned jam session to celebrate things like Wild Wednesday or Maddening Monday. We've built a dedicated studio, with professional PA gear, double DJ turntables, a V-drum kit, MIDI keyboards, sequencers, and a computerized mixing and recording console. The music flows and everybody rocks. Together.

Chapter

11

How to Train and Motivate the Sales Team

We hear this argument from retailers all the time, "I can't afford to invest in sales training for my staff. What if I train them and they leave?"

Well, what if you *don't* train them and they *stay*?

Training your sales team is one of the best investments you can make, because it will pay dividends for the rest of the year. If you have a staff of ten or more, consider using a professional sales trainer. Your staff is much more likely to listen to an outside expert and even the expensive ones are a bargain. The Container Store invests 235 hours of formal training in every first-year employee, vs. the industry average of only seven hours. Turnover is only 8% among full-time employees and only 20% for part-time. Compare that to the average retail turnover of 120%.

Retailers often overlook a free and readily available source of sales training, your suppliers. These are full-time sales professionals, after all, who already know about the product. Ask them, as a condition of taking your order, to volunteer once a month to come in and do a one-hour, pre-opening sales meeting on their products. The up side for them is that salespeople tend to sell the products with which they're most familiar. The more they know about a particular line, the faster it will move. That means more volume and more market share for your supplier.

Routinely quiz your people on your products and reward them for superior knowledge. Financial incentives will encourage them to study. Pay a $10 spiff to anyone who gets a perfect score on the test.

Build a corporate library of sales training materials, including books, tapes, videos and audio CDs. Make these available to your people on a library basis and they'll take them home and study them on their own time. In some stores, it may be appropriate to build a master catalogue of product manuals for ready reference. When a customer asks a question about a product that the sales clerk can't answer, instead of saying "I don't know," they can say, "Great question. Let's look it up." Now they can present technical features right off the spec sheet or owner's manual. Your investment is minimal and reusable.

Bookmark all of your suppliers' websites on a computer that's easily accessible to your sales associates so that they can easily find product specifications and information. Also, use the web to gain access to information about competitive products that you don't sell so you can quickly show customers the advantages of your merchandise.

Never let your salespeople practice their new sales techniques on customers. It's just too costly and too dangerous. Let them practice on you, or better still, on each other.

Video Role-Play

A simple and very effective method is video role-play. Selling is a behavioral skill, like skiing or hitting a tennis ball and seeing yourself on TV is an eye-opening experience. A video camera can expose subtleties of sales-killing body language or voice tones that may not be obvious from casual observation. Set up a simple role-play, with one staffer playing the customer and agree on the customers' issues, concerns, budget, or objections in advance. Type up a short character sketch on a 3x5 card and hand it to the "customer," so that the "salesperson" is going into the situation cold, just as they would with a real customer. Then roll the camera, while the rest of the team stands back and watches *quietly*. There should be *no* commentary until the playback.

There are some important rules to follow when viewing the playback. Remember that people are more fragile than tropical fish and this can be a very stressful experience for them. That's why most salespeople *hate* doing role-play. It's awkward and potentially embarrassing, particularly if their co-workers use this opportunity to cut up or take pot shots. Scenarios should be kept short and realistic, focusing on one particular skill at a time: greeting, qualifying, presenting, summarizing, accessorizing, or closing. Players are required to stay absolutely in character at all times. Warn them that this is not a game, and that they're up next. Let the presentation run for not more than three or four minutes, then rewind and review.

During playback and this is *very* important, ignore *all* mistakes. People tend to be over-critical of their performance when watching themselves on camera, so you don't need to reinforce the negative. Instead, use the pause button on the remote to stop and comment only on the things they do right. Likewise, in discussion of alternatives, colleagues are only allowed to comment on what they liked about the transaction and avoid, "Well what I would have done is. . ." suggestions. Instead, let them demonstrate by example when it's their turn in front of the camera.

Another effective training technique is the Tag Team. Set up your new salesperson to "shadow" one of your star veterans and take turns serving customers while the other looks on and listens without speaking. After each customer, they debrief the exchange, make suggestions, then reverse roles.

Guerrilla retailers can also produce accelerated training success by pairing salespeople into teams. Each agrees to split all their sales (and commissions) with a partner and they work together to serve customers. One might pull the product out of stock while the other writes up the paperwork. They cover for each other on days off, and if one is working a customer and the chemistry isn't working, he can hand them off to his partner, whose personality may be more compatible. This works especially well for resolving rivalries between star salespeople, putting their competitive energies into constructive behavior that increases sales and sets an example for the rest of the staff.

Building Enthusiasm

It starts with real quality and genuine value. Sales associates get excited about products when they understand and appreciate how the customer benefits.

Schedule regular staff meetings to review each employees' successes for the previous week. Cover new products and promotions.

Look for opportunities to celebrate as well. This includes staff birthdays or other special events, as well as record sales days, weeks, or months.

Information is also a great enthusiasm builder. Think of a subject about which you know little or nothing, like bee keeping or exploring caves. Even though they don't sound very exciting, there are hundreds of people who are enthusiastic about these same activities. When you talk to them about their interests, their enthusiasm is contagious. Caught up in their excitement, you listen with interest to stories about how the queen bee signals her daughters or how the dripping water deposits stalactites, stalagmites and flowstone curtains in a cave.

To warm up to any product or service, you must first gather information. You will gain confidence and enthusiasm by learning how the product works and how to use it. Study until you become an expert. Learn as much as you can about every aspect of your product, your competitors' product and any other product that could be substituted for yours. Learn about every possible application of your product and every kind of customer that uses it. This expertise will make you more enthusiastic, more confident and more anxious to tell others. It also makes you more interesting to talk to and more fun to do business with. Enthusiasm is the bunker that protects you from the depression that can come with occasional failure.

McGuckin Hardware stocks 128,000 SKU's, enough to keep an army of stockers busy every night. Instead, every employee, all the way up to the GM, spends one day a week stocking shelves. The result, you can ask anyone where to find anything and they actually know. Imagine that!

Study professional selling! Doing something well is always a lot more fun than doing it badly. Think about how much you enjoyed being triumphant on the tennis court or golf course. Remember the rush of elation when you climbed a mountain, ran a rapid in a river kayak, or had a story published in the newspaper. What ever you do, the better you are, the more fun it is.

Warm up to your customers in the same way, by getting to know them. They will be much more likely to take an interest in you and your proposition when you show sincere interest in them.

➤ Create Your Own Training Programs

There are a number of experts available who can train your sales staff and even the expensive ones are a bargain. Expert retail sales training is always a worthwhile investment and you'll see it paying dividends right away. But you can also create your own training program. The most effective format is short, regular and structured around a specific product line or sales technique. Consider having everyone come in an hour early before opening on Saturday, or one evening a week. Invite your suppliers to come in *regularly* to talk about their new items and trends they see in their line.

1. Set clear instructional objectives. What's your goal for the session? What skills do you want your trainees to learn? What behaviors do you want them to change?

2. Assemble information that supports your goals. Eighty-five percent of retailers don't have clear selling plans. So be careful about using training sources that just *report* what the majority of retailers do. Focus on those sources that *recommend new ideas* that will work for you.

3. A great way to change negative selling behavior is to ask your sales staff to think back to the last time they went shopping and discuss behaviors that they wouldn't want to see in their own store. All the no-nos will come out. Write down the answers on a flip chart. Get the staff to commit to avoid doing these things. Since the list of what is and what is not acceptable came from the sales staff, personal pride and peer pressure will help change behavior.

4. After introducing new sales tools, have your staff role-play customer scenarios. Write an imaginary customer's name on the front of a standard sticky-label name badge. On the back, write the character's personality, buying style, some brief information about needs and wants and so on. Create a variety of customers, buying styles, objections and so forth. Hand these badges out at random and have your people role-play custom-

ers and sales associate in round-robin fashion. After the role-play, ask for comments on what went well and what they could improve.

5. Better still, videotape the role-plays, then review them as a group, using the remote control to freeze-frame the tape and point out every time you see a member of the sales staff doing something *right*. And this is *very* important; do not comment on the negatives; people will pick them out for themselves and dissecting the sale in front of peers only makes everyone uncomfortable.

6. Wire your stars. Have your most effective salespeople wear a wireless microphone or simply carry a micro cassette recorder so you can record their conversations as they're working the floor. Have these tapes transcribed into a word processor and then edit the resulting files into scripts. Train your new hires to use the same effective phrases and questions that your superstars use.

Just as you would never let a theatre troupe rehearse in front of the audience, never let sales associates practice new techniques on customers until they have practiced them backstage with each other.

➤ How to Select a Professional Sales Trainer for Your Team

Content

A professional sales trainer should educate, motivate and entertain and in that priority. Unless this event changes your sales associates' behavior in some measurable way, you're wasting their time and your money. New skills, new information and new insights produce new customers, new sales and increased profits for your business.

Authority

Wouldn't you rather take advice from a published expert, who has invested the time and effort to thoroughly research his field and written a book, or two, or three? Ask for autographed copies.

Originality

Beginners often pirate other speakers' examples and content, sometimes even telling a story as if it had actually happened to them. I recently heard a meeting planner complain, "If I hear the 'starfish' story one more time I will *scream!*" If you've heard it before, so have your people.

Delivery

Are you looking for a topical expert (who may put your people to sleep) or a stand-up comic (who's act could play a nightclub)? Look for a pro who can engage *and* entertain, delivering powerful content with passion and pizzazz. After all, you want your people to remember the *point*, not just the punch line.

Customization

If a trainer is going to presume to tell you how to run your business better, she better understand your business. Select a speaker who will take a *personal* interest in your industry, your store and your people. Will she visit your office, review your collateral, shop your competition, or spend a day mystery shopping your salespeople? Will she fly in early to attend the *whole* meeting? An outsider's insight may prove priceless. A real pro is a quick study and will customize until she sounds like she's from home office.

Certification

There are two certifications recognized worldwide by the speaking profession: the Certified Speaking Professional (CSP) and the Council of Peers Award of Excellence (CPAE). The CPAE is an *honorary* designation, a lifetime achievement award, while the CSP requires a minimum of 250 presentations over a five-year period, for at least 100 *different* clients, at a substantial minimum fee and must be renewed every five years. The CSP is your assurance of the *highest* standards of professionalism and excellence.

Technical Mastery

The days when a speaker could stand behind a podium and just read from notes are long gone. Top pros supercharge their training with multiple multi-media tools: computer animation, upbeat music, sound effects and video. And they bring their own computers, projectors and microphones. After all, when you take your car to a mechanic, don't you expect them to own their own tools?

Access

Does a live person answer the phone when you call? Successful trainers travel constantly, but are always accessible through their staffs. They use cell phones, voice-mail and e-mail to keep in touch. The real pros check both at least twice a day and respond promptly, personally.

Video

They *did* include a video didn't they? The pros all have at least one; or two, or more. Ask for the what-you-see-is-what-you-get (WYSIWYG) version, shot live and *unedited* (except perhaps for opening trailers). And while the WYSIWYG version may be technically flawed, anyone can look good in front of a studio full of friends and family.

Audition

Are they coming to your area? The pros get around and will gladly arrange for you to sit in. If that's not an option, interview them by phone. Think of it as a live one-on-one audition. Ask them to advise you on a particular business challenge or issue, then ask yourself, "Does this sound like the kind of advice we want our people to hear?"

References

You should never have to ask for them. A professional will automatically include them in the press kit, along with a client list and multiple testimonials. Read the letters. Look at the dates. Are they current? Then call at least two.

Deliverables

What will your people take away to help them recall and implement what they've learned? Extras, such as a textbook, a workbook, a CD or two, an action list, a checklist, a laminated wallet card, or a free web e-zine add major impact and multiply the take-home value of the message. Ask about them.

Fees

Worry less on what the speaker will charge; worry more on what your people will get. Does the fee include pre-event consultation, research, customization, travel time, travel expenses, handouts, workbooks, AV equipment, pens, markers or other supplies? A bad program is no bargain.

➤ Performance-based Compensation Strategies

Michael LeBeouf, in his book *The Greatest Management Principle in the World*, contends that, "Any behavior which gets rewarded will tend to be repeated." He advocates paying close attention to how employees get rewarded for performing (or *not* performing) the various aspects of their job.

Incentive, or *performance-based* compensation, is nothing new. Commission plans for salespeople are common because their productivity is so easy to document. But small businesses tend to eschew these compensation plans thinking that "we're mom & pop. We're different." In the competitive environment you're faced with today, you have no choice. You *must* use every management tool available to maximize your marketing firepower.

Jack Welsh, the legendary former CEO of General Electric, believed in what he called the "20-70-10 Rule." That is, twenty percent of your people are the superstars, the real performers, who give it their all and produce outstanding results. These are the people who become the strategic leaders and decision-makers, supervisors, managers, or department heads. Seventy percent of your people are the worker bees who do what needs to be done each day. They are good people who do a good job; they're just not leaders. Some of these people in the seventy-percent category eventually rise to greater heights over time, as they accumulate skills and experience. Likewise, people in the top twenty percent can lose their spark and slip back into mediocre performance. Then, Jack believed, there is a group in the bottom ten percent of the organization that will never really even come up to par. Perhaps they don't have the necessary skills, motivation or desire. He felt he owed them the opportunity to be successful, somewhere else. So he actively looked for opportunities to weed out his non-performers. That's why there was always opportunity at GE, they were always hiring.

Guerrillas are not only intolerant of non-performers, but they lavishly *reward* their stars, setting a higher standard of excellence for the whole organization. The problem is how to reward your people *appropriately*, particularly if they're *not* directly responsible for easy-to-measure activities like sales revenue.

Some simple guidelines can put this powerful management tool to work for you. The foundation of an effective performance-based compensation plan is a set of *clear and specific* goals for your organization as a whole, for each functional department and for each individual employee. These goals must be *objective* and *quantifiable.* For example, "Increase walk-in traffic by ten percent or to 650 per month by the end of the year." or, "Achieve an average rating of 4.5 of 5 on monthly customer satisfaction surveys." Subjective factors, like attitude or good work habits may be included in review criteria but if you can't measure them statistically, you can't use them as a standard for performance-based compensation. Then devise methods for *gathering data* to measure progress (or lack of it) toward these goals. What you measure is what you get, so inspect what you expect.

Salary

The advantage is that it's easy to calculate, punch in, punch out, so much per hour. The disadvantage is that it doesn't motivate people to perform.

Commission

Commissions can be computed on the gross sale price (good), or the gross profit margin (better).

One important factor to consider when designing a compensation plan is that it must be simple. Paying commissions on straight gross sales is easy, and if you put the table in fig. 11-1 up on the wall in the break room, everyone can quickly estimate what they're earning, given the overall gross margin of the store.

Should you really pay no commission on gross margins below 13%? Absolutely. If your sales staff is selling at less than 13% margin, they're giving away the stock and putting you out of business.

Generally, the lower the gross margin, the easier the product is to sell, and the higher the gross margin, the harder it is to sell. So we recommend paying commissions based on gross margin, to reward your sales people for working harder to maintain profits, not just sales.

Commission based on Gross Sales:

Overall Gross Margin on Sales for the Month	% of Gross Sales Paid as Commission[2]
All above 27%...2.8%
26.0 – 26.99...2.6
25.0 – 25.99...2.4
24.0 – 24.99...2.2
23.0 – 23.99...2.0
22.0 – 22.99...1.9
21.0 – 21.99...1.8
20.0 – 20.99...1.7
19.0 – 19.99...1.6
18.0 – 18.99...1.5
17.0 – 17.99...1.4
16.0 – 16.99...1.3
15.0 – 15.99...1.2
14.0 – 14.99...1.1
13.0 – 13.99...1.0
Below 13.0%...none

Figure 11-1

It's harder to track and compute, but it motivates salespeople to sell higher priced or higher profit items, add accessories and extended, follow up prospects and follow up customers for referrals after the sale.

Commission based on Gross Margin:

Overall Gross Margin on Sales for the Month	% of Gross Profit Paid as Commission
All above 27%...	15.5%
26.0 – 26.99..	15.0
25.0 – 25.99..	14.5
24.0 – 24.99..	14.0
23.0 – 23.99..	13.5
22.0 – 22.99..	13.0
21.0 – 21.99..	12.5
20.0 – 20.99..	12.0
19.0 – 19.99..	11.5
18.0 – 18.99..	11.0
17.0 – 17.99..	10.5
16.0 – 16.99..	10.0
Below 16.0%..	none

Figure 11-2

Basing commissions on gross profit also discourages discounting. It can drive the pushy attitude that doesn't take the customers' interests to heart. It can also produce competitive rivalries between salespeople, (which is not necessarily a bad thing, unless it leads to bad blood).

Bonus

Bonuses can be paid on a monthly sales quota, or on reaching a target profit margin. The whole sales team can qualify for a bonus for reaching a collective goal. Managers often receive bonus for exceeding key performance targets. Some retailers offer year-end bonuses, but these are not really very motivating. Bonuses should cover shorter periods. People need to be able to envision their progress, either on a regular report, a reader board, or a United Way style thermometer.

Spiffs

An acronym for "sales promotional incentive funds," spiffs are paid for specific sales behaviors. Some spiffs are funded by manufacturers to move specific SKUs. Or they can be paid by the store for selling a specific old, obsolete or damaged item.

Guerrillas don't allow the manufacturer to pay spiffs directly to their salespeople. You want to get the credit for paying the reward. Also, you don't want the manufacturers to control what products sell on your floor. You need to manage that mix based on your niche, your identity and your business model.

Sales Contests

It's important to include all the support people, the back office, the warehouse, cashiers and delivery.

You can run a sales contest on any number of different metrics. First Sale of the day, Biggest Ticket of the day, Most Line Items in an order, Most Orders written in a day, Order with Highest Gross Margin. You can also run contests on product knowledge. Devise a simple test and give a certain sum for every question they get right.

Steak and Beans dinner. Divide the team into two groups. At the end of the contest everyone goes out to dinner. The winners get steak while the losers eat beans. It's a blast.

The best sales contests combine performance with an element of chance. For example, every qualifying sale wins a ticket dropped into the hat. A weekly drawing determines the winner of a cash prize, a merchandise prize, or the trip for two to Hawaii. The more you sell, the better your odds.

Draw card. Every qualifying sale gets a playing card from the deck. The best poker hand at the end of the contest wins all.

Wiltshire TV, in Thousand Oaks, California, has developed an unusual variant of Bingo. Each month, each square on the bingo is assigned a different product. Instead of letters and numbers, their Bingo card is laid out with brands across the top and model numbers down the side. Sell a qualifying product and you mark that square on the card. Sell any five qualifying items in a row, and BINGO!

➤ Benefits

Salespeople need health coverage too. In the world of retail, ten-hour days and working every Saturday is the norm. Vacation days, employee discount plans, a company-paid cell phone, tuition reimbursement plans, or scholarships for advanced training sessions are all welcome benefits.

➤ Combination Plans

Hourly rate plus a commission on sales: you'll get the most consistent performance and see the lowest turnover if sales associates are compensated as if they are career professionals. Eight bucks an hour will get you a night shift clerk in a 7-Eleven who speaks English as a second language, if you're lucky.

The first level of your plan should be directed at the *individual*, by isolating the particular *behaviors* that will produce the desired outcome. For example, pay a $10 spiff to an employee for selling an open-box or demo unit off the floor.

The second level of compensation is directed at the *group* or *unit* level. Staff in administrative positions can be set up to share a periodic bonus upon completion of *particular benchmark objectives.* For example, the benchmark may be reducing delivery damage to zero. Earmark $500 for a bonus pool, and any damage claims paid out to a customer for, say scratching the front door or nicking the merchandise, are deducted from the pool. Whatever remains at the end of the month is split among all the delivery drivers.

The third level of your plan is structured to reward *the collective.* Set aside a fund to pay a quarterly bonus to everyone *if the business meets its overall quarterly goals.* In this way, you reward collective effort as well as individual initiative and foster an environment of cooperation and teamwork. Peer pressure becomes a powerful force in keeping everyone on their toes.

Gain-share incentives are often very effective for cutting costs. Challenge employees to keep their own work area clean, reducing the costs of the janitorial service. Put half the savings back into their pay envelopes.

Consider *non-monetary* rewards as well. Recognize employees *publicly* at every opportunity for creativity, leadership, or innovation. For many, a certificate, plaque or small trophy is more motivating than cash. Thank you notes from the manager are huge. They end up on bulletin boards. Or tie helium balloons to the chair of someone who's done something great. Encourage *competition* for these awards by posting individual and departmental performance statistics where everyone can see them. Heated rivalries often develop over the coveted "Employee of the Month" parking space. Even seeing the sales "thermometer bar" moving up each week can be a powerful incentive.

And reward mistakes. Create a rotating gag prize for the employee who makes the biggest mess, the most costly mistake or the dumbest error. This award should be presented in an atmosphere of friendly fun, never to punish or embarrass. Laughing these things off serves two purposes: first it encourages people to take risks by letting them know that it's OK to fail and second, it allows them to "pay their dues" with co-workers, appease their conscience and get on with their jobs.

Finally, *never argue with results.* If a team member goes about achieving his objective in an unconventional way, reward him anyway. What works for you may not work for him. Encourage your people to take responsibility for achieving their objectives, reward them progressively and stand back. They will amaze you with their ingenuity!

➤ Invest in Your Stars

Guerrilla managers also lavishly reward their stars. They set high standards and goals and are constantly on the lookout, trying to catch someone doing something right. They encourage independent thinking and innovation and they *never* argue with results. They are ruthless enforcers of the new ethical standards and highly intolerant of non-performers who would bring down the curve. They do not abide racist or sexist language in the office, on the shop floor, or even on the docks.

If you have more than fifteen people working for you right now, *fire* one of them. That's right. Fire someone. There's *someone* in your operation right now who is unhappy with her job and you're unhappy with the job that she's doing and you *already* know who she is. Do her a favor by giving her a new opportunity, somewhere else. Chances are she won't be missed and the rest of your organization will breathe a sigh of relief at her exit.

➤ Make Production Public

Would you like to see a ten percent increase in sales on a $10 investment? Go to the office supply store and buy a white dry-erase marker board and a couple of rolls of border tape (skinny, black vinyl tape for making lines). Make a line for each salesperson and a column for each day of the week and hang in on the wall in the warehouse, break-room or back office. Each day, post the sales figures for each sales associate where everyone can see them. This works on two levels. First of all, your stars will set the pace for the rest of store and that alone will give you the ten percent increase we promised earlier. Nobody wants to be the lowest producer consistently, so they will work to improve their product knowledge and sales skills. And you know that one person you have on staff who you wish you had fired? After a few weeks he'll get the message and leave on his own.

➤ Raising the Bar

Salespeople are competitive by nature. Great sales trainers and coaches capitalize on that trait to help team members improve their skills.

One great trick is to track all of the associates' performance on several different variables. At end of the month, calculate their total sales volume, their average ticket amount and their gross margin, then compute the average for each variable measured and compare each associate's performance to the average.

Monthly Sales Performance

	Total Sales Volume	Number of Transactions	Gross Margin %
Jeannie	$16,550.00	25	31.1%
Ted	$20,196.00	26	30.2%
Aaron	$24,952.00	30	29.3%
Chris	$19,252.00	32	32.1%
Pat	$22,532.00	31	34.9%
Michelle	$21,036.00	25	26.0%
Ryan	$26,382.00	19	31.0%
Average	**$21,557.14**	**26.86**	**30.7%**

Figure 11-3

Congratulate those who beat the norm, then meet individually with each associate to discuss his or her individual performance. "You're doing a good job over all, but last month, your (parameter) was just a little bit below average. How could we work together to help get you up to the average (on this parameter)?"

Nobody wants to be "below average," but suggesting that you just expect them to work up to the norm will always be perceived as reasonable and achievable. It should be easy enough. After all, you're not asking a low performer to shatter any records, just to improve enough to make the middle ground.

In the example above in figure 11-3, the average sales volume per associate for the month was $21,557.14. So you might take Ted aside and ask him to suggest ways that he might sell an additional $1300 this month. After all, he *only needs* $1300 to get up to *average*. You'd have the same conversation with Jeannie, Chris and Michelle, and suggest ways that they could increase their overall sales. Maybe they just need to put in more hours, or take a Sunday shift or two. Perhaps they need to pay closer attention to customers when they're in the store, or be more proactive about suggesting companion products or accessories.

In figure 11-3, the average number of sales per associate was 26.86, but Jeannie, Ted, Michelle and Ryan all fell below that average. You can talk to them about qualifying customers more carefully, or about asking for the order. They *only* need to make a *few more* sales next month to move into "above average" territory.

Similarly, where the average gross margin was 30.7%, Ted, Aaron, Linda and Ryan were below the bar. Perhaps they're over-emphasizing sale merchandise on the floor. You might coach them on selling up to full-feature products, or about adding high-margin accessories.

From time to time, you can change the parameters to help associates improve in other areas such as closing ratios, total accessories sold or extended warranty penetration.

Very quickly, you'll find that the averages start to climb, as each associate gets exactly the right coaching.

---

[2] Lee, Bill. *Gross Margin : 26 Factors Affecting Your Bottom Line.* New Oxford Publishing, 2002. p. 150.

Chapter

Selling Effectively on the Retail Floor

Remember sitting through those dreaded, boring, sales training sessions where some over-caffeinated guy drilled you on the famous "Seven Steps Of Selling?" Greeting, Qualifying, Presenting, Closing, Overcoming objections, Turn over, Closing.

Now let's get real. When's the last time you went to the mall and actually expected to find a retail clerk with the initiative to come up and "greet" you?

Then you eagerly listen, waiting for him to ask those "qualifying questions"? Yeah, right.

Guerrillas still have a selling formula, although they more often follow the subtle clues in the customer's speech, that show you where the customer is headed. Instead of having a pat formula, they look at every opportunity through the customer's eyes.

It starts with recognizing what the customer needs. We know that every customer is shopping for a different item, and even customers buying the *same* item are often buying it for a *different* reason. And there should be as many reasons to shop at your store as there are items on your shelves.

While customers may be shopping for something different, they all *need* the same five things: they need to feel *welcome*, they need to feel *comfortable*, they need to feel *important*, they need to feel *understood and* they need to feel *appreciated*.

➤ Five Basic Needs All People Share:

The Need to Feel Welcome

Customers aren't always comfortable when they walk into a store or a department, so you'll *build rapport* when you make your customers feel *welcome*. Always take the initiative to help the customer feel welcome *right away*. Don't wait while they wander around aimlessly, anxiously trying to find the right aisle. Acknowledge them as soon as possible.

Guerrillas *greet* their guests just as if they were friends arriving for a cocktail party. Great sales associates try to catch their customers' attention as soon as they come in, with a wave, a smile and a friendly "good morning." This initial contact sets the energy level of the interaction, so strive to project an upbeat attitude. Shake their hand. Give them a warm greeting. Guerrillas *never* use the trite cliché, "May I help you?" because it inevitably triggers the reflexive, "No thanks, just looking."

Ready for Action

Look alert, ready and willing to do business. Body language is very important to attracting customers. A relaxed, comfortable stance will prevent you from feeling tired and will make you look more approachable. Stand with hands at your sides or lightly clasped in front, feet several inches apart. Never lean on walls or fixtures.

Face the aisle

Show that you're open and ready to help by turning to face your customers as they approach. When there is slack time in the store and you're busy stocking shelves or having a discussion with colleagues, turn to face towards the aisle and keep an eye out for customers. Always stop your work immediately when approached. When you hesitate, even for a moment, it sends the message, "I'm busy; go away."

Don't guard the display when the traffic is light by standing at I-dare-you-to-enter-this-department parade rest. Move slowly around the area. That gives you a chance to stretch, and you'll appear more approachable.

When you're sitting down, even on a barstool, customers are inclined to "not interrupt" what you're doing, even if you're doing nothing. It is easier for a walking prospect to relate to and establish rapport with a standing salesperson. If you need to sit, take your break *off* the sales floor.

If you have sales associates who have physical disabilities and must sit down, order tall stools or taller director's chairs. This way they can be seated at the same level as your standing customers.

Smile First

Even if you don't feel like it, smile. You'll start to feel better and you will look and sound friendlier. We're not talking about a Cheshire-cat grin, but a pleasant, inviting look on your face. When you smile at prospects, they'll smile back.

If you're already smiling when a customer first looks at you, the customer gets a completely different feeling than if she notices you putting on a smile when you see her coming. Since she doesn't know you, she doesn't know what you're smiling about and may turn away. If you're smiling first, the customer tends to return the smile, giving you the instant opening you need for a greeting and getting down to business.

A bored expression is uninviting. Do you feel inclined to seek out and to talk to bored-looking people at parties? No! You want to talk to happy-looking people. You want your expression to tell your customer, "I'm eager to talk with you and help you find the right item."

Try this. Imagine that you just paid off all your bills for the month and discovered you had $500 left in your bank you didn't know about. Feel that smile? That's the kind of smile you want on your face. It's a *real* smile.

Always have a smile on your face while you're in the store. Just think about all the business you're taking away from your competition!

Maintain Eye Contact

If you make eye contact with a customer and then look away without saying anything, you've just dismissed him. Once you make eye contact, you have to do something to initiate a greeting.

Once you've greeted the customer, maintain eye contact. This doesn't mean you have to stare the customer in the eyes the whole time; just don't be looking around like you're looking for someone more important to speak with.

As you first greet a customer, observe his or her eye color. Noting eye color will make you look naturally interested, and your eye contact will be *electric*. This will give you a very caring and sincere expression.

Another way to make your eye contact really connect is to think, "This is probably the most important person I'll meet today!" as you first reach out to greet the customer.

Guerrillas know that it's a lot easier to sell something to a friend than to a stranger, so they *invest time* to make their customers feel *comfortable*. If you're busy with another customer, or on the telephone, simply making eye contact and a nod of the head and they will feel acknowledged and important. If you *invest energy* in the customer, they will reciprocate that energy by seeking you and buying from you.

The Need to Feel Comfortable

Take a few minutes to start a conversation about something that has nothing to do with the products you sell. You'll increase sales and profits when your prospect is *comfortable*. Show hospitality by providing for their needs, both physically and psychologically.

On a hot July day, you would be greeted at the front door of SoundTrack by a young man in a sport coat offering chilled bottled water. You can offer coffee, water or other refreshment, perhaps from a bowl of fruit. Offer them seating. Offer them use of the telephone. Ask them about the temperature of the room. Direct them to your sparkling-clean restroom.

One of the best ways to make someone feel comfortable is to *find some common ground.* You may notice that the shopper is wearing a local team's shirt or ball cap. Start a conversation about the last game. Or, you can sincerely ask how the traffic was, or if the rain has stopped or if the mall is crowded.

People like people who are like them. The phrase, "Birds of a feather flock together" is absolutely true. The fastest way to create rapport is to be like your visitor. And the fastest way to do this is to match the person you're meeting.

You can initially match the intensity level, voice tone and volume of your customers. If they are active and outgoing, you can be active and outgoing. If they are reserved, you can be reserved. This doesn't mean that you should match regional accents, mannerisms or unusual behavior, but do match general energy levels. This will help them to trust you. Be easy to converse with and willing to talk about their problems with ease.

Very quickly, you'll have established enough rapport to introduce yourself and get the customer's name. Names are the first foundation for any relationship. After all, even blind dates start with an introduction. Dale Carnegie said it best back in the 1930's, "If you want to win friends, make it a point to remember them. If you remember my name, you pay me a subtle compliment; you indicate that I have made an impression on you. Remember my name and you add to my feeling of importance." A man's own name, to him, is the sweetest-sounding word in any language.

The Need to Feel Important

If you've ever seen your name in the newspaper, you've experienced the thrill of feeling important. Treat each customer as if they're the most important visitor you'll have all day. Give them your undivided attention, listen carefully and use their name. Never make them feel wrong or stupid (even when they *are*).

The quickest way to build trust is to actively *listen* to your customer. It's not enough to be able to prattle on about all the world's news. Guerrillas make the customer feel important by listening carefully, even actively.

Nod your head as you listen. This subliminal signal says, "I'm listening, I understand and I agree."

Use verbal attends to verify that you're listening. These are just grunts and phrases like, "Umm-humm," "I see," "Wow!," or "I understand." They telegraph the message, "Please continue, tell me more."

A fail-proof way to get the shopper's name

After you've asked a couple of questions and gently gotten the customer to speak to you, simply extend your hand and say, "by the way, my name is…..and yours is……? Keep your hand out, your eyes focused on the customer and smile warmly. Everyone will shake your hand and introduce himself.

Rapport is lost when someone feels unimportant. Look at your customers when they're speaking to you. Step back a moment and take them all in. Take notes to let them know that their needs are important to you. Go first class when bringing in refreshments.

Ask LOTS of questions

You're always safe asking the typical, who, what, when, where and how questions. "Who are you shopping for?" "What can I help you find today?" "When is your wife's birthday?" "Where will you be using this table saw?" "How would that printer work for you?" But don't ask "why." When you ask *why* questions, you trigger what psychologists call the "dextify" response. It forces your customers to *defend, explain,* or *justify* their need.

Imagine if we asked you, right now, "Why are you reading this book?" Do you feel the accusatory undertone? Guerrillas avoiding making the customer uncomfortable by rephrasing their questions to avoid asking "why."

If you've asked the right questions, the customer is already sold. To avoid the big question, ask little ones. Each time you demonstrate something the product does, ask for the customer's opinion. "Would that work for you?" "What do *you* think?"

"This treadmill has a floating suspension system, so it's easier on your knees when you run and you'll be able to stay on it longer and go farther without aches and pains. Won't that be good?"

Don't be afraid to ask "Is this what you had in mind?" or "will that color work in your bedroom?" If it's not the right item, you can easily move on to the next one.

When the customer has answered "yes" a few times, she's sold. She may just be waiting for you to finish.

The Need to Feel Understood

People don't feel understood until they know that you understand.

You can make your customers feel understood by listening carefully, then plucking key words or phrases from the conversation, and turning them into questions. This is a lot like paraphrasing, except instead of restating their idea in your own words, you use *their* words to build your next question. This is a very powerful way to build rapport.

We call this tactic, "Their-a-Phrasing." It's not quite like paraphrasing. It's quite the opposite, actually. When you paraphrase, you are restating their thought in your words. It's far more powerful to use *their* words to express your ideas.

The key to this tactic is to use *their* vocabulary as much as possible, instead of your own. A customer might ask, "I'm looking for a *flat* light fixture to go in the *stairwell*." The clerk *could* respond with, "We have several *wall-mounted* fixtures that you can choose from." But it would be much more effective for the clerk to *ask*, "You want something that mounts *flat* on the wall? We have several *flat* fixtures that could work well in a *stairwell*. Let me show you...."

The psychology at work here is that people *already know what they mean* when they use a particular word or phrase. Even if the technical term is more accurate, communication is enhanced when you use the *same* terms as your customer, because they will always communicate the *same meaning* for that customer. When the customer hears *their* words coming out of *your* mouth, they know you've been listening and they know you understand.

When customers hear *their* words coming out of your *mouth*, they can hear that you're tuned into them. They appreciate the extra effort you've taken to understand. From time to time in the conversation use the magic affirmation, "I understand," and you'll create a very strong emotional bond with your customer.

This may feel a bit awkward at first, even insincere. Remember: every new sales idea will feel uncomfortable at first. But soon you'll discover the joys of listening to all those stories of all the people you serve. People are remarkably different from each other, and each has their own story to tell. This is one of the most exciting aspects of the selling profession.

To get comfortable yourself, practice before you try it on your customers. Start now; walk up to your fellow sales associate, your family members, your friends and say, "by the way, my name is..., and yours is...?" It won't take long before it rolls of your tongue easily.

Follow your *introduction* by using the customer's name and *transition* into a discussion about the product by asking them, "What can I do for you today?" (Never the dreaded, "May I help you?")

The Need to Feel Appreciated

The most frequently cited reason why customers leave is "lack of contact or follow-up." Everyone loves to be appreciated.

At a Saturn dealership in Chicago, the lot boy brings the car around front direct from detailing and parks it in front of the dealer's sign. A digital camera captures the Kodak moment as the salesman hands the new owners the keys. Then he prints two 8x10 color prints on an inkjet photo printer and slips them into inexpensive plastic frames. One gets mailed to the new customers. The other goes on the salesman's "Wall of Fame." Imagine the impact on the NEXT customer when they walk in and see all these happy, smiling customers with their new Saturns.

Here's what we may have so far. See how natural it sounds.

"Good morning! It was pouring when I came in, is it still raining?" (Remember your manners. Wait for a response. Your next question might just pop up by itself. If not, keep going.) "I see you're a 49ers' fan, did you see the game last week?

Again, wait for the response and listen carefully.

Continue with, "By the way, my name is Sally and yours is…?" (Remember that "patient" is one of the characteristics of a guerrilla. Patiently wait for the customer to answer.)

"Nice to meet you, Bill. What can I help you find today?"

It's just an easy conversation between friends.

Now comes the hard part. Most sales associates immediately run to the products that the shopper has asked about and start showing the options.

Good ones, though, particularly in higher ticket sales, will help the customer make a selection by narrowing down the choices. Ask your customers if you can ask a few questions so that you can save them time by getting some information.

"We've got every kind of recliner imaginable. Can I ask you a couple of questions so that we can find the perfect one for you?"

At that point, take a pen and a small note pad or the back of a business card and write down the answers to the questions. Since there aren't very many guerrilla sales associates in retail, your customers will immediately see that you are really interested in making them happy and know that you are paying attention. Taking notes makes them feel *understood* and has the added advantage of keeping you from talking excessively.

Ask as many questions as it takes until you can pinpoint the one or two products that will work for the customer.

If you sell products that people don't buy often, they may not know about changes in technology or about the newest features available. You can teach them about those things by asking "leading questions" that essentially explain the feature as you ask about it.

"Would you be interested in a mattress that you'll never have to turn?" Or, "some of the new fabrics we have feel just like silk, but never wrinkle. Do you ever travel?" Or, "would you be interested in a dishwasher with a timer so that it can go on late at night when energy rates are lower and you can save money on your utility bills?"

By suggesting features that will save the customer time, energy and money, the obvious answers — and the reason we call them "leading questions" — are "yes!"

We all like talking about ourselves, so customers will usually answer more questions than associates are willing to ask. The more questions you ask, the easier the sale will be. Remember, you're trying to *narrow the selection* so that you only show the merchandise that will suit the customer's needs. Working to pinpoint your prospects' exact needs makes them feel *important*.

At that point, you can say "I know just what you want," and take the customer right to the item you have in mind.

One of the most important guerrilla tactics in retail sales is showing the customer the *right* stuff the *first* time. When you *show the right stuff*, concentrate on pointing out those features that the shopper was most interested in when you asked them questions.

➤ Handshakes

Guerrillas reach out to their customers and offer a welcoming handshake. It formalizes the introduction and starts building rapport. The act of touching a stranger does more to establish a relationship in a few seconds than anything else you can do. If they don't respond, gently drop your hand to your side and carry on.

Handshakes telegraph a tremendous amount of information about the personality and intent of your customer. In Western cultures and particularly in the business world, it's appropriate for both men and women to initiate a handshake.

People have been greeting one another by shaking hands since the last Ice Age and no doubt, this ritual originally meant, "See, I'm unarmed, you can trust me." But over thousands of years the handshake has evolved to convey a number of subtle messages, each telegraphed by slight differences in touch, pressure and force. These subliminal signals are easy to decipher, *if* you know the secret code. Used carefully, these micro gestures can send subtle messages that will put your customer at ease and help to neutralize differences in age, status, physical size, or gender.

Web-to-web

A wimpy, fingertip handshake is sure to make an impression — a bad one. Make sure that you get hold of the customer's hand correctly. Most four-finger handshakes happen accidentally, because you're looking the customer in the eye, walking, talking and *not* paying attention to how you're clasping the customer's outstretched hand. Extend your open hand with the palm rotated slightly counterclockwise and then, at the moment of contact, push away gently against the fleshy part at the base of the thumb until it's made a good web-to-web contact. Then fold your fingers gently around the other person's hand. This slight delay communicates confidence and avoids the accidental dead-fish slip-grip. Shake hands only for as long as it takes to exchange names and then let go. An overextended handshake is uncomfortable for most people — they feel like they've lost control.

Grip

One of the most frequent questions we're asked in our Guerrilla Selling®[8] seminars is, "How hard should I squeeze the prospect's hand?"

The answer: match the pressure offered by your customers. They may grip your hand lightly, or firmly. A firm grip is asserting dominance and this customer wants to ask the questions and control the interview. A light grip communicates passivity and this customer will appreciate your taking the initiative to guide the discussion. Excessive pressure communicates insecurity. The exception is never reciprocate an excessive grip, but strive to relax and make the customer feel more comfortable.

Tilt

Differences in *status* are communicated by tilting the handshake. Some customers will rotate their elbow out slightly and roll their hand over, putting their hand on top of yours, taking the one-up position. You may even feel them press the top of your hand slightly with their thumb. This tilts the handshake down slightly on your side, tipping you a tad off balance and creating the impression of them being taller. Subconsciously they are literally putting you down, elevating their own status at your expense.

We've observed that older men often do this with when shaking hands with younger men, and high-status managers may shake hands this way with subordinates. Men usually take the one-up position when shaking hands with a woman, and a well-dressed sales rep may even do this unconsciously with a customer dressed in a T-shirt and jeans.

You might think that an aggressive, assertive greeting communicates confidence, but this is really a kiss of death. The customer *always* has higher status, regardless of age, gender, or position. Whoever signs the check has the status.

Guerrillas do the opposite of what feels natural, reversing the tilt of the handshake and creating an advantage by relaxing their arm, gently rotating their hand underneath and lifting their fingers slightly, tilting the handshake down on their side and up on the customer's side. This sends the signal, "I acknowledge your higher status and I am here to serve you!"

Push Pull

A handshake quickly sets limits of personal territory. Most people will settle into comfortable distance during the handshake. This distance can vary from customer to customer.

Some customers will literally push you away when they shake hands, while others will gently draw you in as they step up to you. This indicates the customer's comfort with intimacy and tells the guerrilla where to start the conversation.

The pusher is subliminally saying keep your distance. This person doesn't want to become overly friendly and the conversation should focus strictly on business issues. Ask straightforward questions like, "Have you used this product before? What has been your experience?" Never compliment clothes, hair, or jewelry with this prospect and do not inquire about their family or personal matters, at least not right away.

The puller is literally inviting you in to the inner circle of his personal space. He'll want to get to know you person-to-person and if you connect on a personal level, then he'll feel comfortable talking business. With this customer, it is essential to *establish common ground*. You might open with, "I see you're from San Diego. My wife went to school at UCSD. Maybe you know her?"

Ancillary Touch

A simultaneous touch with the left hand denotes familiarity and acknowledges history. The most common form of ancillary touch is the two-handed handshake, which communicates intimacy. The degree of intimacy is communicated by moving the touch further up the wrist. With someone you have known a long time, you would touch higher up the forearm, at the elbow or even on the shoulder.

Guerrillas never use ancillary touch with strangers because there is no history to acknowledge. They know it will be interpreted as insincere, the politician's handshake."

Ancillary touch can be helpful when being introduced by a mutual third party to create an atmosphere of immediate intimacy. You're bringing the history of their relationship into yours. And the farther up the arm you touch, the more familiar the message. Just a brush on the elbow is all it takes.

Stance

How you stand during your handshake is also significant. Stepping forward with your right foot is the most common form. It communicates parity, or equality with the prospect, mirroring the forward motion of his approach. This is good, but, for a change, try stepping into the handshake with your *left* foot. Practice on a friend, and you'll feel the subtle difference it makes. It makes the other person reach into your personal space with an outstretched hand and communicates a degree of warmth, acceptance and trust, which is even better.

Special Considerations

A colleague of ours, W Mitchell, is an effervescent fellow who always wants to shake hands and he often offers his hand first. The problem is that Mitchell is confined to a wheelchair and his hands are severely disfigured, with most of his fingers missing from a tragic motorcycle accident. What should you do?

If your customer is missing several fingers, or even wearing a prosthesis, clasp the hand as best you can and respond as you would normally. If he offers you his hook, treat it as if it were his everyday hand; for him, it *is*. And most important, *maintain your eye contact*, resisting the temptation to stare at the disfigurement. These people really appreciate being treated just like everyone else. The more you treat them as if they are just like you, the more likely they are to like you and do business with you.

➤ Active Listening

How well do you hear what people are saying?

When conducting an interview with a prospect or customer, do you:

	Usually	Sometimes	Seldom
Prepare yourself physically by facing the speaker and making sure you can hear?	❑	❑	❑
Maintain eye contact with the speaker?	❑	❑	❑
Assume what the speaker has to say is worthwhile regardless of her dress or appearance?	❑	❑	❑

	Usually	Sometimes	Seldom
Listen primarily for ideas and underlying feelings?	❑	❑	❑
Encourage the speaker to continue by using verbal signals like "Uh huh," "I see," and "I understand?"	❑	❑	❑
Keep your mind on what the speaker is saying?	❑	❑	❑
Encourage the speaker to elaborate when you hear a statement that you feel is wrong?	❑	❑	❑
Use gestures like smiling, nodding your head and leaning forward in your chair to encourage the speaker to elaborate ?	❑	❑	❑
Paraphrase and demonstrate your understanding of what you've heard?	❑	❑	❑
Make a conscious effort to evaluate the logic and credibility of what you hear?	❑	❑	❑

Give yourself 10 points for each answer of Usually; 5 points for each answer of Sometimes, 0 points for each answer of Seldom.

90+   You're a very good listener.

75–89   Not bad, but could improve.

74 or less   You definitely need work on your listening skills

➤ Becoming a Better Listener

Listening is a process of hearing, understanding, remembering and observing what people are telling you.

Hearing

Hearing is the physical process of having the sound waves reach your ears with enough loudness for you to recognize what your customer is saying. Make sure your exhibit is quiet enough and that you're close enough to your customer to hear them clearly. If not, move the conversation to another location.

Understanding

Understanding is the mental process of grasping the ideas your customer is trying to communicate. The key is never assume that you know what the customer will say. Although you may have asked the same question and heard the same answer a thousand times, you never know when it might be different. It's the same when you ask your customers questions. You may know *your* answer and you may have heard nine others answer the same way, but you don't know *their* answer. Don't assume anything. Repeat back what they said to make sure you understand them correctly. Ask further questions to clarify important points.

Your customers don't *feel* understood until they *know* you understand. Demonstrate your understanding with questions that clarify what they've asked and by repeating back what you've heard in your own words.

Remembering

With all the activity going on and all the people you'll meet, remembering details can be difficult. You *intend* to remember an important detail and then someone interesting comes along, your attention is redirected and you forget.

It's critical to remember what your customer says so you can make the appropriate recommendation and take the correct follow-up action. The best way to do this is to take notes.

Observing

Observe your customers' body-language clues that can tip you off to their internal state.

➤ Non-verbal Communication Signals

Signal	Possible meaning
Folded arms	Defensive, no compromise
Hands covering mouth	Insecure, not sure of what is being said
Tugging at ear/nose/throat	Impatient, usually wants to interrupt.
Fingers of both hands touching	Supremely confident
Tightly clenched hands, wringing hands, excessive perspiration, rocking/swaying	Nervous to varying degrees
Feet or body pointing toward exit	Ready to leave

Hands supporting head when leaning back	Thinking, unsure of ground, stalling.
Hands to face	Evaluating, listening
Clenched hands locked ankles	Nervous or upset
Legs comfortable and arms open	Interested and involved
Avoiding eye contact	Ill at ease

➤ Take Notes

The dullest pencil works better than the sharpest memory. You don't have to take extremely detailed notes, just a word or two will suffice to remind you of the key points.

Taking notes accomplishes five things:

1. You better focus your attention on what the customer is saying

2. Your customer knows you're paying attention and listening

3. You don't have to stare the customer in the eye the whole time

4. You have written details that you can use to resume the conversation the next time the customer comes in, or if you call to follow up by phone.

5. When you have a record of the conversation, your customer is less likely to change his mind.

When asking qualifying questions like, "What do you want in a _____?" write down the customer's criteria words *verbatim.* You will want to use this *exact* vocabulary later when you do your presentation. Guerrillas understand that every prospect feels that "these ears believe most what this mouth says." When you truly understand your prospect's needs and can describe your offer in familiar terms, your offer becomes irresistible.

Your customers don't *feel* understood until they *know* you understand. Demonstrate your understanding with questions that clarify what they've asked and by repeating back what you've heard in your own words.

➤ Follow up

Customers really appreciated a simple follow up. A "thank you" note may be appropriate. (Guerrillas use Hallmark because we really do care enough to send the very best.) Let your customer know that more information will follow in the mail, or that you'll be in touch soon.

The added contact of a personal note will take you miles ahead of your competition.

Use the Guerrilla THANKS approach to remember :

T — *Today!* Write your thank-you letter the same day if at all possible and get it in the mail. An e-mail thank you note is fast, easy, inexpensive and arrives instantaneously.

H — *Handwritten.* A handwritten address stands out in a stack of mail. It will probably be the first piece read. A barely legible scrawled sentence has more impact than a typewritten page. The exception: a same-day E mail.

A — *Active.* Write in active voice. Don't start out, "Dear John." Instead, say, "It was great to speak with you today, John!"

N — *Next Step*. Remind them what is scheduled to happen next. "I'm really looking forward to seeing you in that new dress. Alterations will be finished on Tuesday for your final fitting. See you then, Mary." Make sure your reader knows what to anticipate, what date to check and when to expect action.

K — *Keep It Short*. You only need 25 words or so. A few sentences are enough to make the point and the impression. Write the note in 90 seconds or less.

S — *Specific*. Be very specific on why you're writing the note. For example, "I have a new consignment of vintage clothes come in and I have several things that I know you'll really like. Perhaps you can drop by after work and take a look?"

Investing time in follow up will make your customer *feel appreciated*. Being invited to shop is like being invited over to a friend's house for coffee.

Demonstrate your genuine concern with a simple phone call. Touch base to check and see if there were any service issues with the installation, and that everything is in perfect working condition. If not, deal with these issues immediately.

"How is that washer-dryer combination working out for you, Mrs. Wilson?"

"Hey Bill, what did your friends at work say about your new suit?"

The guerrilla at a high-end consumer electronics retailer kept a 4x6 file card for each of his customers. If he sold you the big screen TV, he would soon be calling, saying, "We're having a truckload sale this weekend, and I'll have this surround-sound system on special. This would be a *great* time for you to *think about* adding home theatre audio. If you can be here before 10:30 on Saturday morning, I'll pull one aside for you...." By the end of Friday's business, he had personally invited a dozen customers, and on Saturday morning there's a line waiting for the doors to open.

New Customer Brochure

This tactic will triple your word of mouth advertising. The New Customer Brochure is a one-page, typewritten summary that tells the story of your business. You hand it out or mail it only to *new* customers. People are most likely to talk about you to their friends in those first few days immediately after their purchase. If they're happy, they'll recommend you to three of their friends. The purpose of the New Customer Brochure is to make them feel more confident telling your story. By putting the right words in the right mouth at the right time, they will tell *nine* people.

Important Anniversaries for Follow-up

Within the first 48 hours, send your thank you card. If you don't send it right away, you likely won't send it at all.

On the 30-day anniversary of the purchase, send a letter inviting them back.

After 90 days, send a letter offering new products, or an invitation to a preferred customer sale.

At six months, call and ask for three names for your mailing list.

At nine months, send a Customer Questionnaire.

At one year, send an anniversary card.

■ THE ADD-ON

Here is a guerrilla tactic that will increase your average ring by ten percent, overnight. It's the add-on, the suggested accessory. Guerrillas use the phrase, "You'll also need…" and suggest additional related items. At the hardware store, the clerk helped me pick out an electric string trimmer/edger. "An extra roll of string is only $7 and you'll need it eventually." I said, "Sure," even though I could see it sitting on the shelf in the garage for the next several months, I've already saved myself another trip to the hardware store and saved the inconvenience of trying to find exactly the right item next time.

In the paint department, we asked the clerk for advice about paint brushes, and when we explained that we were painting a bedroom, he suggested these large, thin, disposable plastic drop cloths, "Only $2." We bought two.

Keep suggesting add-ons until the customer says "no." The beauty of the add-on is that it doesn't matter if the customer accepts the suggestion or not, by saying "yes" to the smaller item, they've signaled their readiness to buy the larger one. When the clerk suggested a six-amp extension cord for the trimmer, I said, "No thanks. I have a hundred-footer already."

"Great," he said, "so you're all set then," and led me to the register.

Don't waste your customer's time. Walk to the computer or get out your order book. Asking, "Let's see how many we have in stock" or "when do you want to have it delivered?" or "which one do you like best?" will tell you if the customer is ready to take out his or her wallet.

If your shopper isn't ready to buy, needs to see more options, or wants more information, he or she will tell you. In that case, you can easily keep showing more features or different products.

➤ Don't give up

Sometimes, customers just aren't sure if they want to make the purchase. Guerrilla sales associates don't give up and hand them a business card, but instead, will keep drilling down to *help solve the customer's problems.* They listen, agree with the customer, and then give the customer another reason to buy.

"You're right, John. It is a lot of money for a matress. But like you said, you kept your last mattress for ten years. If you do the same with this one, it's less than a quarter a night. That's a small price for a good night's sleep."

Go over your notes with the customer to remind them why you showed the items you did. "Let's see if I forgot something. You wanted something that had…." Remind the shopper why you picked out the product you were showing. Reinforce your presentation.

Guerrillas know that making the sale isn't the same thing as making a customer. They tell their customers that they're going to call them in a few days to make sure their happy and to answer any questions they may have.

As a rule, associates don't want to call customers after they've made the sale. They're afraid that something might be wrong and they don't want to open a can of worms. They'd rather wait for the customer to call them.

But guerrillas are different. They want to create long lasting relationships with their customers. If there is a problem, they'd rather have the buyer tell them instead of their 250 friends, relatives and business associates. If there is a small snag, it can usually be fixed with a quick explanation.

Guerrillas don't just promise to *keep in touch*, they do! Guerrillas know that calls made within two weeks after the purchase are different than the now-illegal cold calls that came at dinnertime. These are "warm calls" because of the relationship they've established.

The best tell their customers that they'll call in a few months to see if they need accessories or additional products. Or, they tell their customers that they'll let them know when they get special purchases or other merchandise that they think they might like.

The guerrilla sales presentation goes like this:

- Greet customers to help them feel welcome

- Introduce yourself to help them feel comfortable

- Listen to the customer to make them feel important

- Narrow the selection

- Show the right stuff

- Ask little questions so you don't have to ask the big one

- Help solve the customer's problems

- Their-a-phrase to make the customer feel understood

- Keep in touch to make the customer feel appreciated

It's warm. It's easy. It's real. It works.

Chapter

Selling at Higher Prices

■ A GOOD DEAL

Orvel Ray tells a story about buying suits. "I was traveling in Asia as part of a world tour of seminars for IBM, and I asked Jon Olendorf, one of the trainers on the team, about the possibility of buying a bespoke suit during our stop in Hong Kong. 'Oh no,' he said. "*Thailand* is the place to buy clothes. The quality is better there because the competition is not as cutthroat as it is in Hong Kong. And besides, we'll be in Bangkok for four days, so you'll have time for two or three fittings. We'll only be in Hong Kong for two days.'

"So when we got to Bangkok, I went strolling downtown looking for a tailor shop. The first one I stopped into was dark and dreary, and the floor was dirty. It had a third-world sweatshop feel to it, so I moved on. The next shop was clean, brightly lit and stacked floor-to-ceiling with beautiful bolts of fabric. Several jackets hung on a rack near the door, only half-finished, with their chalk marks and basting stitches showing still. Several finished suits hung next to them, awaiting delivery.

"A tall, dark-skinned man with a trim salt-and-pepper beard, impeccably dressed in a dark suit and the blue turban of a Sikh, was fitting another customer (whom I later discovered was the French Ambassador). Within moments a young Siamese woman wrapped in a royal blue silk sari invited me to have a seat on a small sofa, and offered a cold beer. When the tailor finished his work, he approached me with a broad smile and greeted me in perfect British-accented English, 'I am Raja and this is my father's shop.' I explained that I was interested in ordering a custom suit, but that I would only be in town for a few days. He assured me they could accommodate my schedule. 'We have seamstresses who work through the night, because our customers are sometimes very demanding. We can have your order ready before you leave on Thursday.'

"I started seeing dollar signs, so I asked, 'What price range are we talking about?'

"'You will find that we are one of the most expensive shops in Bangkok,' he said, without apology. 'We use only the finest materials: Egyptian cotton, English cashmere, New Zealand wool and Chinese silk. We fit you very carefully, several times, as the garment is being assembled, and every garment is finished by hand.' He pulled a half-finished jacket from a hanger and pointed out the unique features and fine detailing. So you can imagine my shock when he went on to say, 'We can sell you two suits, two shirts and two ties for $500.'

"I was stunned. I've paid twice that, and gladly, for a single department-store suit. Even so, Jon had warned me about third-world vendors and encouraged me to negotiate. 'Well, what kind of deal can you give me if I pay cash, in US dollars?' I asked.

"'I will give you a *very* good deal,' says Raja. 'Two suits, two shirts, two ties. Five hundred dollars.' Of course he knew he was right. It was a very good deal indeed. So good, that when I boarded the plane to Singapore, I had negotiated to buy two suits, two sport coats, two pairs of slacks, four shirts and six ties. A thousand dollars. Now I can dress like a diplomat."

As it turns out, Raja's Fashions is world famous. Celebrities, businessmen and even a doctor we know in Las Vegas routinely travel to Bangkok just to have their clothes made Raja's in shop. Every item is marked with a unique serial number that is matched to your measurements on file, so if you ever want to say, order more shirts, all you have to do is send Raja an e-mail, and they'll be ready in a few days.

Guerrillas establish value before they quote their price, and then never flinch. If a customer ever asks you, "Why are you so much more expensive?" just smile and reply, "Because our prices are *higher.*"

➤ Don't Get Mad. Get Even.

Greenland Foliage Company is a very, very successful guerrilla retailer. The owner, Harry Elder, negotiated the use of corner of a mostly vacant parking lot at a Sears store for practically nothing, and put up a 2,500 square-foot, green-and-white circus tent at the city's second-busiest intersection. Long aisles of timber-and-wire benches are blanketed with a colorful assortment of flowering bedding plants, hanging baskets, tress, shrubs, nursery stock and supplies, all at premium prices.

One Thursday morning, as the crew was watering and grooming the stock and getting ready to open, Harry arrived at the store holding a full-page color newspaper insert. A local box store was offering geraniums in four-inch pots for only 89¢. "Did you see this?" Harry shouts to the staff, waving the insert. "I can't even *buy* four-inch geraniums at that price. How can they sell them for that?" See, four-inch geraniums are a very popular item that Greenland sold all day for $1.29. Beautiful, lush, already-in-bud geraniums in four-inch pots. Then Harry realized that he had just answered his own question.

"Here," he says, thrusting the insert at one of the staff. "Take the pickup over there along with this ad and buy as many of them as you can. Pay cash." An hour later, they returned, with more than 250 plants.

Then they built a side-by-side display, with the box-store's color ad on an easel, next to the 89¢ geraniums on the left, and Greenland's $1.29 premium geraniums on the right. The cheap plants looked great on the truck, but next to the more expensive plants the differences were blatant. Now they seemed pale and spindly by comparison, with only one stem and just a few leaves, planted in vermiculite.

The more expensive plants were more robust, already splitting into multiple branches, with larger, darker leaves and many sprouting flower buds. These plants were raised in soil, already sun-hardened and ready to plant. The sales staff explained, "If you want four-inch geraniums for 89¢, you can buy them at [the box-store], or you can get the same thing right *here* for the same price. You'll have to be careful, because you'll have to harden them off for a few days and even so, some of them will not survive transplant-ing." Of course, given a choice, most customers bought the higher quality product.

Harry explained his rationale. "First of all, even if I only break even on the cheap ones, I've kept the customer in *my* store, where they also buy baskets, fertilizer and other high-margin products. And they won't be disappointed if they see the same plant for less money somewhere else, because now they realize it's not the same plant."

➤ Claim the Commonplace as a Differentiating Advantage

Retailers like furniture and appliance stores who make deliveries routinely try to call the customer before the truck leaves the warehouse to confirm that someone will be home and to let them know that they're on the way. The delivery crew doesn't waste time driving across town to find that the customer isn't home. More aggressive guerrillas use a cell phone to call again en route, to confirm the next stop of the day. The cost of the cell phone call is far less than the expense of sending the truck out only to discover that the customer didn't wait for the delivery.

Although it's an obvious benefit to the store, it's an even better benefit to the time-starved customer. The problem is, most stores don't remind their customers of that great benefit.

H.H. Gregg, a 49-store appliance and electronics store chain headquartered in Indianapolis, IN has made a huge promotion out of their call-ahead policy.

Mike Kerlik, Division Manager in Atlanta, says, "Since no one knew us when we first opened in Atlanta, we had to do *something* to get customers' attention. Our 40-minute call-ahead promotion has been a home run. We have television ads showing our truck drivers making the call and cardboard stand-ups in all the stores depicting the delivery crew calling ahead. Customers love it and now they think that we're the only ones who offer that service."

The promotion has enabled H.H. Gregg to gain significant market share within the first six months of opening there.

Sure, customers have expectations and you have to be able to exceed them to win the retail war. But because of poor retailing all around us, those expectations are often not as high as you might think.

Guerrillas all do great things. Great guerrillas shout about those customer benefits all the time.

■ GETTING UNSTUCK ON PRICE ISSUES

Price is always more important in the mind of the seller than in the mind of the buyer. The customer has a problem to solve and is willing to part with hard-earned cash to solve it. A study conducted by the North American Retail Dealers Association found that only 14% of consumers base their purchases solely on price.

➤ Don't Discount

According to a fifteen-year study conducted by the Atlanta based sales training firm VASS, 67% of salespeople will *volunteer* to cut their price, *without being asked*. Usually it's because the salesperson doesn't feel the product is actually worth the price. When a salesperson needlessly cuts price, they're liquidating inventory to benefit the customer.

All things being equal, customers will select the lower price. Guerrillas make sure that *nothing* is equal. Counter this trend by constantly training your sales staff on the unique features and value of the products you offer. When a prospect understands the *value* of your product, price is *seldom* the real issue.

Discount Requests

Savvy shoppers look for a discount because it's their *job*. If they don't ask, they won't get a better price. They have nothing to lose and everything to gain by asking for a lower price. Try this sometime, walk into your competitor's store, pick an item and ask a salesperson, "Can you put this on sale for me?" You'll be amazed how often the answer is, "Sure."

Expect to be asked to lower your price, and have weapons at hand to defend your value.

Higher Prices Imply

When a customer says, "Your price is too high," the guerrilla will say, "Thank you!" A product priced higher than the competition usually means better quality or value.

Try this response: "We have no argument with people who sell for less. They know best what their products are worth."

What's Too Expensive?

When a prospect says, "Your price is too high," the guerrilla will find out what *too high* means with the *about face*. "Too *high*? When you say 'too high,' what do you mean? 'Too high' compared to what?" Find out if you're two cents too high, two dollars too high, or two hundred dollars too high.

■ 23 REASONS WHY CUSTOMERS WILL PAY MORE

Your customers will make decisions for *their* reasons and those reasons may be different than what you think, and are often the very reasons that you don't take seriously. Here are just a few of the many reasons your customer may be willing to pay more to shop at your store. Use this as a checklist as you define your mission and your niche:

People will pay more for **higher quality** of course, but these days, quality is only the price of admission. Hallmark made quality their theme line, "When you care enough to send the very best!" So has Maytag.

People will pay more for **authenticity**: the original, the genuine article, the real deal, even when a knock-off looks identical, even when newer, more modern technology is superior.

Harley-Davidson is known for "selling 1940's technology at 1990's prices," yet the waiting list for new bikes is now more than a year, and their used bikes are worth more today than they sold for new.

People will pay more for **stability.** They want to do business with a company that is financially sound, as well as technically sound. They want to know you'll be around if there's a problem.

People will pay more to do business with a company that is **reliable**. Be careful what you promise to customers and always keep your promises.

People will pay more for products that give them **fewer headaches**, that come pre-assembled, that are easy to use, easy to clean and easy to maintain. *Easy to do business with* is a guerrilla credo.

People will pay more to do business with a company that has **knowledgeable salespeople**. Shoppers get frustrated when a sales clerk doesn't know the product. It gets worse if your customer thinks they have been given incorrect information. Gain an advantage by making all your salespeople experts on your products.

People will pay more to buy from a company with a favorable **reputation**. When your customer is uncertain of their decision, say when buying a major appliance, they tend to select the vendor with the best reputation.

People will pay more for **partnership,** and will spend more to do business with companies that do business with them. Guerrillas always try to buy from their customers. Savvy retailers know that the best vendors become partners in their mutual success. How can you create a partnership with your suppliers to add customer value?

People will pay more for **consistency**, always the same from batch-to-batch, order-to-order. Consistent quality, delivery, service and constant innovation create perceived value in the mind of your customer. When your customer knows what to expect from you, they will trust your recommendations and suggestions.

People will pay more for **authority**. If you're the category leader, the inventor, or the authority in the industry, you have additional power and influence. Gain an advantage by becoming a published author and thus an authority.

People will pay more for **popularity**, to buy the most widely accepted brands. Many people are influenced by what's fashionable. They decide, "If it's so popular, I can't go wrong." They want to be part of the in crowd, so they choose the latest fashion. As the saying goes, "No one ever gets fired for buying IBM."

People will pay more for **exclusive features** that they can't get anywhere else. Feature what's different about your store, your merchandise and your organization. What is the one thing that only *you* can do?

People will pay more for **scarcity**, for items that are in short supply. Anything that is considered scarce is considered more valuable, even when it's not more functional. The DeBeers cartel keeps the price of diamonds high by restricting the worldwide supply.

People will pay more for **disposal**. What's a customer to do with their old mattress, their obsolete computer, threadbare carpet or worn out tires? Customers are more likely to buy from you if you provide disposal or recycling, even if you charge extra.

People will pay more for **intrinsic value**. Does your product have value at the end of its useful life span? This could be the scrap value, or the secondary market value, or that you'll take it back with a guaranteed trade-in price if they upgrade. Or is it a collectable that is likely to appreciate in value.

People will pay more for **short delivery times**. You can send a document via FedEx, or you can put it in the mail. How do you justify the big difference in price? They want it now. Heck, they want it *yesterday*. When you shorten delivery times you add value.

People will pay more for **advanced technology**. Do you stock the newest, latest most up-to-date. Dell revolutionized the marketing of computers by *building them to order*. That way, every customer gets the latest technology and Dell benefits because there is no inventory sitting around becoming obsolete by the day.

People will pay more for **vintage** products. Furniture, cars, collectables, wine, musical instruments, even vintage clothes, are in wide demand and ever-shrinking supply.

People will pay more for a product that **arrives in perfect condition**. It's very frustrating to unwrap something you've ordered and find it damaged or defective.

People will pay more for **problems to be fixed quickly**. It's not product failure that causes problems. It's repair delays that are costly. Rapid reaction reaps rich rewards. A survey by TARP found that when a customer *perceives* that an organization responds *instantly* to their request, the customer will do business with that organization again 95% of the time.

People will pay more for products that are **environmentally friendly**. Being green is good marketing. Eighty-five percent of Americans said that they would pay more to help the environment. Anita Roddick's Body Shop chain aggressively supports environmental causes and is a good example of green guerrilla marketing.

People will pay more to **benefit a third party**. The local Jaycees Christmas Tree Lot sells trees at a 25% premium and they flaunt it with signs throughout, "All profits support your community." Your Labor Day Sale will be more successful if you pledge a percentage to Jerry's Kids. Special event promotions can help raise money for the local Boy Scouts or the volunteer fire department and raise community awareness of your store.

People will pay more to shop a store that is **more fun**. In a national survey of purchasing managers, 83% said they would switch vendors if they could find someone more fun to deal with. This is more true than ever, when men and women alike consider shopping a form of entertainment.

➤ Show the Best First

At an annual dealer conference for Brunswick Billiards, two store managers got into a rather heated argument. The first insisted that salespeople should start at the bottom of the line and up-sell the prospect until they met the limit of their budget, then close the sale. His colleague argued that salespeople should show the most expensive table first and explain all the various features and upgrades that were available, then work down the line, taking features away, until the customer settled on the product that was right for them. Each tried to recruit converts to their side, the first beseeching, "Why would you want to waste your time selling a product that the customer can't afford. You'll just frustrate them." His colleague argued, "Buying a billiards table is a once-in-a-lifetime purchase for most people. They're clueless. How can they make an informed decision unless you take the time to educate them?"

Finally, the National Sales Manager intervened and vowed to settle the argument once-and-for-all with a test. He divided the dealerships into two, more-or-less random groups, according to whether their zip code numbers were even or odd. He then announced that for the next month, all the stores in the first group would sell from the bottom up and all the stores in the second group would sell from the top down. At the end of the month, the Brunswick stores in the second group, that showed the best first, had a higher average sale, by more than $1,000. More importantly, their margins were almost double.

The psychology of this approach is easy to understand. People are much more motivated to hang on to something that they already have than they are to go after something new. Guerrillas show the best first, establish quality and value, then systematically take features and benefits away. The net affect is that the customer starts to rationalize the higher price, even if it's over budget, in order to get the best quality and therefore, the best value.

➤ Attire

How your people dress on the job sends a powerful message and guerrillas consider it part of their marketing. The impression the staff makes on your customers is essential. Don't even think twice about sending someone home to change their clothes; you'll only have to do it once. The same goes for haircuts.

Dress for visibility

The most important consideration is that customers should be able to immediately spot and identify the people who work there. This is most easily accomplished by putting everyone in the same "uniform." And they needn't be expensive. For example, an upscale restaurant and bar requires all the wait staff to wear white shirts or blouses over black slacks or skirts, with a matching necktie provided by the restaurant. A garden center provides bright green aprons, screen printed with their logo in dazzling white, that sales staff can wear over a T-shirt, jeans, or even shorts. A boat service center puts everyone in the same baseball cap.

Dress for success

Staff should dress like your customers and perhaps just a little bit better. After all, this is not a law firm, so we don't expect everyone to dress like Ally McBeal (unless, of course, you run an upscale apparel store that caters to young urban professionals).

Some retailers "strongly encourage" their employees to wear the same brands that the store stocks and while there's a certain rationale in that policy, it can sometimes get expensive on a clerk's salary. Rather, encourage your staff to dress well by offering a (tax deductible) "uniform allowance," or deep employee discounts on in-store apparel.

Dress for excess

You can also have a lot of fun by dressing totally over-the-top. Costumes can add seasonal flair. A young couple working together in a sporting goods store come to work one day dressed up as King Kong and a safari-ready Fay Wray. Fay would explain the features of a product like a new backpack or tent setup, while her gorilla-suited partner chimed in with nods, grunts and the occasional demonstration. The act drew quite a crowd, and they often sold the same item to two or three customers at once.

A husband-and-wife team created simple costumes by cutting arm and head holes into two cardboard boxes. They painted them in bright colors, like a child's blocks, with an "H" on one and an "R" on the other, and walked the mall at tax time to promote their local H&R Block franchise.

At a costume and vintage dress shop, the staff routinely sports items taken from the racks, including neon-colored wigs, pink feather boas and hand-painted four-inch heels. Imagine how much fun it would be to work in a store where you get to play "dress-up" all day.

Creating a Culture of Service Excellence

The definition of customer service includes factors like location, access, speed, product quality, communication, competitive pricing, knowledgeable sales associates, store hours, return policies and price guarantees.

In her book, *Ordinary Acts, Extraordinary Outcomes,* Betsy Sanders defines customer service as "what the customers are willing to pay for."

Linda Hyde, with PricewaterhouseCoopers defines customer service as, "Enabling the customer to have an efficient, productive and enjoyable shopping experience," while Mark Larson of KPMG defines it as "providing customers with what they want when they need it."

All retailers pledge to give good customer service, but guerrillas understand that customer service quality is defined by the *customer*, and not by the store's owners, management, merchandisers or sales team. They understand that customer service is not a department.

It takes five times as much time and effort to attract new customers as it does to keep current ones.

Sometimes it doesn't seem like it, but 96% of unhappy customers won't complain, but nine out of ten won't come back. Each unhappy customer will tell nine others about their experience, and thirteen percent of them will tell as many as 20 others about your poor service.

It's really not fair, because happy customers will only tell five others about your great service, and only one of those will become a customer. It's a whole lot easier to lose customers to poor service than it is to keep them.

Good service is meeting the customer's expectations; great service is exceeding it.

➤ COMMANDMENTS OF CUSTOMER SERVICE

The cover story, "Saving Customer Service: Are Retailers up to the Challenge?" in *Stores Magazine,* cites the 10 Commandments of Customer Service:

Put Your Customers First

Guerrillas understand that without customers, they'd have no business. Customer service needs to be the first priority and all other store departments revolve around it.

Make It Easy

Life is complicated. Customers want their shopping experiences to be entertaining, efficient and productive. They want to buy what they want, where they want when they want it. For guerrillas everything from access to checkout is done with the customers' best interest in mind.

Know Your Customers

Guerrillas target their merchandise, their service, their pricing and even their business hours to their customers. In order to do that, they use surveys, focus groups and third party calling to find out what consumers in their market look for in exceptional retailers.

Keep It Simple

Simplicity is the antidote for our complex world. Don't make customers jump through hoops to get a sale price or a refund. Avoid a small print mentality and make your policies customer-friendly.

Cultivate a Service Culture

Service, service, service may even be eclipsing the old location, location, location mantra as a way to market to your customers. Today's retailing is more about customer satisfaction than about product quality, price or convenience. What do you sell?

➤ It's all about the Customer

Customers always go where they get good value. Value is the perceived relationship between quality, quantity and price. Value is our customer's perception; that is, it is not what *we* think, but what *they* think.

Customers always go where they are treated well. "Whatever-it-takes customer service" will increase your customers' perception of value and improve their shopping experience at your business.

When the value isn't obvious, or when the level of service slips, the customer slips away. Your customers simply walk out the front door and take their business elsewhere. They don't tell you that they are going; they just disappear.

Successful business owners understand these laws and use them to maintain a strong customer focus.

■ PROCESSES ADD TO THE SHOPPING EXPERIENCE

Shopping is no longer the leisure activity it's been in the past. Twenty-first Century shoppers want it to be easy to get in and out of the store, easy to find a sales associate, easy to find the right department, easy to select the right item, easy to get to a cashier and easy to negotiate their checks. You have to simplify every step and every process that affects the customer's experience at your store.

When Elly was conducting an in-store consultation for a client, she watched as cashiers meticulously copied the numbers from two credit cards *and* a driver's license every time they accepted a check. If the account was new, the cashiers would call the bank to verify that sufficient funds were available. Meanwhile, customers were subjected to hassles and delays at checkout. One check was rejected because it was a temporary check, and lacked the customer's name and address imprint.

Although the community was small and it seemed as if people knew each other well, Elly thought that the retailer must have had a serious problem with bad checks. As it turns out, the store manager said that, "no, they didn't get many bad checks." She asked if the information that the cashier's took from customers helped to collect on the checks that did bounce.

No, most of them were from accounts that were closed or from customers who couldn't be located. If, in fact, putting the customer through the wringer didn't help collect bad checks, why do it? The answer: because that's the way we've always done it.

➤ Create a Consistent Experience for Every Customer Every Time

Elly has been a loyal Lands' End shopper for years. Never the cheapest merchant, Lands' End products were always terrific and the service impeccable. When she first walked into the Land's End outlet store in Lombard, Illinois, an entire wall full of their famous canvas luggage caught her eye. There was an amazing display of briefcases, athletic bags and garment bags. Walking closer, she noticed that much of the merchandise had already been monogrammed. She assumed that the products were defective or perhaps factory seconds.

She approached the store manager asking why merchandise that had already been embroidered with names, initials, and even company logos, was on display.

The store manager said, "No, they are all first line products, but have simply been returned by customers who changed their minds."

Elly expressed her surprise that the company would refund products after they had been personalized. The manager's reply was matter-of-fact.

She pointed to the sign on the wall and said, "'Guaranteed. Period.' That's our motto and we live by it. It doesn't say 'Guaranteed Until it's Monogrammed.' or 'Guaranteed Until You Wear It,' or 'Guaranteed Until You Alter It.' It says 'Guaranteed. Period.'"

Shortly after Sears bought Lands' End in 2003, Elly ordered some shoes through their website, but they didn't fit. "No problem," she thought, "I don't even have to box them up and mail them back. I can just run into Sears and exchange them for the right size."

But no, it was too good to be true. The clerk at Sears explained that although they carried Lands' End merchandise, they couldn't take back products that were purchased over the telephone or on the web site. It just couldn't be done because the computer systems weren't compatible.

And so, Sears turned a loyal, long-time Lands' End customer into a new L.L. Bean customer.

People expect your service to be consistent throughout your channels, and from store to store. Toys 'R Us, for example, increased their sales by 22% in one year by marrying their brick-and-mortar and Internet operations. Shoppers who buy on the Internet can return or exchange those products at any store in the country. Eager grandparents can buy toys online, and then direct their children to the local store anywhere in the country to pick up the toys in time for their grandchildren's birthday party.

➤ Play Fair

We shouldn't have to attend classes on business ethics. Business should be a matter of following the Golden Rule.

Bait and switch shouldn't have to be illegal, because no good retailer would even consider advertising a product for the sole purpose of pitching a more profitable item.

Do what you say you're going to do. Deliver on your promises. If you're out of stock on an item you've advertised, give the customer a rain check or offer them the next best product at the advertised price, no questions, no hassle.

The competition can't out-spend you on things that don't cost money, and this new ethical high ground can give your organization the competitive edge you need to succeed, and it costs you nothing! Fail to elevate your standards and the competition will eat you alive.

➤ Empower the Front Line

Let's say a customer comes in, slams a product down on the counter and demands a refund. In many stores, the cashier would immediately ask for the receipt and call for the sales associate who had sold the product to the customer.

The customer would explain the complaint to the associate and demand a refund. The associate would reply, "No we don't give refunds. I can either exchange it, or have it repaired for you." At that point the customer demands to see the store manager.

The customer explains the problem a third time to the manager and again demands a refund. The manager backs up the associate and explains the policy again. At that point the angry customer demands to see the owner.

The owner hears the customer's sad tale, takes the item back and refunds the purchase price. Is the customer happy? Does that shopper become a loyal fan? Does he or she recommend the store to friends? No!

An empowered team says "yes" from the get go. "Yes, Mr. Wilson, I can give you a refund if that's what you want, but why don't you tell me what's wrong here and we'll see if there's something else I can do to help."

It may turn out that the problem was a misunderstanding about the product's benefits or that the customer really didn't know how to use it. It may turn out that it won't help solve the buyer's problem and that another product will work better.

And if the only answer truly is to refund the money, at least the customer hasn't gotten the run around. His problem is solved quickly and efficiently. Most important, he knows that he can buy from the dealer again because it's a store committed to providing quality customer service.

➤ Use Technology

There are great tools available to enhance the customer's shopping experience, but too often, new technology is used to replace customer service, not add to it.

Automated telephone systems can be great for productivity. It eliminates the need for a receptionist, and doesn't tie up sales associates if the customer only needs store hours or directions.

At the same time, though, it takes the customer a step away from the people side of the store. It may not reflect your commitment to good service, your well-trained associates, your warm store ambience and the way you value each customer.

Point of sale register systems help reduce inventory shrinkage and provide accurate sales information. But customers are not well served if the system or the user is new and it slows down the checkout process.

Recover Quickly

Mistakes happen. Prices get misquoted. Merchandise doesn't arrive in time for a sale event. Sale tags get mixed up.

No one remembers a mistake if it's resolved quickly, efficiently and properly.

Remember the great Coke debacle? After years of experimenting and investing millions of dollars, Coca Cola announced the debut of New Coke. Long-time Coke fans ran out and bought the new drink eager to taste the improvement in their favorite soft drink. For most, though, it was an immediate disappointment. They complained that it was too sweet. Some even said it tasted like Pepsi!

The folks in Atlanta might have stuck by their guns. After all, they'd made a tremendous investment in their new product not to mention the additional expense of the huge marketing campaign to roll it out. They may have just hoped that, in time, we'd all forget the taste of their old product and we'd get used to the new taste.

But no, Coke didn't take that risk. Instead, they issued a big Mea Culpa and brought back, with great fanfare, our beloved Classic Coke.

In one of the biggest marketing coups in history, Coke brought their fans back to their camp by quickly admitting that the new product wasn't going to sell and listening to the hue and cry of their customers.

What a great lesson!

■ MOMENTS OF TRUTH

Jan Carlzson became the CEO of SAS airline at a time when it was one of the worst airlines in the industry. Flights were often late, the food was inedible, the crews were rude and surly and bags were regularly lost. Some in Europe at the time said that if their only choice was to fly on SAS they took the train. A short time after Mr. Carlzson took the helm, though, the airline became one of the best.

Management guru Tom Peters interviewed Mr. Carlzson and asked him about the steps he took to turn the airline around.

Carlzson said there wasn't any one single thing that improved the airline's performance. Instead, he said that he looked for, and found, 1,000 things that could be improved by one percent.

In that process, he identified what he called Moments of Truth. Moments of Truth occurred anytime a customer or a potential customer came in contact with the airline. They began to closely analyze each of those encounters to find ways to improve them.

In retail, there are dozens of times you touch a customer. You touch them with each of your marketing weapons, with your storefront when they drive by, in the way your staff answers incoming telephone calls, in the way customers are greeted and so on through every step of the shopping, buying and after-sale service experience.

You can improve your service by closely analyzing each of your own Moments of Truth to see how they might affect your customer. Better yet, have your customers tell you how they feel when they first walk into the store, when they call on the phone, when they can't make up their minds or when they have a complaint.

Guerrillas combine that information with the Japanese philosophy of *Kaizen*—continuous incremental improvement—to ensure that the service they offer make their stores the hands down first choice of shoppers in their communities.

➤ Information is Power

The Nordstrom chain is famous for their outstanding customer service. Near the main door of their store on Westlake Plaza in Seattle, a tastefully dressed young woman stands behind a massive oak service desk. Above her head, on the wall, four-inch brass letters spell out "ASK ME I KNOW."

Unable to resist this challenge, we approached the information desk. "Excuse me. We were wondering if you could help us with some information?"

"Certainly!"

"How long do you bake an eleven-pound turkey?"

Without batting an eyelash, she answered, "Three hours and forty minutes, or twenty minutes a pound, at 350 degrees. Uncover it for the last half-hour so it can brown." We were astounded.

This guerrilla knows her stuff! The service desk is stacked with directories and phone books about two feet high. It's actually her job to answer *any* question that any customer might ask, not just about anything in the store, Westlake Plaza, the Pike Street Market, downtown Seattle, or Washington state in general. She also gives away complimentary parking tokens (normally a dollar).

You don't have to be small to be a guerrilla. The success of the Nordstrom brand is testimony to the power of attending to tiny details.

➤ Brooks Brothers to the Rescue

After flying to Houston to do a large seminar, that was also being shot for a video, Orvel Ray opened his suitcase to discover, to his horror, that a pen left in the inside pocket of his suit had burst, leaking blue ink all over everything.

It was already 9:30 and dark when he approached the front desk clerk in a panic. "I need to buy a suit and a shirt and *right now*. I have a TV shoot at 8:00 in the morning and all my clothes are ruined."

"Well, you're in luck. There's a big mall just on the other side of the freeway, about a mile from here."

He flagged a cab and jumped in. In his best Sean Connery impersonation, he said, "Take me to the mall, and *step* on it."

By ten-'til-ten, the mall echoed like a tomb. Most of the stores were already closed, their dark doorways covered by steel gating. Orvel ran from one end to the other, desperate to find an open department store or menswear shop. The Brooks Brothers was closed, but lights were still on inside, and a tall man in a white shirt and tie was pushing a vacuum up and down the aisle. Orvel Ray took a coin from his pocket and rapped on the window, hoping to get his attention. The man with the vacuum stopped his work, unlocked the door and opened it a crack.

"Look, I know you're closed for the night," Orvel said, "but I have something of an emergency. I have to shoot a TV show tomorrow and my clothes were ruined in transit. Can you just sell me a light-blue long-sleeve shirt, and maybe a tie?"

"No problem. Come on in."

He closed the door and locked it behind them, then led Orvel to the shirt display. "You're about a 32?"

"Yeah. That's right."

"Here you go," he said, as he pulled a perfect powder-blue shirt off the shelf. "My clients tell me that this particular shade is best for TV work. Now, let's find you a nice tie."

As he rummaged through a table of brightly-colored ties, he turned over his shoulder and said, "You know, all our suits are on sale right now."

"Yeah? But how am I going to get something fitted and altered and ready by seven AM?"

"That's not a problem. Our tailor is still here finishing up an order for another customer. If we get you fitted with a jacket off the rack, he can hem the pants and send them with you tonight."

Now Orvel Ray is the proud owner of not one, but *two* Brooks Brothers suits, each with a matching shirt and tie.

■ TRUE VALUE

McGuckin's Hardware in Boulder, Colorado, has a reputation for being expensive. You can find it cheaper at the box stores, but if you just can't find it anywhere else, go to McGuckin's.

Our client was restoring an antique drum set and had broken a lug-screw. This screw was an odd shape to fit a drum-wrench, with odd threads. Companies stopped making these things fifty years ago; everything today is metric. Rummaging through parts bins in the dusty back rooms of a dozen music stores proved a major exercise in frustration.

As a last resort, he went to McGuckin's. The shock walking in the place was overwhelming! It was huge, brightly lit and spotless. Everything neatly labeled, priced and exquisitely merchandised.

He had barely walked in when a young man in a freshly pressed green apron greeted him with raised eyebrows and asked, "Are you looking for something in particular?"

"Well, yes," he said. "I've just about given up hope, but maybe you've got something in the way of a bolt or something that will work." He showed the clerk the broken lug and resigned himself to enduring the usual runaround. He was growing accustomed to being shuffled from to one clerk to another for an hour or so before being dumped out on the street.

"Let's take a look," says the clerk, turning down a long, narrow aisle, walled in by high steel shelf units, each containing hundreds of small drawers. The first drawer he opened revealed an assortment of four-sided-head-with-a-three-eights-inch-diameter-chrome-plated-shaft-with-English-threads lug bolts!

"Now what length did you need?" he asked.

Three register clerks stood by, waiting to ring up this sizeable order. Our friend paid forty cents, which when you think about it, is an outrageous price for one lousy bolt. But he would have gladly paid twenty dollars or more to repair this drum. He had already invested weeks looking for the broken part. The McGuckin's clerk found it in two minutes. That's why our friend goes back to the store and as a homeowner, he spends a lot of money in Mr.

McGuckin's higher-priced-than-anyone-else-in-town hardware store.

The reason is simple. You can't walk down an aisle without bumping into one of those green-aproned guerrillas. Two thirds of McGuckin's employees are dedicated to full-time floor walking and every employee stocks shelves until everyone knows where every one of more than 128,000 items can be found. They are prohibited by company policy from ever using the phrase, "No, we don't have that." Instead they say, "We'll be happy to order it for you," while serving more than 3,000 customers a day, seven days a week.

The success story of this hometown hardware can be boiled down to three common sense things that guerrillas understand.

First, they anticipate the customers' needs by having a wide selection of merchandise and options available. In addition, the guerrilla is always prepared to suggest some solution or alternative, even if it means brokering an item, or personally introducing them to a competitor.

Second, they give customers only one person to deal with. These guerrillas know the territory. If you want to win the respect and loyalty of your customer, take personal responsibility for solving the problem without handing it off to someone else. If this means you have to do research, check with another department, or ask a supervisor, fine. Guerrillas will set up a three-way conference call and keep the customer at their side and on the line as they investigate.

Third, they add value to commodity hardware items through display, merchandising and service. Guerrillas know that people make buying decisions on the basis of value, not price. And everyone at every level can find ways to add value, regardless of the product. Whether it's tracing the status of an order, investigating an invoicing error, or pricing out a custom job, guerrillas remember that customer service is everyone's responsibility.

The bad news is that American business is increasingly being dominated by coupon printers, discounters and offshore manufacturers. In this economic environment, service is the only arena where the guerrilla can compete effectively.

The good news is that people will gladly pay and pay handsomely for exceptional treatment. That means rendering service that never sends them away frustrated, service that surpasses the norm, service that surprises and delights, service that solves their problems. Such service will be the key to profitability for the handful of guerrillas who get it right.

Chapter

Retailing in The Experience Economy

An ad for a flea market touts that it's the perfect place for the "overstuffed." Let's face it, with the exception of the occasional quart of milk, we really don't need to buy much. Americans have achieved a level of abundance, or even over abundance, never seen before.

Because of that, research conducted by Yankelovich reveals that consumers now value quality over quantity and time over money. Today's shoppers are looking for comfort and connection.

Consumers are in the hunt for a shopping experience that provides an escape. They go into stores to explore, stalk, pursue, touch, feel and interact with products that might fit into their lives.

Stacks of products lined up in neat rows may satisfy customer "needs" but not their "wants."

Today's buyers have been to Walt Disney World, IMAX and the Rain Forest Café. They've seen Paris from the top of the Eiffel Tower and ridden the fabled cable cars of San Francisco. They've sat in the front row at Sea World and been kissed by a killer whale. You can only capture their attention if you tickle their imagination.

➤ Von Maur

Even though department stores are struggling to find their niche between discount stores and boutiques, Iowa-based Von Maur is expanding. In their new Ann Arbor, Michigan store, customers can try on shoes sitting by a fireplace. In the men's department they watch a football game on the big-screen TV or relax on sofas placed strategically through out the store.

Instead of locked behind glass showcases, cosmetics in Von Maur are displayed in open shelves where customers can reach them easily.

➤ REI

Outdoor specialist REI has a large vertical climbing wall to teach would-be climbers the basics of the sport. Shoppers can try on gear like shoes and harnesses for fit and comfort as well as performance.

The bike path outside the flagship store in Denver encourages bicycle purchasers to try before they buy. The path puts the bike through its paces with tight turns, asphalt, gravel and dirt surfaces, water bars and rock jumps. Customers can compare ride, handling, braking and suspension.

Two large auditoriums are used for clinics and classes and to show adventure and travel films featuring extreme sports. Climbers, kayakers, skiers and mountain bike enthusiasts can feel the thrill of the sport as they ready themselves for each new season to finally arrive.

➤ Insperience Studio™

Appliance manufacturer Whirlpool has become obsessed with the purchase experience. The Insperience Studio™ in Atlanta is not a showroom or an appliance store. It's a studio of solutions and a resource for great ideas. Customers are encouraged to turn up the heat on a high-powered cooktop, experience the elegance of a stainless steel refrigerator, or test a KitchenAid™ stand mixer on their favorite family recipe. Although the Studio sells no products, consumers are invited in to wash clothes, cook and bake on the latest Whirlpool and KitchenAid brand appliances.

The Insperience Studio has a full complement of cooking classes so that customers can test drive professionally performing stainless steel home appliances and cultivate design ideas. Classes conducted in partnership with *Cooking Light* magazine drew nearly 100 eager aspiring chefs.

All products are displayed in vignettes staged to depict one of six lifestyles, from the young family in their first home, to empty nesters craving to become weekend gourmets. Customers team up with selection consultants to help choose the products most likely to mirror their lives and referred to local area retailers to complete their purchase.

Whirlpool also uses the Studio to train sales associates in the Atlanta area about the benefits of their products. Customers are only referred to those who have completed the courses and become certified because of their expertise.

➤ Gymboree

Gymboree sells clothing, gifts and toys in sizes for newborns to children's size seven, a pretty small niche for pretty small tykes.

Since 1976, the retailer has been a leader in parent-child play, music and arts programs. Joan Barnes, a California mother, attempted to find a safe, fun and nurturing place for new parents and their children to play together. Unable to do so, she did what any guerrilla would do, she started her own.

From newborns through kindergarten, children and their parents have come to the store for classes like GymBabies, GymCrawlers, GymWalkers, GymRunners, Quarternotes, Halfnotes and Wholenotes in colorful playscapes.

Crayola has teamed up with Gymboree to offer art classes to children from eighteen-months to five years old. Children expand their creativity as they learn to paint, draw and sculpt.

Classes and birthday parties range from 45 to 75 minutes long and are taught by trained teachers while parents relax, meet other parents, play-along or shop the store's brightly-colored, stylishly designed, well-made clothing, gifts and toys.

Where else can parents of a toddlers shop for them without worrying about a bored, crying or fussing child?

Mall fatigue isn't just for the holidays anymore.

People are going to shopping malls less than they did a decade ago. When they do, they're visiting fewer stores, spending less money and leaving sooner.

No longer seduced by sheer variety, shoppers are increasingly turning to strip malls and "power centers" – medium-size shopping centers anchored by big-box retailers.

With retail industry data indicating that less is more, the operator of San Diego's largest mall has fashioned a somewhat counterintuitive response: More is more.

Taking a cue from the tourism industry, Westfield Corporation is employing a strategy more often used by resorts and amusement parks to keep people on the property and spending money: more amenities, more personal services and more entertainment.

"We fundamentally believe that we can create a branded destination experience the likes of Disneyland or Universal Studios," said Todd Putnam, Director of Customer Service and Marketing for the Los Angeles-based company. The key to this new initiative, which Westfield is test-marketing in seven San Diego properties, is knowing what keeps people from going to malls.

The hassle of parking, dragging cranky children around and getting lost in a sea of specialty stores is enough to drive one to Wal-Mart or the Web. Westfield's response is to offer valet parking, dedicated parking spaces for expectant mothers and free strollers shaped like cars with pretend steering wheels. Each mall will have a small playground with seating for parents to take a break while children play. Malls also will have family lounges, like the one already installed at Plaza Bonita, with large changing tables, bottle warmers and free baby wipes, as well as a seating area with a television airing cartoons. The lounges also have breast-feeding areas with curtains for privacy and family bathroom stalls with both a regular and a child-sized commode.

Just as important as luring shoppers to malls is keeping them there longer and increasing the number of stores they visit. Industry-wide numbers indicate 44% of shoppers today leave a mall without a single non-food purchase.

A study by the International Council of Shopping Centers, an industry research group, showed today's typical shopper spends 20 to 25 minutes in a mall and visits an average of one-and-a-half stores. This is a far cry from the typical mall shopper of the 1980s, who stayed two hours and visited four stores.

A given in retail is that people only have two hands to carry bags. This means shopping often stops when those hands are full. Westfield's solution: carry-out service by uniformed "concierges" who will come to a store at a clerk's request and take packages to a customer's car. These concierges, who Putnam said are being recruited heavily from the hotel and tourism sector, are charged with interacting with retailers to find out what sort of promotions and new merchandise are in the stores, then using that information to help shoppers. Carrying balloons for children and a shoulder bag filled with bottled water, aspirin, lip balm, mints and disposable cameras to give away, these employees try to determine customer needs, and then point them in the right direction.

Within the next year, Westfield plans to have each concierge carry a hand-held computer to print out coupons for a particular store on the spot.

Merrill Lehrer, president of Retail Samurai Sales in San Diego, said the Westfield initiative is a smart way to address retailing's holy grail.

"Retailers forever have been trying to figure out how to make shoppers stay longer," Lehrer said. "This should entice people to stay longer and return more frequently." But Lehrer said he's cautiously optimistic that the idea ultimately will become part of the company's plan for all its 65 U.S. properties. Too often, he said, the "financial wizards" become impatient for a return on investments and abandon costly efforts to improve service.

Building out the physical structures, recruiting and training the additional personnel and quadrupling the mall staff has been about a $15 million investment in San Diego, Putnam said.

The strategy is to differentiate mall shopping from other shopping experiences, which will lead to more and happier customers. That is meant to generate higher sales for retailers, eventually enabling Westfield to raise rents.

"The shopping center industry, at least in big shopping centers, is fairly homogenous," Schroder said. "What is, realistically, the difference in the tenancy in Plaza Camino Real versus Plaza Bonita? Not much. So you have to try to differentiate them using other strategies."

George Whalin, president of Retail Management Consultants in San Marcos, said anything that enhances the mall experience will help. He cited the success of the fountain play area and merry-go-round at Newport Beach's Fashion Island as an example of added amenities acting as a draw.

But what Whalin sees as the critical challenge U.S. malls are facing–and what' driving customers to power centers and strip malls–is that most people simply have less time to shop.

"I think this is probably a good idea," Whalin said. "But I'm not sure it's going to change the problem of people with time constraints."

➤ Ed Debevic's

"Eat at Ed's" says a sign which greets the customers of Ed Debevic's, a popular diner in downtown Chicago operated by Bravo Restaurants. But really, it isn't the food that makes Ed's unique. The menu is typical of a traditional diner, or Denny's for that matter.

The restaurant is themed in the 1950's style, and the waiters and waitresses dress and act the part. *Life* Magazine called it, "a cross between a bowling alley and a neon-lit drive in."

Oddly enough, what brings people to Ed's is the service. It's a great spot for kids and the under-21 crowd, who dig the smart-aleck decor and wait staff (in the insult-the-customer vein). The servers are all well-rehearsed in mock-rudeness, and start barking a stream of orders and insults as soon as you walk in. After slapping menus on the table and sloshing water glasses all around, they start prompting you to "Make up your mind already!" Their smirk tips off even newcomers that it's all an act, but it soon escalates. "Order the meatloaf. We're trying to get rid of it because the health department's comin' tomorrow." Or, "Now YOU. You don't look like you should be eatin' no more cheeseburgers! I'll just bring you a nice salad, and maybe a Diet Coke." This is fast-food plus stand-up comedy delivered while juggling a tray of root-beer floats.

The Chicago Tribune voted Ed's #1 in Casual Dining in 1994, and the food is consistently solid, though much of it lies between hot dogs with fries and open-faced hot roast beef with mashed potatoes.

Adding to the experience are the frequent bar dancing outbursts performed by the staff, none of whom seem to be enjoying the experience, although you know they're having a ball. Ed's has a backlog of more than a hundred applicants who have to actually *audition* to wait tables there.

Ed's is a fun joint, especially if you're entertaining friends from out of town. It takes a few minutes for them to catch on, especially if you play along, and hey, who doesn't like to watch their friends being made fun of? But avoid the peak lunch rush, even on a weekday, the place will be jammed. On summer evenings, the parking lot is filled with patrons awaiting tables.

It's a guerrilla retailing operation through-and-through. They've turned an ordinary restaurant into a unique experience, even a tourist destination, by using nothing more than imagination and a spirit of fun.

Chapter 16

Getting Customers Back Again and Again

■ BEING EASY TO DO BUSINESS WITH

Although it's much more difficult and more expensive to get new customers than to keep old ones coming back, most marketing efforts are spent on acquiring new customers instead of getting existing customer base to come back. This plays to the great advantage of the Guerrilla retailer.

Guerrillas have learned that a key to retail success is to get a bigger share of each customer's wallet, and they have developed an arsenal of weapons to keep them coming back for more.

Regulars are more profitable, return fewer products, need less customer support and buy more accessories and add-ons.

They're more profitable because of the trust level you've already established with them. Since they felt like they received a good value when they bought from you before, they are less likely to be price-shoppers and ask for additional discounts.

Their trust in your expertise enables you to sell them up to more profitable, fully featured products and to include accessory items in their purchases.

Repeat customers have less buyer's remorse creating fewer returns because they feel comfortable with their continuing experience with you.

➤ Make it Simple

If you're going to get customers to come back, you've got to do everything you can to make it simple, convenient and easy to do business with you.

Life is complicated. Customers are time-constrained and shopping is no longer a leisure time activity and today's consumer has lots and lots of choices.

The Internet has enabled prospects to access products just like those you sell 24/7—that's every hour, of every day, all year. Your cyber competitors are open nights, weekends and holidays. While you may not be able to go head to head with that, what you can do is let customers know that you'll gladly meet with them at any time convenient for them.

Not open? Guerrillas make appointments to see their customers. Have your outbound telephone message let customers who call after hours know it. "Thank you for calling ABC Sales. We're sorry we missed your call. Your business is very important and it would be our pleasure to make a private appointment to help you make your purchase when it's convenient for you to come in. Please leave your name and your telephone number and a good time to reach you so that one of our associates can contact you to schedule an appointment."

The price of long distance calling drops almost daily. Encourage customers who may live outside of your immediate marketing area to contact you by installing a toll-free telephone number. Be sure to put that number on your business cards, in your ads and in all of your marketing materials.

Credit Cards

Guerrillas encourage their customers to use their major credit and debit cards in their stores. The small discount you'll pay will be more than offset by the increase in your business.

Better yet, establish your own store card. The cards serve as additional marketing material subliminally reminding your customers of your store each time they open their wallets. Customers with your cards are far more likely to shop your store first the next time they need to purchase products that you offer.

Studies conducted by GE Capital, one of the largest providers of private label credit cards, have proven that customers carrying those cards spend more than cash customers do. Knowing that they can extend their payments or even make minimum monthly payments, customers are more likely to step themselves up to better, more expensive products.

Customers with private-label credit cards shop those stores more frequently.

Private label credit is so valuable that it's well worth your while to pay your sales associates a spiff for taking the customer's credit application. Encourage customers to keep their credit lines on their major credit cards open for emergencies or travel and to use your store card to buy from you.

Guerrillas use their private label credit card programs to schedule promotions like One Year Free Financing, 90-Days Same As Cash, or No No No sales, where customers make no down payment, make no payments, and accrue no interest for a certain length of time.

A word of caution, the credit business is risky. Unless you can afford to risk your assets, be sure to use programs offered by companies like GE, BankOne, Household Finance or even your own bank. In those programs, the retailers don't assume the risk, don't have to make credit decisions or do collections, and don't tie up their own cash in outstanding receivables.

➤ Find Out What Your Customers Are Thinking

A study conducted by the consulting company Yankelovich showed that 68% of consumers said they were more likely to do business with a company that had asked their opinions.

If more than two-thirds of your customers want to talk to you, Just Do It!

➤ Telephone Surveys

Electronics and Appliance retailer H.H. Gregg has built their company from a small chain in Indianapolis into a regional powerhouse by keeping close to their customers.

Each month, an independent telemarketing company calls 100 randomly selected customers from each of their stores to find out how they felt about their experience.

The results of those calls are given to each store manager so that they can coach their teams and make improvements. What's more important is that one-third of each store manager's monthly bonus is based on the results of the survey.

Although customers hate telemarketing, they love follow-up phone calls after making a purchase. Calls made within the first seven days after the sale reinforce the customer's buying decision and gives them a chance to ask any questions they may have.

Sales associates fear making calls to their customers because they're afraid that if they call their customers they'll hear a complaint, or they might have to answer difficult questions. But think about it. If a customer has a serious problem—like that the product is dead out of the box, or doesn't do what they thought it would—wouldn't the customer have already called you? And if the customer has a real problem, wouldn't you rather they tell *you* about it, rather than their 250 friends, relatives and business associates?

Follow-up phone calls also give you the opportunity to make add-on sales. You can use the call to remind the customer about some of the additional accessories that are available for the product.

Be sure that your callers have a script for the call and that they ask the customer if it's a good time to call.

Kerry Olson, the great sales associate from Valas TV and Appliance, used follow-up calls to ask customers what purchases they planned to make next, offering to watch for sales and specials on those particular items. She also asked about upcoming birthdays and graduations, suggesting appropriate gift items. Then she'd tickle her calendar with notes to get back to those customers. Any time she was in the store, Kerry had a line of "her" customers waiting patiently to buy from her.

The only time Kerry wasn't making calls to her customers was during the busy holiday selling season. She'd jokingly complain then that because she didn't have time to make calls, it would probably hurt her February business. Kerry is a real pro.

➤ Written Surveys

Surveys are another great way to find out what customers are thinking. Shorter surveys, the size of postcards, are most likely to be returned. To increase the number you get back, enter the names of all those customers who return cards (and who fill in the optional customer name) in for a drawing each month.

Use the information on the survey cards for coaching and to give special recognition to those who have gone the extra mile for their customers. Post the ones complimenting your service on a bulletin board for your whole team to see.

➤ Five Rules for Customer Surveys:

Limit 1

Customers hate long questionnaires, so limit your questionnaire to fit on one side of a postcard, or at most, one sheet of 8 ½ x 11 paper. Anything longer is too daunting.

Limit 10

For the same reason, limit yourself to not more than ten questions. Seven is better. Five is ideal.

No Fill in the _____

Customers are not stupid but they *are* lazy and when it comes to answering questions, they hate filling in blanks. So give them a checklist, or a check-all-that-apply list, or rank order these five things, or a Lickert scale (put an X on the line somewhere from 1 to 10) so they can respond with a single stroke of the pen.

Fax Back

Pre-pay the return postage, or better still, encourage customers to fax back the results. You'll get a higher rate of response and it's cheaper than enclosing a self-addressed stamped envelope.

Share

Offer to share the results of your survey with all who respond. Curiosity is a powerful motivator and people will often complete the questionnaire just to see what other people are saying. Another benefit: if your customers are giving you a 98.6% Excellent rating, well then, you can tell all your customers without feeling like you're exaggerating or bragging.

➤ Board of Directors for a Day

Once a year, a small local clothing chain sends out slightly longer surveys to all of the customers holding their private label credit cards.

The one-page survey asks their customers to spend a few minutes on their "Board" by answering questions about their store locations, the merchandise they carry, their sales associates, their pricing, their return policies, their advertising and promotion and whatever other questions are pertinent at the time.

Customers who bring their surveys into the store anytime the following month get a $25 gift certificate.

The survey not only generates great information that the store's management uses in developing the coming year's business plan, but creates excitement and traffic in the store as the "Directors" flock in to turn in their surveys and get their gift certificates.

➤ Focus Groups

Although it's best to have an independent person facilitate focus groups, Guerrillas without big marketing departments are successfully running them for their stores. One of the best and least expensive ways to get someone to run your focus groups is to approach the business school at a local College or business school. Professors are always looking for good "hands-on" projects for their students.

Invite groups of five or six customers to come to a neutral meeting place like a hotel conference room and talk about the experience they have had in your store. Provide participants with beverages and snacks and ask them to be available for about two hours. Reward participants with a gift from your store, $100 in cash or even a gift certificate for a nice local restaurant.

Make sure your facilitator is familiar with your store and your products before he or she conducts the focus group meeting. Give the leader a list of questions you'd like them to ask during the session. Videotape the session so that you can not only transcribe it, but also capture the body language used by the participants.

➤ Thank You Notes

Nothing works better in getting customers back to your store than thanking them for their business. There are never too many ways to say thank you. Since we now live in a world of telephones and email, the handwritten thank you note is a particularly welcome touch.

Elly was taking clients to dinner in Atlanta and the group said they wanted to go to Bone's, because they'd heard it had the best steaks in town.

She went to the hotel concierge and asked him to call for reservations for 12 people at 7:30. The concierge said that since it was Saturday night, he probably couldn't get them into Bone's and suggested several alternatives.

Elly asked him to call Bone's first and listened to the conversation.

Unfortunately, it was Saturday night and there was nothing available until 9:30. She pled her case to the manager, Bobby, who said to come in, have a drink at the bar and he'd do everything possible to seat us as quickly as possible. He was careful, though, to say that the 9:30 seating was probably the best we could hope for.

The group got to Bone's just after 7:30 and two of them went to find Bobby. In introducing themselves, they tried to slip $20 to him to help insure that they'd be seated quickly.

Bobby was almost offended by that effort. He gave their money back and insisted that his tables weren't for sale but that he really would try to do what he could to accommodate us. They felt somehow they were now doomed to the dreaded two hour wait.

Instead, just as their first round of drinks was served, Bobby came to the bar and told them their table was ready.

The food, service and atmosphere were wonderful and their expectations were exceeded.

If the experience had ended there Elly would have been a very happy camper and eager to come back to Bone's.

But, wait, there's more! As she walked to the parking lot to get our car, Bobby ran out to say goodbye and make sure they enjoyed the evening. They exchanged cards and she assured him she'd be back the next time she was in Atlanta.

Here's the best part. A week later, Elly got a hand-written note on Bone's stationery. The message was simple.

"Dear Ms. Valas: It was a pleasure to meet you this week when you had dinner at Bone's. We appreciated the opportunity to serve you and your guests during your stay in Atlanta. The Bone's staff would be honored to serve you again on your next visit from Colorado. Kindest regards, Bobby Donlan."

Bobby didn't write that note because he thought she would tell people all over the country about his restaurant. He didn't know that we would write about his restaurant in a book that will be read by tens of thousands of people around the world. He probably didn't even fully appreciate the impact his note would have on her.

He was simply doing his job as a good businessman, managing an independent business, competing with the chains and trying to build customer loyalty.

Elly has gone to Bone's every time she's gone back to Atlanta.

There's a footnote to this story. Bobby Donlon has recently gone off and opened his own restaurant in Buckhead, called New York Prime. Mark Stewart has taken Bobby's place, but he still knew who Elly was when she came in, and he sent her another thank you note after her last visit to Bone's.

Now, Elly's eating steak twice every time she goes to Atlanta.

➤ Clubs and User Groups

People are social animals. Anytime you help build community among your customers you increase their loyalty to you. If, at the same time, you can provide additional opportunities for them to come into your store, you've doubled the benefit.

Quilting bees were traditionally great opportunities for neighbors to get together to chat, trade stories, learn new sewing techniques and from time to time, work together to make a quilt for a wedding gift or for someone in need.

When Barb Perry and Regis Boire bought Aurora Sewing Center in East Aurora, New York, they wanted to bring back some of the traditions of the sewing bee. They looked to one of their suppliers, Bernina of America to help provide some answers and their Bernina Club was off and running.

Bernina Club members pay an annual membership fee, receive a monthly newsletter and get special discount rates on the store's wide array of sewing and quilting classes. Each month, they invite their customers in for special Bernina Club events. At Club events, members show their projects and learn about new techniques, new fabrics and other new products. They get discounts on products they buy during the meeting.

Owner Perry says, "We always do incredible business on nights when our Club meets. We sell lots of notions, accessories, machine feet and fabric. I can't tell you how many times one of our members looks at a new machine and walks out with it after the meeting. Usually, they're replacing machines that are just a couple of years old."

Several times each year they invite in guest teachers who are well-known industry experts. Club members get first priority in making reservations for these classes.

➤ In-store Clinics and Classes

Technology is moving at warp speed. Even the biggest geeks can get left in the dust. The surest way you'll lose a customer is to send them home with a new product they can't use well.

Guerrillas have an on-going calendar of clinics and classes so that their prospects can see new products and customers can learn to use them.

Guiry's Paint Wallpaper and Art Supplies has a full complement of classes covering everything from faux painting to stenciling to wallpaper bordering. Their customers become expert decorators coming back over and over to buy supplies and enhance their skills.

Guiry's often brings in representatives from suppliers like Ralph Lauren Paints to conduct seminars about their particular products.

The things you can offer classes on are limitless. People love to learn. Classes on gardening, digital photography, flower arranging, computing, quilting, travel, fitness and health fill up quickly. Poetry readings and book signings can also bring your customers back.

Runner's Roost stores are race headquarters for every big 5k, 10k and marathon race in the area. Runners signing up for races will frequently buy socks, shorts or even new shoes for the event.

If you have a good meeting space in your store, open it to local service clubs and homeowner groups for their meetings.

➤ Loyalty and Frequent Buyer Programs

Airlines may have started the first frequent buyer programs, but guerrilla retailers have run with them.

To compete against Starbucks and Caribou Coffee, many local coffee sellers offer punch cards offering a free drink or a free pound of coffee beans after ten are purchased.

Monaco Shoe Repair sells a discounted punch card for 12 shoe shines. The best part is that they keep the card in an alphabetical file to guarantee that their customers remember to use them.

Birthday Clubs

The restaurant business may be the toughest retailing of all. Only the best attract new customers, appeal to a broad cross section of the public and survive the onslaught of new formats. Palettes are continually changing and people are naturally drawn to the most adventurous tastes in town.

The Fresh Fish Co. in Denver just marked its twenty-fifth anniversary. Started long before the latest high-protein Atkins or South Beach diet crazes, the restaurant has lured customers with the freshest fish available grilled to order on smoky mesquite grills.

Birthdays are big events at the Fish Co. So much so, customers are encouraged to join their birthday club. Club members receive postcards inviting them to celebrate and receive their age as a discount on their entrée.

Manager Timothy McNamara says that the birthday club is so successful, 25% of the customers in the restaurant each evening come in to receive their birthday discount. On most nights, the restaurant serves birthday dinners to 100 guests.

Entrees average about $24, so the average discount is about ten bucks. Is it profitable? Consider this: How many people go out for dinner alone on their birthdays? Most celebrants come with parties of four to eight. They usually order appetizers and drinks, pushing the average sale per customer to $40.

Most important, the restaurant has built a loyal customer base. Every year, 36,500 unique customers come in just to mark their birthdays. One woman actually gets money back. She collected $7 from the restaurant on her 107th birthday! The birthday club list grows every year ensuring the success of the Fresh Fish Co. for another twenty-five years.

Gift Cards

Gift cards are no longer considered impersonal or "lazy man's" gifts. In fact, people love to receive them.

Nearly half of all consumers planned to purchase at least one gift card during the 2003 holiday season. The National Retail Federation predicted that their buyers would spend more than $17.2 billion on gifts cards during that same period.

Consumers love the cards because they can combine several cards to make one large purchase. They don't have to hassle with returning unwanted gifts and they can make purchases whenever they want to—like during a sale, or after inventory when a wider selection of merchandise may be available.

Cautious retailers are careful not to book gift card sales until they are redeemed, instead carrying them as a liability on their books. Dormancy can run as high as six to eight percent. At some point of time, retailers get a real bonanza as they begin booking a portion of the dormant cards, until the balance is depleted.

Retailers love gift cards because it draws consumers into their stores. Although there is some breakage in unused cards, most companies find that people actually spend more than the gift card amount, which increases sales even further.

Gift cards are really win-win-win opportunities. They are easy to give and fun to receive, but the big winner is the retailer who ensures that customers come in over and over to both purchase and redeem the cards.

Keep the Money in Your Store

When a customer returns or exchanges an item at Lowe's, instead of back-crediting the customer's credit card, the clerk offers to simply transfer the credit onto one of their own store Merchandise Credit cards. Not only is the credit easier to process, it guarantees that those same customers won't spend that money at Home Depot or Ace Hardware.

➤ Preferred Customer Sales

Everyone likes to feel like they're a part of a special group. There's nothing like a preferred customer sale to bring your old friends back. The invitation could be to a private sale the evening before an anniversary sale or clearance event opens to the public.

Mike Moore of Townhouse TV in Lisle, IL perfected the art of the private sale as early as the seventies. Not much has changed from his original formula.

Private sales can be done two to three times each year as long as they are credible and offer real values. Done right, the preferred customer sale can generate a store's monthly sales volume on a Sunday afternoon or from noon until 9 on a weekday evening.

Some dates that work well are the week before Thanksgiving and the week before Mother's Day or holidays like Veteran's Day when a significant number of people have the day off.

➤ The Townhouse Formula:

Before the sale:

Develop a database of all of your customers. Verify accuracy and delete duplicate entries.

Ask vendors for special purchases and for giveaway items like hats, mugs and t-shirts.

Buy inexpensive gifts to give to each customer coming in.

Arrange for beverages and invite a scout troupe to grill hot dogs as a fundraiser for their troop.

Schedule the promotion date and ask suppliers to have representatives there to demonstrate their products.

Schedule a full complement of staff and additional cashiers and credit clerks.

Arrange for special financing terms like 1-year free financing.

Ask vendors for additional promotional funds.

Write private sale letter; design envelope and admission tickets. Don't forget to mention the free gifts, limited hours, brands on sale, discounts up to x% and that you are including extra tickets so that they can bring friends or relatives as their guests.

Mail letter to arrive 3 to 7 days before the sale.

Remind staff not to quote sale prices but to remind customers that the prices will only be good during the sale hours.

Day of sale:

Place small ad in newspaper saying that the store will be closed to the public and only be open to those with invitations. Guerrillas will make a limited number of tickets available to those who come to the store anyway but remind those customers to keep their "secret."

Until opening, paper the windows with butcher paper and put a sign on the door stating the hours of your private sale.

Put special Private Sale tags on all merchandise even if you can only discount it a few dollars. There may be products that you cannot discount because of your agreements with your suppliers.

Put a security guard or off-duty policeman at the door to collect tickets.

Hold staff meeting to remind associates of special prices and policies. Remind them that prices are only good during the hours of the sale. When customers aren't sure of themselves, instruct sales associate to write up the order for pickup later. If your store is on commission it's often a good idea to pool commissions for all products sold during the event. Feed the crew before the opening bell. They may not have time to eat later and you don't want anyone going out for dinner. Make sure there are plenty of sales invoices and additional staff to write orders.

Open the doors and enjoy the crowds.

Day Following the Sale:

Remove Private Sale tags. If the sale preceded a public event, put up new price tags on sale items. All prices should be higher than during your Private Sale.

Go to the bank. Make a large deposit.

Dealing with Upset or Angry Customers

No retailer opens the door hoping to disappoint customers. Yet no matter how hard dealers try to offer legendary service, some customers will still get upset or even angry.

It shouldn't really be too hard to satisfy today's buyer. The formula for customer satisfaction is simply to exceed their expectations. Time and again, though, some aspect of the customer's shopping experience leaves them disappointed.

➤ Total Product Concept

One might assume that the rapid growth of warehouse clubs and self-service superstores means that consumers have lowered their standards in regards to service, but the opposite is true. Today's customer demands more than ever before.

Resolving customer problems quickly and expeditiously actually creates customer loyalty and word of mouth advertising. A customer who has had an issue successfully resolved is four times as loyal as a customer who never had a problem. It's well worth the effort to design a process to seek out and manage customer complaints.

Making a Molehill out of a Mouse

A colleague of ours went into a Computer City store to exchange a mouse that wouldn't work with his system. He'd received it the previous day as a gift from a friend. Told that he'd have to go wait in line at the Customer Service Department, he couldn't help but notice the back-lit sign on the wall portraying the company's CEO saying, "We won't judge the quality of our customer service by how well *we think* the customer was treated but instead by how well *the customer thinks* they were treated."

The clerk in the Customer Service Department pointed to the appropriate aisle in the store and told her customer to find one that would work with his system.

After cruising the aisle for ten minutes, the customer returned to the service desk to see if someone could help him find the proper mouse.

A sales associate finally took the customer back to the department and spent another ten minutes trying to find the proper mouse, before throwing up his hands and admitting that they didn't seem to have one in stock.

The customer returned to the Customer Service desk and asked the clerk there if she would special order him the proper mouse. Her frustration with the customer became apparent as she explained that the company was a large national chain and couldn't do special orders for every single customer.

At that point, the customer asked for a refund.

When the clerk asked for his receipt, the customer explained, yet again, that he'd received the mouse as a gift and didn't have a receipt, but that the friend had bought it at that very same store the previous day. Since they had asked his friend for his name, address and telephone number as part of the credit card transaction, surely they had a record of it.

Now the clerk looked like she'd had enough of this particular customer as she explained, again, that they were a huge national company and couldn't possibly keep a record of every single transaction at every single store location. No receipt, no refund.

The customer ultimately got his $29 back from the store manager. The company was soon acquired by its largest competitor and the CEO in the picture was fired.

If 20 customers feel they have been treated badly, only one will complain. But at least fourteen of those dissatisfied customers will instead choose to do business with someone else.

In fact, 96% of dissatisfied customers do not complain to the store about poor service and inattentive salespeople. At the same time, 74% of dissatisfied customers will become loyal customers again if their complaints are handled competently and quickly. The American Society for Quality Control has determined that loyal customers are worth ten times their initial purchase.

Consumers whose problems are resolved to their satisfaction are actually *more* likely to do business with that retailer in the future than people who shopped at the same store and had no complaints. Those who left happy in the first place only had their expectations met—they came to the store expecting to find the products they bought and they found the experience efficient and reasonably pleasant. But those with complaints expect a fight to the death before their problems are resolved. They expect to be shuttled from department to department and from manager to manager before finally settling for a compromise that doesn't really make them feel like they've won.

Disgruntled customers who leave fully satisfied are the *most* loyal because their expectations have been wildly exceeded. No fight.

No battle. None of this, "We can't do that. It's *policy*." Guerrillas exploit this principle of psychology at every opportunity.

There are a number of reasons why customers might be unhappy. The obvious ones are product failure or poor service by a team member. The human psyche is complex and a number of other factors may come into play.

Customers who have had poor experiences with other retailers come in pre-disposed to do battle. If other sales associates, even those in another industry, treated them rudely, their expectations are set by those experiences. They will test every buying opportunity to see if they will be treated badly again.

Families are time-constrained trying to balance dual-income households, with the demands of childcare, carpools, meals, entertainment and hobbies, there just isn't enough time for shopping, much less for a return trip to make an exchange or get more information.

Buyer's remorse is a major cause of customer dissatisfaction. An expense that seemed appropriate in the store last night may look extravagant in the light of day. A change in employment or family dynamics might make a major purchase that was appropriate just days ago suddenly seem overwhelming and burdensome. A new color that brought a smile to a customer's face might have made her husband grimace.

A little bit of empathy goes a long way in building customer satisfaction. Too often, retail associates error in assuming that customers trying to return products or complain about service are really just covering their own mistakes. Yeah, and so what if they are?

People are basically honest. Most buy products with the full intent of using them and enjoying them. Studies show that many returns are actually a result of poor selling. A failure to ask the customer the right questions and present the most appropriate product often leads to their purchasing something that doesn't meet the needs.

Whether the customer's problem is caused by disappointment in the product purchased, the service received or something else going on in his or her life, Guerrillas understand that the most important part of the solution is a truly empathetic ear.

Just like selling, there's a tried and true plan to effectively solving customer complaints and dealing with disgruntled people. In order to solve a consumer's problem so that he or she becomes a banner ad for the company, it's important to fully understand the complaint, let the consumer tell his or her story and vent frustrations, rephrase the concern, explore all possible solutions and reach an acceptable conclusion.

Customer service is not a department. Running from irritated patrons only adds fuel to the fire. Retail consultants have videotaped sales associates who spot a buyer coming into the front door or into their departments carrying bags or boxes of what is obviously merchandise to be exchanged or taken back. Clerks who scatter in these situations only reinforce the customer's expectation of the impending battle to find resolution. Guerrillas that have learned to embrace complaints and to make lemonade out of those lemons are way ahead of their competitors.

The most powerful word to use when dealing with a dissatisfied customer is "*yes.*" "*Yes* we will solve the problem." "*Yes* I will fix it, exchange it, make it right, listen, answer your questions and anything else needed to make you happy." Time spent reassuring customers that you don't think they're too fussy, and that their complaints are really valid, is a great investment.

As quickly as possible, the associate must assure the customer that the problem will be resolved. He or she must listen to the consumer's complaint carefully and actively. Taking notes shows the customer that you are truly interested in helping. Making eye contact and nodding from time to time shows the patron that you are still listening. Don't interrupt and let the customer finish explaining his or her concern. Move loud or angry customers away from others.

The next step is to restate the problem including all of the key points, whether right or wrong, accurate or not, that the consumer felt were important. Acknowledge the customer's feelings. "You felt that the clerk wasn't accurately scanning your order" or "you were disappointed that the item didn't last as long as you had expected." Avoiding judgment helps put Guerrillas on the side of customer.

Let the customer suggest a resolution to the problem. If asked what would satisfy their complaint, most will ask for far less than retailers would be willing to offer. Letting the customer make the first offer makes them feel empowered and in control.

Explore all possible solutions with customers. The easiest solution, offering a refund, is not usually the best for the consumer. Where shopping was once a leisure time activity, it is now more often done to achieve specific goals and satisfy needs. Most purchases are made because the patron really wanted a product. Simply offering a refund may sound like a good resolution but it still leaves the customer with the item they needed.

Finally, empower the front line to become advocates for their customers. Sending consumers up the ladder from one manager to the next only irritates them. Disgruntled customers become increasingly more irritated as time passes without satisfaction. Trained sales associates at all levels should be able to solve all but the most unusual customer problem.

Statistically, each person influences 250 other people. What customers tell their friends, relatives and business associates depends more on how they are treated when things go wrong than when things go well.

Things will go wrong. Systems will fail. As a guerrilla, you must make sure that when your customers are dissatisfied they tell their 250 friends that you were polite, efficient and courteous, that you treated them with respect, and above all, that the problem was resolved to their satisfaction.

Customer loyalty builds great retail companies. Unhappy customers do not come back. The Bain Company has done extensive research on customer retention and has found that every five percent improvement in customer retention can add up to ten percent in additional bottom line profits.

Complaints are gold mines. Guerrillas seek them out, learn from them and try to improve processes so that they don't reappear. Customers who voice their concerns tell companies when products fail and suppliers need to be replaced.

Customers have a wealth of information about what they want to buy and how they want to be served. Reading between the lines of consumer complaints provides store management with the ammunition they need to win the retail wars.

Chapter 18

Guerrilla Marketing Online

No discussion of retailing would be complete without exploring the exploding use of the Internet.

The newest, biggest, most mysterious, most misunderstood and most promising marketing opportunity in history is the one offered by the advent of the Internet. Every day, online marketing gets bigger, better and more helpful, both for marketers and for consumers.

Forrester Research predicts that e-commerce will continue to grab a larger slice of the retail pie. The consultancy predicts that online sales will hit $95.7 billion in 2003 and climb to $229.9 billion in 2008.

Although that figure seems small at only about 3% of retail sales, the projection is roughly equal to about two and a half times Sears, Roebuck & Co.'s total annual revenues, or about 40% of Wal-Mart's sales. By 2008, e-commerce will represent as much as 8% of total sales.

Still, all who would hope to become online guerrillas must understand three facts:

1. Online marketing will only work if you understand marketing.

2. Online marketing means a lot more than having a website.

3. Online marketing is only 1% of all marketing.

The multi-channel shopper, who is using both storefront and online venues, is driving the rapid growth of e-Commerce. Remember that there are at least 100 marketing weapons, and that online marketing is only one of them. In most cases, you can't market online only with any expectation of success. Yet, the entire media world is becoming fragmented. There are regional editions of magazines, zone editions of newspapers, cable TV stations that reach local communities, local radio stations, targeted mailing lists. Where does everything come together?

It all happens online. Slowly but certainly, people are learning that the whole story exists online — that all the details they must learn before making a purchase are ready to be studied online. The entire Internet phenomenon is part of human evolution and humans learning how to interact in cyberspace is also part of evolution. You don't have to be reminded that evolution takes place over a long period of time. The Internet is here and everybody knows it, but not everybody is online yet and not everybody online is ready to make purchases yet. They will, but not quite yet.

The number of households online has risen from 43.8 million in 2003 to 67.5 households in 2003. Roughly half of online households have bought online.

The number of categories shopped online is rising quickly from 4.4 per household in 2000 to 8.1 in 2003. Early buyers bought books, music and videos but as their comfort level increased, they began to buy big-ticket merchandise.

The best news lies in the rapid proliferation of broadband services. According to Forrester, 61% of those who buy online use broadband service. While dial-up users spend an average of $324 in the three months prior to the study, those with high speed service purchased $552 in the same period.

Click-and-brick merchandising rolls together online and in-store selling. Customers can use your website to collect information and to compare product features and benefits. They come to your store just to see the products that they've already decided to buy. Savvy consumers have learned how to easily buy and ship gifts from e-tailers.

As consumers move stealthily between stores and their web sites, retailers need to pay equal attention to the service provided in all channels. Prices, selection, quality, policies and support services must be mirrored wherever your customers find you.

The insight is that you've got to continue marketing with traditional media, but don't overlook the power of the keyboard. Even when the Internet has achieved a market penetration comparable to that of the telephone, you must continue marketing using time-honored methods. TV revolutionized the marketing scene in it's day, but most of the big TV advertisers also market their offerings in places other than the tube.

When marketing with the traditional media, you're going to have to devote time and space to heralding your website because many people will want to know where they can get more information. Your website is where. No media offers you the comprehensiveness of the web. That's why you need it to flesh out your marketing. The world is learning to buy things in a new way and that way is online. But the learning process is still in process.

For a detailed treatment of this topic, read Jay's book, *Guerrilla Marketing Online.*

Chapter

Managing for Growth and Profitability

■ Metrics and Business Intelligence

Successful Guerrillas develop good financial controls, reporting and budgeting. They understand the relationships between inventory, sales, cash and receivables. They know that their stores are not museums and that merchandise is meant to turn profitably, because profit is the only legitimate measure of success in retail. Retailers who thoroughly analyze all the factors in developing their sales, merchandise and profit plans will be much more profitable.

➤ Merchandising Budget

A merchandising budget is your formal outline of merchandising objectives. It is a plan of projected sales, how much merchandise will be needed to support those sales, what profit will be made on that inventory and how quickly it will be sold.

Budgets may reflect the plan for the entire company, a single store, a division, or a department.

➤ Anticipated Sales Budget

To begin the budgeting process, analyze your previous year's actual sales. Because most retailers have seasonal fluctuations throughout the year, it's best to make a spreadsheet that shows the sales in each product category for each month.

In projecting sales for the coming period, you'll need to factor in projected increases in the cost of your inventory (plus your planned

■ FINANCIAL CAUSE & EFFECT

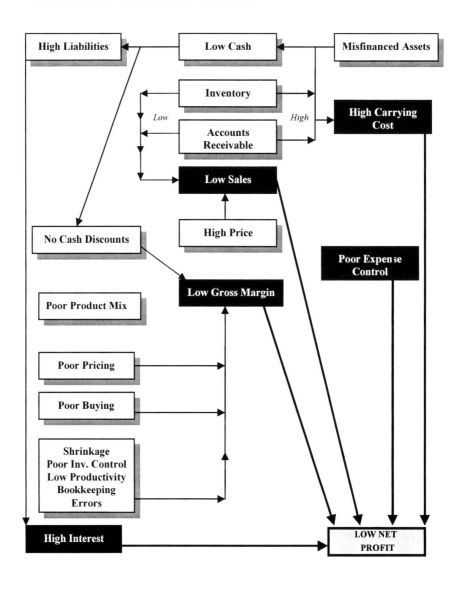

profit on the increase in cost), the general economic outlook, the forecasted growth in your sector, and your company's targeted growth.

Let's consider the sales budget for a department that sold $100,000 last year. First you'll need to determine the gross margin on the goods sold in the previous period. Gross margin is determined by dividing the cost of the goods sold by the dollar amount of sales. In this example, let's assume that the cost of the merchandise was $75,000

$$\$ 75,000/\$100,000 = 25\%$$

If you were planning for a ten percent increase in sales based on both economic forecasts and planned internal growth, that department's budget would be $110,000.

$$\$100,000 \times 110\% = \$110,000$$

Compute the target gross profit by dividing profit dollars by total sales. To obtain a 25% profit margin on the new sales projection, the profit would need to be

$$\$110,000 \times 25\% = \$27,500.$$

If the department's cost of merchandise was also expected to rise by 3%, that should be factored in as well. Since the cost of merchandise increased from $82,500 ($75,000 x 110%) to $84,975 ($82,500 x 103%) with the price increase, sales projections will need to be increased by $2,475, plus a projected 25% profit on the price increase. You would need to increase your sales projection an additional $2,539 to make the planned three percent price increase and a 25% gross profit margin on the increase.

$$(\$2,539 - \$2,475)/\$2,539 = 25\%$$

or $\$64/\$2,539 = 25\%$

Including the price increase and the profit on it, the new sales goal would be $112,539. The budgeted cost of goods would be $84,975, and the budgeted gross profit at 25% would be $27,564.

Sales – Cost of Goods Sold/Sales = Gross Profit Margin %, or

$$(\$112,539 - \$84,975)/\$112,539 = 25\%$$

or $\$27,564/\$112,539 = 25\%$

➤ Inventory Turns

The faster your inventory moves through the store, the more likely you are to be profitable. Japanese companies coined the term "Just In Time" to describe their philosophy of taking delivery on raw materials just in time to use them in the manufacture of finished goods. Sitting on idle inventory is costly.

Similarly, retailers strive to receive their merchandise just as it's needed. No one wants to have inventory intended for holiday sales arrive in June. It's expensive to warehouse, ties up cash or available credit lines, can get damaged and may become obsolete. Guerrillas try to have new merchandise arrive just as they run out of older goods.

Membership clubs like Sam's or Costco turn their inventory so quickly that they don't even need warehouse space. All merchandise is displayed on the selling floor because new orders arrive as quickly as it's sold. Some products are on the floor less than a week—which would equate to merchandise turning more than 52 times each year.

In the example above, the company is planning to sell $112,539 in goods, and the cost is $84,975. Since not all of that inventory will be sold at the same time, there's no reason to buy it all at once.

Inventory is an investment, and guerrillas maximize that investment by buying and selling their merchandise as quickly as possible. So how much inventory should you keep on hand?

Much depends on how much warehouse and display space your store has, how long it takes suppliers to get the goods to you, how frequently it changes during a year and the terms offered by your suppliers. There's a delicate balance between having too much inventory and being short of stock.

Most retail segments publish standards for inventory turns. These are computed by dividing the cost of inventory sold during the year by the typical on-hand inventory. Depending on the products, they may vary from 3 to 8 turns per year.

In our example above, if your inventory level were $20,000 you would be turning your inventory 4.2 times each year.

Cost of Goods Sold (annualized)/Average Inventory = Inventory Turns, or

$84,975/$20,000 = 4.2

To increase the number of turns, you would have to carry less inventory or increase sales while keeping inventory at the same level.

➤ How to Diagnose and Solve Financial Problems

Financial Statement Analysis

Analyzing your store's financial statements can be quite intimidating. It often involves concepts that are only vaguely familiar to most business owners. In addition, most owners tend to focus on only one line on their financial statements: Net Profit After Tax. Unfortunately, this information by itself tells you very little about the true financial condition of your business.

Understanding all of the key indicators found in your financial statements and how they relate to the management of your business is critical to your long-term financial success.

To completely analyze your financial statements, follow the steps listed below. The key to making this easier is to take one step at a time.

Spread your Financial Statements

You must first collect the financial statement data for the last several years. Then put the data from three to five years of balance sheets onto one page. Then repeat the process for the income statements. This process, called "Spreading the Financial Statements," allows you to look at accounts side-by-side over several years. By doing this, you will be able to spot trends in your financial statements that you might not otherwise notice. It also makes the information much easier to work with.

Calculate Common Size Percentages

Now common size the income statement and balance sheet. For the balance sheets, each asset, liability and equity account is divided by total assets. For the income statements, divide all expense accounts by total sales. This is called a common size analysis because it allows you to compare your income statement and balance sheet to others in your industry on a percentage basis.

Calculate Key Indicators (Ratios)

Using the formulas from the Glossary of Financial Information in this chapter, calculate some key indicators that are called ratios. The idea is to look not just at the numbers by themselves, but what are they in relation to something else. This way, you can measure specific areas of your business such as liquidity, safety, profitability and balance sheet management.

Interpret the Ratios and Analyze Trends

Interpret and review the ratios for each year, one ratio at a time. Note any fluctuations or declines in the ratios over time. Spend some time reviewing common sized financial statements for your industry, available from your trade association, or the RMA Reports from Robert Morris Associates.

Conduct an Industry Comparison

To get a sense of how your business is performing compared to the market, compare your ratios and common sized financial statements to the data found for comparable stores. Look where your performance is better or worse than the industry standards. Ideally, use the high profit standards as the basis of comparison. If you don't feel comfortable with the statistics in the RMA report, use your store's best year as your basis of comparison

Identify Problems

You will be surprised and pleased to discover that you don't need an MBA to spot problems. Make note of any areas of concern. Be sure to include areas where performance is declining, even if it is still above the statistics found in the report.

Calculate Financial Impact

Calculate the financial impact for each of the problem areas you have identified using the formulas in the How to Diagnose a Financial Problem section of this chapter.

Diagnose Problems through Cause & Effect Analysis

Use the Financial Diagnostics to determine both the causes of the problem and its possible solution.

Develop a Plan

Document the problems and the steps necessary to fix each of them. Identify who will be responsible for implementing the solutions and set deadlines to analyze the results.

Variance Analysis

Compare actual performance to planned performance each month. Carefully analyze the variances and take the appropriate action to return to the plan.

➤ How to Diagnose a Financial Problem

There are four basic steps to diagnosing and solving a financial problem in your business:

1. Conduct Financial Impact Analysis

2. Determine the Cause of the Problem

3. Determine Possible Solutions

4. Implement a Plan of Action

Use the Financial Impact Analysis formulas below to calculate how big the problems are in dollar terms. The word 'target' in the formulas refers to the goal you've set for your store. This may be the median or the high profit median from the industry norms, your store's best year, or some other type of industry-specific goal.

If a store has low net profits, there are five general causes:

1. High Carrying Costs

2. Low Gross Profit

3. Poor Expense Control

4. High Interest

5. Low Sales

Each of these causes is in turn caused by something else. For example, high carrying costs are driven by high inventory levels or large accounts receivable.

To determine possible solutions, use these Financial Diagnostic Formulas.

➤ Financial Impact Analysis

Total Liabilities

Target Liabilities = Net Equity x Target Debt-to-Equity Ratio

Actual Liabilities – Target Liabilities = Financial Impact ($)

Gross Profit

Target Gross Profit = Sales x Target Gross Profit Margin (%)

Target Gross Profit – Actual Gross Profit = Financial Impact ($)

Pretax Profit

Target Pretax Profit = Sales x Target Pretax Profit Margin (%)

Target Pretax Profit – Actual Pretax Profit = Financial Impact ($)

Sales

Target Sales = Total Assets x Target Sales to Assets

Target Sales – Actual Sales = Financial Impact ($)

Total Assets

Target Total Assets = Sales/Target Sales to Assets

Actual Total Assets – Target Total Assets = Financial Impact ($)

Net Fixed Assets

Target Net Fixed Assets = Sales/Target Sales to Net Fixed Assets

Actual Net Fixed Assets – Target Net Fixed Assets = Financial Impact ($)

Accounts Receivable

Target Accounts Receivable = Sales

Target Accounts Receivable Turnover

Actual Accounts Receivable – Target Accounts Receivable = Financial Impact ($)

Accounts Payable

Target Accounts Payable = Cost of Goods Sold/Target Accounts Payable Turnover

Actual Accounts Payable – Target Accounts Payable = Financial Impact ($)

■ Glossary of Financial Terms

We strongly recommend that you review this section carefully before completing an analysis of your business.

➤ Liquidity

Liquidity ratios are ratios that measure a dealership's ability to meet its short-term obligations.

Current Ratio

Formula: Current Assets / Current Liabilities

The current ratio shows a dealership's ability to pay obligations due within twelve months with assets that are expected to turn to cash in twelve months. For the most part, a dealership that has readily collectible accounts receivable can operate safely with a lower current ratio than a dealership whose cash flow is less dependable. The key factors that influence the current ratio are asset productivity, leverage and debt structure.

Quick Ratio

Formula: (Cash + Short-term Securities + Net Receivables) / Current Liabilities

The quick ratio is intended to take the current ratio one step further. It gives an "acid test" of the retailer's ability to meet its current debts using only the most liquid of assets. In periods of stress, other assets such as inventory would not bring their assigned value or turn into cash very quickly. Therefore, only cash, securities and receivables are considered. Assuming good accounts receivable collections, a quick ratio of around 1.0 is usually adequate.

Cash to Current Liabilities

Formula: Cash / Current Liabilities

This ratio is intended to take the quick ratio one step further. It gives an instant "acid test" of the retailer's ability to meet its current debts using the *most* liquid asset, cash. In periods of stress, other assets such as inventory, receivables, or other current assets would not bring their assigned value or turn into cash very quickly. Therefore, only cash is considered. A cash/current liability ratio of around .20 to 1 is usually considered adequate.

Safety

Safety ratios are ratios that measure a dealership's ability to withstand adversity.

Debt-to-Equity

Formula: Total Liabilities / Total Equity

Debt-to-equity, also known as leverage or debt-to-worth, compares the amount of funds invested by creditors to the amount of funds invested by owners. Although it is necessary to incur liabilities to do business, this ratio should not be allowed to become too large, because the higher the Debt-to-Equity ratio becomes, the more the business is at risk. A larger amount of debt increases a dealership's ability to grow during good times; however, it also decreases the dealership's ability to withstand a downturn in profitability. The key factors that influence the size of the debt-to-equity ratio are your dealership's borrowing, profitability and capital structure (i.e. sources of funds other than debt).

➤ Profitability

Profitability ratios are ratios that measure a store's profitability at various levels.

Gross Profit Margin %

Formula: (Gross Profit / Total Sales) x 100

The gross profit margin equals your gross profit divided by sales. This is a ratio representing what percentage of each sales dollar is available after paying for the cost of goods sold or direct expenses. The gross profit margin measures the effectiveness of your pricing policies and your efficiency in producing/delivering your product or service. Conducting trend analysis and industry comparisons are very important for determining the adequacy of this ratio.

Operating Profit Margin %

Formula: (Operating Profit / Total Sales) x 100

The operating profit margin is the percentage return on sales after all operating expenses and before other income and expense. Conducting trend analysis and industry comparisons are very important for determining the adequacy of this ratio.

Pretax Profit Margin %

Formula: (Pretax Profit / Total Sales) x 100

The Pretax profit margin is the percentage return on sales after all expenses, except taxes. Conducting trend analysis and industry comparisons are very important for determining the adequacy of this ratio.

➤ Balance Sheet Management

Balance sheet management ratios measure the financial strength of a dealership's balance sheet.

Sales to Assets

Formula: Total Sales / Total Assets

Also known as the Asset Productivity Ratio, this ratio indicates the amount of sales generated from each dollar invested in total assets, or the efficiency with which the assets are being used to drive sales. The key factors that influence asset productivity are accounts receivable management, fixed asset management, management of all other assets and the total sales volume.

Sales to Net Fixed Assets

Formula: Total Sales / Net Fixed Assets

The sales to net fixed assets ratio indicates the amount of sales generated from each dollar invested in fixed assets. As with the sales to assets ratio, the sales to net fixed assets ratio measures the efficiency with which fixed assets are being used to produce sales.

Operating Return on Equity %

Formula: (Operating Profit / Total Equity) x 100

The operating return on equity, also known as operating return on investment, indicates the amount of income from operations generated for each dollar of equity. The net equity represents the equity of the proprietor, partners, or stockholders in the dealership. This equity usually consists of the original and subsequent investments or stock issues plus retained earnings. By calculating this ratio you can determine how effectively the owner's money is being used.

Operating Return on Assets %

Formula: (Operating Profit / Total Assets) x 100

The operating return on assets gives a measure of the return obtained on the total assets of the dealership. Since the assets are the tools with which a dealership must work to make a profit, this ratio gives a measure of how well management is utilizing these tools.

Return on Equity %

Formula: Net Profit / Total Equity x 100

The return on equity, also known as return on investment, takes the operating return on equity one step further. This ratio shows the amount of profits generated, after other income and expense, for every dollar of owner's equity.

Return on Assets %

Formula: (Net Profit / Total Assets) x 100

The return on assets is like the operating return on assets, except that it shows the amount of profits generated, after other income and expense, for each dollar invested in assets.

chapter 20

■ Parting Shot

Retailing is more art than science. It exposes the warts and reveals the pimples of every business. Retailing is the pure essence of trade, so it magnifies the difficulties and amplifies the advantages. Retailing is sales in it's purest form; just put the goods out there and people buy them. If only it were that simple.

Everything in the scope of marketing comes out in the open on the retail floor: manufacturing, distribution, salesmanship, signage, shelving, lighting, packaging, pricing, customer service and most of all, buyer behavior. All the facets of marketing are focused on that behavior, attempting to influence it at every turn. The sales process is collapsed into an eye blink, as shoppers respond to some deep impulse to buy.

It's not an easy job, which is why so many aspiring retailers fail. You picked up this book, so we certainly don't have to tell you that retailing calls for the acumen and energy of a guerrilla.

Where does retailing begin? Not on the sales floor. Not in the window. Not in the newspaper ads.

Retailing begins in the mind of the eventual buyer. The ember of a need or a want is ignited by the spark of a good idea, spread by the crackling of advertising or a friend's chance comment, fanned to a flame by a glance at a sign, and spread by a hand reaching for a package.

In between the steps leading to a purchase, many factors enter the equation, and you, as a guerrilla retailer, are in charge of all of them. More important, you, as a guerrilla, are aware of all of them.

A guerrilla retailer is fully aware of how many factors there truly are. Consider the true tale of a retailer in Canada.

Once upon a time there were two retailers in the same business, the furniture business. One was located in the Denver area and had grown from zero to more than 20 showrooms. Let's say his name was Jake. The other was from the San Francisco Bay area and had grown from zero to one gigantic 80,000 square foot showroom. We'll call him Ralph.

Jake and Ralph were not competitors, though each one was extremely competitive. They would meet a few times a year at tradeshows and trade war stories.

One year, they met at a conference and talked about a furniture dealer in Edmonton, Alberta, Canada, a dealer who was ringing up more than *eight times* the sales per square foot than either Jake or Ralph. Just as amazing, the Edmonton dealer's showroom was no larger than Ralph's and he had been in business no longer than Jake.

Yet, he was doing eight times the business. Hmmm.

Jake and Ralph put their heads together, and in the true spirit of fusion marketing, decided to visit the Edmonton showroom as a team to learn the secrets of its success. Their plan called for three days in Edmonton, visiting the showroom and talking to its owners, looking around and checking the books.

The retailers were not only joining forces, but also taking precious time to visit a rip-roaring success with the admirable goal of determining why it was doing so well.

They returned three days later. We were anxious to talk to each of them and get their take on the situation. After all, they were both doing very well, but doing only one-eighth the business of the Edmonton furniture store.

We asked Ralph first, "What was their secret?"

"They didn't tell us," said Ralph. "Oh, they answered all of our questions, showed us their records, took us into their office and explained everything. But you know what? They didn't tell us one single thing, really. They kept it all secret. I spent three days there and didn't learn one thing, except that they were secretive. Nice guys, but very closed."

Next, we spoke with Jake. "What was their secret?"

"They didn't *have* a secret," he countered. Everything they did was obvious and open. They gave us all the details. While I divide my business into five sections, they divided theirs into forty-five. They were aware of personnel, parking, prices and selection. They paid close attention to greeting customers, keeping their showroom spic and span, walking customers to their cars and making certain their employees attire reflected their identity. In truth, they spilled all the beans and told us or showed us everything we needed to know. I was so embarrassed by my cluelessness as a retailer that I vowed to totally revamp my way of doing business."

Today, Ralph slaves away at his showroom, while Jake is happily retired in his Hawaiian getaway.

The moral is a religious one. The Devil is in the details. The Edmonton operation was aware of all the details of running a business and paid very close attention to each one of them.

Ralph was oblivious to them. Jake was made painfully aware. Now, you're aware too. There is no secret.

That is the real secret of success.

Appendix A

■ FINANCIAL DIAGNOSTICS

➤ Problems, Possible Causes, and Solutions

I. Low Current Ratio

    A. Cause: Current liabilities too high

        1. Solution: Move some short-term liabilities to long-term

    B. Cause: Using short-term funds (current liabilities) to fund long-term assets

        1. Solution: Sale/lease back some fixed assets

II. Low Quick Ratio

    A. Cause: Current liabilities too high and using short-term funds (current liabilities) to fund long-term assets

        1. Solution: Move some short-term liabilities to long-term

        2. Solution: Sale/lease back some fixed assets

    B. Cause: Inventory is too high.

        1. Solution: Reduce inventory

III. High Debt to Equity

    A. Cause: Net worth too low.

        1. Solution: Add to capital (sell stock)

B. Cause: Liabilities too high

    1. Solution: Slow growth in order to let profits reduce liabilities instead of purchasing additional assets

IV. Low Gross Margin

  A. Cause: Poor pricing

    1. Solution: Don't offer discounts

  B. Cause: Poor buying

    1. Solution: Take trade discounts

  C. Cause: Poor product mix

    1. Solution: Change sales mix

  D. Cause: Poor productivity

    1. Solution: Reduce acquisition costs

  E. Cause: Spoilage, shrinkage, etc.

    1. Solution: Monitor Inventory more closely

V. Low Pretax Margin

  A. Cause: Low gross margin

    1. Solution: See IV.

  B. Cause: Overhead too high

    1. Solution: Reduce overhead

      a. Calculate appropriate overhead by multiplying sales by industry average overhead percentage

VI. Low Sales to Assets

  A. Cause: Low sales

    1. Solution: Increase sales by increasing accounts receivable (loosening credit terms)

  B. Cause: High assets

    1. Solution: Reduce inventory

    2. Solution: Reduce accounts receivable

    3. Solution: Sale/lease back of fixed assets

    4. Solution: Sell unneeded property

VII. Low Return on Assets

  A. Cause: Low Pretax Profit

    1. Solution: Increase sales

    2. Solution: Reduce expenses

  B. Cause: High assets

    1. Solution: Sale/lease back of fixed assets

    2. Solution: Sell unneeded property

VIII. Low ROI

   A. Cause: Low Pretax Profit

      1. Solution: See IV

      2. Solution: Reduce overhead

         a. Calculate appropriate overhead by multiplying sales by industry average overhead percentage

   B. Cause: High net worth

      1. Solution: Expand the business using borrowed funds

IX. Low AR Turnover

   A. Cause: Accounts receivable too high

      1. Solution: Reduce accounts receivable

         a. Calculate appropriate accounts receivable by dividing sales by the industry average accounts receivable turnover

         b. Tighten credit terms

X. Low Inventory Turnover

   A. Cause: Inventory too high

      1. Solution: Reduce Inventory (Sale)

XI. Low Sales per Employee

   A. Cause: Too many employees

      1. Solution: Reduce the number of employees

Appendix B

■ Job Descriptions Directory

This Appendix includes job descriptions for:

General Manager

Sales Manager

Store Manager

Office Manager

Warehouse Manager

Sales Associate

Delivery Supervisor

Delivery Driver/Installer

➤ General Manager

Reports to: Company President

Basic Function:

The basic function of the General Manager will be to work directly with the company President to oversee and direct the operations of the sales, service and warehouse/delivery/installation departments. All activities of the General Manager shall always be carried out in a professional and ethical manner.

Duties and Responsibilities:

By implementing the following duties and responsibilities properly and by performing related work as required, the General Manager will be able to perform his/her job function as outlined.

1. Participate in developing budgets and business plans for the profitable operation of the departments under his/her control and manage to reach or exceed the agreed-to goals.

2. Create and implement job descriptions for his/her subordinate managers.

3. Delegate specific job functions to their respective departments.

4. Hire, train, review and evaluate subordinate managers.

5. Oversee each manager's review and evaluation of his/her employees.

6. Help solve any recurring problem that is beyond the scope of a manager.

7. Supervise the merchandising manager's development of merchandising, pricing, display and sales plans for all products.

8. Supervise the merchandising or advertising manager's development of advertising programs and sales promotions.

9. Review sales and financial performance daily, weekly and monthly (with the Controller) and determine and implement changes that may be needed in order to meet sales, turns and margin budget projections.

10. Develop a business plan in conjunction with the service manager for the operation of the service department as a profit-making division.

11. Provide for the maintenance and security of business buildings and property.

12. Act as a role model for company policies.

13. Take an active role in representing the company in the local community.

14. Attend manufacturer and association training meetings and business schools as required.

Relationships:

It is essential that the General Manager maintain professional communication with all company managers and departments in order to maintain good relationships within the company and assure total customer satisfaction. The General Manager's immediate supervisor shall be the company President. The General Manager will work cooperatively with others who report to the president, which may include the Controller, Office Manager and IT Manager.

Minimum Qualifications:

It will be necessary for the General Manager to have a minimum of five to seven years of retail store management experience and to have completed business management training as set forth by the company President. He or she must be able to pass a pre-employment drug test and a criminal/theft background check.

➤ Sales Manager

Reports to: Company President, General Manager or Store Manager

Basic Function:

The basic function of the Sales Manager will be to oversee the operation of the entire sales portion of the company. This includes but is not limited to training of all Sales Associates, merchandising of products sold by the company and providing professional assistance to customers. All activities of the Sales Manager shall always be carried out in a professional and ethical manner.

Duties and Responsibilities:

By implementing the following duties and responsibilities properly and by performing related work as required, the Sales Manager will be able to perform his/her job function as outlined.

1. Develop a team of customer-friendly Sales Associates.

2. Provide training and coaching to all Sales Associates on qualifying customers, explaining product features, advantages and benefits and closing sales.

3. Provide training to all Sales Associates on the benefits of selling extended service protection and accessories to customers.

4. Provide training to all Sales Associates on offering the company's private label credit card as an alternate source of credit.

5. Institute and manage creative sales contests and incentive programs to maintain a high level of morale and productivity among the Sales Associates.

6. Arrange and oversee weekly sales meetings to keep Sales Associates up-to-date on new products, programs, laws and regulations.

7. Assure that all merchandise is always displayed in an attractive manner. This includes making sure that it is clean, operational (if applicable) and priced with a clearly printed price tag.

8. Work directly with sales representatives from vendors to make sure that all literature is current and to keep abreast of any changes within vendors' lineup of products.

9. Work directly with the company President, General Manager or Store Manager to ensure that all merchandise is priced at adequate margin levels and to monitor margin performance on a daily basis.

10. Oversee the implementation of the company's loss prevention policies on the sales floor.

11. Assist Sales Associates on special order/out-of-stock customer quotes.

12. Provide caring assistance to customers who have special requests or complaints about the company or products. This must always be done in a non-confrontational, non-emotional manner.

13. Attend manufacturer and association training seminars as required.

14. Work with Merchandising Manager to ensure that all products in stock are on display. All empty spaces should either be filled or remaining products spread out to fill the void.

15. Inform company President, General Manager or Store Manager of any issues that arise that could have an impact on the company. This includes competitive, pricing and personnel issues.

16. Review monthly sales quotas with Sales Associates and provide performance appraisal and guidance when necessary.

17. Maintain a program of competitive shopping.

18. Actively participate in the selling of merchandise.

19. Ensure that the store opens and closes at assigned hours and that the sales floor is adequately staffed during peak hours.

20. Act as a role model for company policies and customer-focused sales presentations.

Relationships:

It is essential that the Sales Manager maintain professional communication with all company managers and departments. Only by working together and having respect for everyone's position in the company, will the company be able to accomplish its goal of continued growth and continuity. The Sales Manager's immediate supervisor shall be the company President, General Manager or Store Manager.

Minimum qualifications:

It will be necessary for the Sales Manager to have a minimum of two (2) years' on-the-job experience and to have completed necessary business operation training as set forth by the company President.

➤ Store Manager

Reports to: Company President or General Manager

Basic Function:

The Store Manager is responsible for the overall performance of the store including but not limited to profitability, customer satisfaction, personnel, sales, merchandising, advertising and operations. All activities of the Store Manager will be carried out in a professional and ethical manner.

Duties and Responsibilities:

By implementing the following duties and responsibilities and performing related work as required, the Store Manager will be able to perform his/her job function as outlined.

1. Create and implement job descriptions for all store personnel.

2. Hire, train, supervise, motivate and evaluate store personnel.

3. Manage the daily activity and personnel scheduling of the store.

4. If there is no Sales Manager, perform those duties. (See that job description.).

5. Develop and implement an annual quarterly and monthly budget for advertising, sales, turns and margins.

6. Manage store expenses within the approved budget.

7. Develop and implement an annual, quarterly and monthly merchandising, pricing and display plan for all products.

8. Assure that the sales floor and store appearance are maintained according to the merchandising, pricing and display plans.

9. Continuously monitor inventory to insure that aging products are moved through the system for maximum turns and productivity.

10. Review sales performance daily, weekly and monthly and determine and implement changes that may be needed in order to meet sales, turns and margins budget projections.

11. Assure that cash control policies are followed at the service desk and/or checkout counters.

12. Oversee the implementation of the store's safety, security and loss prevention policies.

13. Act as a role model of company policies.

14. Take an active role in representing the company in the local community.

15. Attend manufacturer and association training meetings and business schools as required.

Relationships:

It is essential that the Store Manager maintain professional communication with all company managers and departments. Only by working as a team will the company be able to accomplish its goal of continued growth and continuity. The Store Manager's immediate supervisor shall be the company President or General Manager.

Minimum Qualifications:

It will be necessary for the Store Manager to have a minimum of three years of retail store management experience and to have completed business management training as set forth by the company President. He or she must be able to pass a pre-employment drug test and criminal/theft background check.

➤ Merchandising Manager

Reports to: General Manager or Store Manager

Basic Function:

The merchandising manager will be responsible for planning the type and quantity of products to be sold and buying and display of merchandise on the sales floor in order to maximize productivity and profit margins for the company. All activities of the Merchandising Manager shall always be carried out in a professional and ethical manner. (This job description may be adapted for use for individuals responsible for specific product categories such as appliances, electronics, etc.)

Duties and Responsibilities:

By implementing the following duties and responsibilities properly and by performing related work as required, the Merchandising Manager will be able to perform his/her job function as outlined.

1. Develop and maintain a comprehensive understanding of market trends, technology and feature developments and vendor programs for products that are sold or could be sold by the dealership.

2. Conduct on going analysis of competitors' product and pricing strategies.

3. Determine which vendors, product categories and models will best accomplish the company's marketing and profit goals.

4. Develop documented price point merchandising plans for determining the assortment and price points of

products to be sold in each category in order to meet established margin goals.

5. Develop documented open-to-buy plans to assure that the appropriate products are available in the warehouse and on the sales floor in order to accomplish the merchandising plan for each category and assortment.

6. Review sales and margin performance daily, weekly and monthly and implement changes to the merchandising and open-to-buy plans that may be needed to assure that margin goals are met.

7. Negotiate purchases and authorize purchase orders as required to fulfill the established price point merchandising and open-to-buy plans.

8. Develop and maintain positive relationships with vendor and buying group representatives in order to receive information on price changes, special offers, product availability, feature and marketing support information necessary to accomplish sales and margin goals and to assure favorable response to special requests.

9. Work with the Store Manager or Sales Manager to assure that products are properly displayed and sold to fulfill merchandising plans and that the store layout, displays and POP create an attractive buying environment.

10. Help train sales associates.

11. Attend manufacturer and association training meetings and business schools as required.

12. Act as a role model for company policies.

Relationships:

It is essential that the Merchandising Manager maintain professional communication with all company managers and departments in order to maintain good relationships within the company and assure total customer satisfaction. The Merchandising Manager's immediate supervisor shall be the General Manager or Store Manager.

Minimum Qualifications:

It will be necessary for the Merchandising Manager to have a minimum of three to five years of retail experience and to have completed business management training as set forth by the company President. He or she must be able to pass a pre-employment drug test and a criminal/theft background check.

➤ Office Manager

Reports to: CEO or General Manager

Basic Function:

The basic function of the Office Manager is to provide for customer satisfaction with the company's services by supervising the activities of the business office to ensure that the transaction and record-keeping procedures necessary to sustain the business are carried out in the most efficient and cost-effective manner possible.

Duties and Responsibilities:

1. By implementing the following duties and responsibilities and by performing related work as required, the Office Manager will be able to perform his or her job functions as required.

2. Create and execute job descriptions for office personnel, which may include cashiers, bookkeepers or bookkeeping clerks, customer service specialists, administrative assistants, general office or clerical workers and others.

3. Hire, train, supervise, motivate and evaluate office personnel.

4. Be responsible for financial transactions including, but not necessarily limited to, accounts receivable, accounts payable, payroll, cash control and banking.

5. Be responsible for records, bookkeeping and reporting including sales, inventory, receipts, disbursements and the general ledger in order to produce accurate daily,

weekly and monthly sales and margin reports and monthly income statements and balance sheets.

6. Be responsible for processing customer sales, purchase orders, delivery tickets and receipts and incoming merchandise receiving receipts, back orders, returns and return authorizations.

7. Prepare the company records for audit and comply with the auditor's requests for records and information.

8. Coordinate delivery scheduling and paperwork with the sales department and Warehouse Manager to assure fast and efficient delivery of products to customers, including notifying customers of any merchandise back orders and anticipated arrivals of special orders.

9. Maintain customer records and an up-to-date mailing list.

10. Oversee the processing of all business and customer correspondence.

11. Be responsible for assuring the security of records and cash.

12. In the absence of a bookkeeper, perform the entry work and processing necessary to produce reports and statements and prepare the records for audit.

13. In the absence of an IT Manager, be responsible for purchasing, maintaining and updating the company's computer hardware and software.

Relationships:

The Office Manager's immediate supervisor will be the CEO or General Manager. It is essential that the Office Manager maintain professional communications with all other departments and managers in order to maintain good relationships within the organization and total customer satisfaction.

Minimum Qualifications:

It will be necessary for the Office Manager to have excellent organizational and supervisory skills, knowledge of operating appropriate computer systems, retail bookkeeping proficiency and five years of retail office management experience. He or she must be able to pass a pre-employment drug test and a criminal/theft background check.

➤ Warehouse Manager

Reports to: Store Manager or General Manager

Basic Function

The Warehouse Manager is responsible for maintaining a safe, secure and efficient warehouse operation including inventory control and receiving, storing, delivering and installing merchandise. He or she will operate in a professional, ethical and courteous manner with the goal of assuring customer satisfaction with the company's services. The Warehouse Manager may perform the duties of the Delivery Supervisor. (See that job description.)

Duties and Responsibilities

By implementing the following duties and responsibilities properly and by performing related work as required, the Warehouse Manager will be able to perform his or her job function as outlined.

1. Manage the warehouse according to an approved budget and business plan.

2. Hire, train and supervise warehouse personnel to assure maximum productivity.

3. Purchase and provide for the maintenance of storage fixtures, material handling equipment and delivery equipment and vehicles.

4. Devise and administer loss prevention policies and purchase appropriate security and loss control equipment.

5. Establish and oversee secure procedures for merchandise receipt, handling and storage.

6. Establish and enforce safety policies and procedures for warehouse and delivery personnel.

7. Follow appropriate procedures or suppliers' policies for notifying vendors and/or shipping companies of incomplete shipments or damaged goods.

8. Establish and oversee secure procedures for removing merchandise from inventory for delivery to customers.

9. Schedule and route the delivery of merchandise to customers in cooperation with the Office or Sales Manager.

10. Follow established inventory control and reporting procedures and systems.

11. Coordinate return authorization procedures with the Office or Sales Manager and be responsible for returning merchandise to suppliers.

12. Dispose of products removed from customers' homes in compliance with the appropriate local, state and federal laws and regulations.

13. Attend business seminars and classes as required.

Relationships:

The Warehouse Manager's immediate supervisor will be the Store Manager or General Manager. He or she will work closely with the Sales Manager and/or Office Manager to assure customer satisfaction with the company's services. It is essential that the Warehouse Manager maintain professional communications with all other departments and managers in order to maintain good relationships within the organization and assure total customer satisfaction.

Minimum Qualifications:

It will be necessary for the Warehouse Manager to have appropriate training in business and warehouse procedures, five (5) years on-the-job experience and to have a commercial driver's license in good standing as required by the state. He or she must be able to pass a pre-employment drug test and criminal/theft background check.

➤ Sales Associate

Reports to : Sales Manager or General Manager

Basic Function:

To help customers purchase the different types of merchandise and services available from the store in a professional, customer-friendly manner and to assure customer satisfaction.

Duties and Responsibilities:

The basic goal of a Sales Associate is to determine which of the company's products or services will best meet a customer's needs and complete the sales transaction in a manner that satisfies the customer and creates a positive impression of the company.

1. Attend scheduled sales, customer service, product training and other meetings.

2. Learn the features of products and what their advantages and benefits are for customers.

3. Appropriately greet and qualify customers, explain product features, advantages and benefits and close sales according to the company's sales and customer service policies.

4. Provide customers with information about how extended service protection, accessories and the company's private label credit card will meet their needs.

5. Maintain daily, weekly and monthly sales and goal sheets and meet or exceed sales goals.

6. Make sure all merchandise is presented in a clean and attractive setting and that there are no empty spaces in the product displays.

7. Make sure all merchandise that needs to be is hooked up and operating.

8. Answer the company telephones according to company policy and in a manner that satisfies the callers' needs and creates a positive impression of the company.

9. Contact customers who purchase products or services within 10 days after delivery to thank them for their business and ask if they are satisfied or have any further needs.

10. Establish a schedule for writing and phoning customers to advise them about new products or sales and events with products that might meet their needs.

11. Attempt to call or write customers who leave the store without buying to find out if a competitor met their needs or they are still looking for a product or service that the company can provide.

12. Return phone calls promptly.

13. Assist in preparing for sales events including re-pricing sales tags and setting out point-of-sale ad material.

14. Learn about and be prepared for advertised sales and special events and featured merchandise.

15. Attend manufacturer sales training as required.

16. Follow established guidelines for Point-of-Sale transactions and inventory procedures.

17. Wear proper business attire when working that meets the company's dress code policy.

18. Represent the company positively both in the store and the community.

Relationships:

A Sales Associate's immediate supervisor will be the Sales Manager or Store Manager. However, it may be necessary to ask the appropriate product specialists questions about the features and benefits of specific products. It is essential that the Sales Associate maintain professional communications and a positive and friendly attitude with other employees in order to maintain good relationships within the company and assure total customer satisfaction.

Minimum Qualifications:

Prior retail sales experience is desirable but not necessary. A successful Sales Associate has good communication skills and enjoys interacting with customers. All Sales Associates are required successfully to complete a training and probation period of up to ninety days after the date of employment. He or she must be able to pass a pre-employment drug test and a criminal/theft background check.

➤ Delivery Supervisor

Reports to: Warehouse Manager

Basic Function:

The basic function of the Delivery Supervisor is to oversee the delivery and installation of merchandise to customers so that the work is done in a professional, ethical and courteous manner so as to assure customer satisfaction. The Delivery Supervisor may perform the job duties of an Installer. (See that job description.)

Duties and Responsibilities:

By implementing the following duties and responsibilities properly and by performing related work as required, the Delivery Supervisor will be able to perform his or her job function as outlined.

1. Train and supervise Installers in proper installation procedures and paperwork, use of material handling equipment, safety precautions and customer satisfaction policies.

2. Assist the Warehouse Manager in the scheduling and processing of deliveries to customers.

3. Oversee the receipt of merchandise into inventory, check for visible damage, make sure that merchandise received matches the vendors' shipping documents and route products to their appropriate locations in the warehouse.

4. Notify the Warehouse Manager of any damaged or missing merchandise before the vendor delivery vehicle leaves the loading dock.

5. Arrange for merchandise to be picked up from vendors.

6. Maintain an adequate supply of installation materials and supplies.

7. Provide for the maintenance of delivery vehicles and equipment.

8. Oversee the placement of merchandise on display in the store.

9. Oversee that all warehouse facilities are clean, organized and secure.

10. Attend necessary training meetings as required.

11. Maintain adequate floor display of merchandise in inventory.

12. Report all injuries to Warehouse Manager immediately.

Relationships:

The Delivery Supervisor's immediate supervisor will be the Warehouse Manager. The Delivery Supervisor is required to maintain professional communications and a positive and friendly attitude in dealing with customers and other employees in order to maintain good relationships within the organization and assure total customer satisfaction.

Minimum Qualifications:

It will be necessary for the Delivery Supervisor to have one (1) year on-the-job experience, a commercial driver's license in good standing as required by the state and be able to perform the above-mentioned duties and responsibilities, including lifting products weighing up to 75 pounds, without restriction. Lift truck certification may be required. He or she must be able to pass a pre-employment drug test and a criminal/theft background check.

➤ Delivery Driver/Installer

Reports to: Delivery Supervisor or Warehouse Manager

Basic Function:

The basic function of an Installer is to deliver and install merchandise to customers in a professional, ethical and courteous manner. The Installer is the last company representative to have contact with customers and it is his or her responsibility to leave customers with a positive impression of the company.

Duties and Responsibilities:

By implementing the following duties and responsibilities and by performing other related work as required, an Installer will be able to perform his or her job function as outlined.

1. Deliver, install and hook up merchandise sold to customers and complete necessary paperwork according to company standards.

2. Notify supervisor of any customer complaint so the company can correct the problem.

3. Drive responsibly and follow all traffic laws when operating a company vehicle.

4. Follow company policy regarding notifying supervisor when a traffic accident or traffic citation does occur.

5. Assist in preparing merchandise for delivery.

6. Assist in receiving merchandise.

7. Assist in distributing merchandise within the warehouse and store.

8. Assist in maintaining and cleaning warehouse locations and merchandise.

9. Assist in maintaining delivery vehicles and equipment.

10. Attend training meetings as required.

11. Pick up merchandise from vendors as required.

12. Notify supervisor of any damaged or missing merchandise immediately.

13. Follow company policies regarding safety measures and precautions.

14. Wear company uniforms at all times while at work and follow established policies governing their use, cleaning and return (or follow company dress code regarding appearance and cleanliness).

15. Put all packing, debris and appliances to be disposed of where directed.

16. Report all injuries immediately to supervisor.

Relationships:

The Installer's immediate supervisor will be the Warehouse Manager or Delivery Supervisor. Installers are required to maintain professional communications and a positive and friendly attitude in dealing with customers and other employees in order to maintain good relationships within the organization and assure total customer satisfaction.

Minimum Qualifications:

It will be necessary for the Installer to have a commercial driver's license in good standing as required by the state and to be able to perform the above-mentioned duties and responsibilities, including being capable of lifting products weighing up to 75 pounds, without restriction. Lift truck certification may be required. He or she must be able to pass a pre-employment drug test and a criminal/theft background check.

The above statements are intended to describe the general nature and level of work being performed by the individuals assigned to this classification. They are not intended to be construed as an exhaustive list of all responsibilities, duties and skills of personnel so classified.

Bibliography

➤ Books

Beckwith, Harry. *Selling the Invisible*. New York, N.Y.: Warner Books. 1997.

Blechman, Bruce, and Jay Conrad Levinson. *Guerrilla Financing*, Boston: Houghton Mifflin, 1991.

Buckingham, Marcus and Curt Coffman. *First, Break All the Rules : What the World's Greatest Managers Do Differently*. New York, NY. : Simon & Schuster, 1999.

Brown, Mort, and Thomas Tilling (contributor). *So You Want to Own the Store: Secrets to Running a Successful Retail Operation*. New York, N.Y.: McGraw Hill Trade. 1997.

Canfield, Jack and Mark Victor Hansen. *The Aladdin Factor*. New York: Berkley; 1995.

Charvet, Shelle Rose. *Words that Change Minds*. Dubuque, IA: Kendall/Hunt. 1997.

Cialdini, Robert B. *Influence: The Psychology of Persuasion*. New York, N.Y.: Quill, 1993.

Dion, Jim and Ted Toppin (contributing) *Start and Run a Profitable Retail Business (4th edition)*. Self Counsel Press: 2000.

Dunne, Patrick and Robert F. Lusch. *Retailing, Third Edition*, Orlando FL. The Drayden Press,. Harcourt Brace College Publishers. 1999.

Goden, Seth. *Purple Cow: Transform Your Business by Being Remarkable.* New York, N.Y.: Portfolio, 2003.

Gordon, R. M. Erik and Barton A. Weitz. *American Retail Excellence — A Key to Best Practices in the U.S. Retail Industry,* The NRF Foundation, 2002.

Geist, Sam. *Why Should Someone Do Business With You Rather Than Someone Else? : A Guide To Discover New Perspectives, Differentiating Strategies to Get and Keep Customers, to Increase your Staff Productivity and Increase Business Profitability.* Bonita Springs, FL : Addington & Wentworth, 1997.

Gross, T. Scott. *How to Get What You Want from Almost Anybody.* New York, N.Y : Mastermedia. 1992.

Jennings, Jason and Laurence Haughton. *it's not the BIG that eat the SMALL — it's the FAST that eat the Slow : How to Use Speed as a Competitive Tool in Business.* 1st HarperBusiness pbk. ed. New York: HarperBusiness, 2002.

LeBeouf, Michael. *The Greatest Management Principle in the World,* New York, NY : Putnam, 1985.

Lee, Bill. *Gross Margin : 26 Factors Affecting Your Bottom Line.* New Oxford Publishing, 2002.

Levinson, Jay Conrad, with Theo Brandt-Sarif. *Guerrilla Travel Tactic : Hundreds of Simple Strategies Guaranteed to Save Road Warriors Time and Money.* New York, N.Y.: American Management Association, 2004.

Levinson, Jay Conrad. *Guerrilla Marketing for Free: 100 No-Cost Tactics to Promote Your Business and Energize Your Profits.* Boston: Houghton Mifflin Company, 2003.

Levinson, Jay Conrad, Rick Frishman, and Jill Lublin with Mark Steisel. *Guerrilla Publicity : Hundreds of Sure-Fire Tactics to Get Maximum Sales for Minimum Dollars.* Avon, MA : Adams Media Corporation, 2002.

Levinson, Jay Conrad. *Guerrilla Creativity: Make Your Message Irresistible with the Power of Memes.* Boston: Houghton Mifflin Company, 2001.

Levinson, Jay Conrad, *Guerrilla Marketing: The Best of Guerrilla Marketing*, [edited by] Ginger Conlon. Boston: Aspatore Books, 2001.

Levinson, Jay Conrad, Rick Fishman and Michael Larsen. *Guerrilla Marketing for Writers.* Cincinnati, OH.: Writer's Digest Books, 2000.

Levinson, Jay Conrad and Kathryn Tyler. *Guerrilla Saving: Secrets for Keeping Profits in Your Home-Based Business.* New York, N.Y.: John Wiley, 2000.

Levinson, Jay Conrad. *Mastering Guerrilla Marketing : 100 Profit-Producing Insights You Can Take to the Bank.* Boston: Houghton Mifflin Company, 1999.

Levinson, Jay Conrad, Mark S.A. Smith and Orvel Ray Wilson. *Guerrilla TeleSelling: New Unconventional Weapons and Tactics to Get the Business When You Can't Be There in Person.* New York: John Wiley & Sons, 1998.

Levinson, Jay Conrad. *Guerrilla Marketing — How to Make Big Profits from Your Small Business,* third edition. Boston: Houghton Mifflin Company, 1998.

Levinson, Jay Conrad and Charles Rubin. *Guerrilla Marketing Online: the Entrepreneur's Guide to Earning Profits on the Internet.* 2nd ed., Boston: Houghton Mifflin Company, 1997.

Levinson, Jay Conrad. *Get What You Deserve. How to Guerrilla Market Yourself.* New York: Avon Books, 1997.

Levinson, Jay Conrad. *Guerrilla Marketing with Technology: Unleashing the Full Potential of Your Small Business.* Reading, Mass.: Addison-Wesley, 1997.

Levinson, Jay Conrad. *Guerrilla Marketing With Technology.* New York: Addison-Wesley, Publishing Company, 1997.

Levinson, Jay Conrad, Mark S.A. Smith and Orvel Ray Wilson. *Guerrilla Trade Show Selling: New Unconventional Weapons and Tactics to Meet More People, Get More Leads and Close More Sales.* New York, N.Y.: John Wiley & Sons, 1997.

Levinson, Jay Conrad. *The Way of the Guerrilla: Achieving Success and Balance as an Entrepreneur in the 21st Century.* Boston: Houghton Mifflin Company, 1997.

Levinson, Jay Conrad and Charles Rubin. *Guerrilla Marketing Online Weapons : 100 Low-Cost, High-Impact Weapons for Online Profits and Prosperity.* Boston: Houghton Mifflin Company, 1996.

Levinson, Jay Conrad. *Guerrilla Marketing for the Home Based Business*. Boston: Houghton Mifflin Company, 1996.

Levinson, Jay Conrad and Seth Godin. *Guerrilla Marketing Handbook*. Boston: Houghton Mifflin, 1994.

Levinson, Jay Conrad. *Guerrilla Advertising: Cost-Effective Tactics for Small-Business Success*. Boston: Houghton Mifflin Company, 1994.

Levinson, Jay Conrad. *Guerrilla Marketing Excellence: 50 Golden Rules for Small Business Success*. Boston: Houghton Mifflin Company, 1993.

Levinson, Jay Conrad, Bill Gallagher, PhD and Orvel Ray Wilson, CSP. *Guerrilla Selling — Unconventional Weapons and Tactics for Increasing Your Sales*. Boston: Houghton Mifflin Company, 1992.

Levinson, Jay Conrad. *Guerrilla Marketing Weapons: 100 Affordable Marketing Methods for Maximizing Profits from Your Small Business*. New York, N.Y.: Plume, 1990.

Levinson, Jay Conrad. *Guerrilla Marketing Attack: New Strategies, Tactics & Weapons for Winning Big Profits From Your Small Business*. Boston: Houghton Mifflin Company, 1987.

Rasmus, James A. and Gerald D. Rasmus. *Winning in Retailing: Success Strategies That Will Increase Your Sales, Increase Your Profits, and Enhance Your Image*. Mechanicsburg, PA: RDA Pub. Group, 1994.

Schroeder, Carol L. *Specialty Shop Retailing: How to Run Your Own Store* (revised) New York, NY. John Wiley & Sons

Segal, Rick. *Retail Business Kit for Dummies*®, New York, NY. John Wily & Sons

Steinmetz, Lawrence L. *How to Sell at Prices Higher than Your Competitors*, Boulder: Horizon Publications, 1994.

Taylor, Don (Donald D.) and Jeanne Smalling Archer. *Up Against the Wal-Marts: How Your Business Can Prosper in the Shadow of the Retail Giants.* New York, N.Y.: AMACOM, 1994.

Underhill, Paco. *Why We Buy: The Science of Shopping,* New York, N.Y.: Simon & Schuster, 1999.

Whalin, George. *Retail Success!: Increase Sales, Maximize Profits, and Wow Your Customers in the Most Competitive Marketplace in History.* San Marcos, CA: Willoughby Press, 2001.

Walther, George R., *Upside-Down Marketing — Turning Your Ex-Customers Into Your Best Customers.* New York, N.Y.: McGraw-Hill, 1994.

➤ Audiotapes[12]

Wilson, CSP, Orvel Ray. *Guerrilla Selling - Live!* Boulder, CO: The Guerrilla Group, Inc, 1996.

➤ Video Training Materials

Wilson, CSP, Orvel Ray. *Guerrilla Selling - Live!* Boulder, CO: The Guerrilla Group, Inc., 1996.

About the Authors

Jay Conrad Levinson

As an author, speaker, workshop leader and owner of a successful marketing firm, Jay personifies the true entrepreneur. Before embarking upon his life of writing and public speaking, he was a vice president and creative director at one of the largest advertising agencies in the world.

With an award-winning career in advertising and a nationally syndicated column, Jay has authored or co-authored 29 books, including the best-selling marketing series ever, with more than 14 million books sold worldwide, translated into 37 languages.

The books have led to the rapidly growing *Guerrilla Marketing Newsletter*, two successful audiotapes, a videotape, columns on marketing in 12 national publications and presentations at major conventions throughout North America.

He served as senior VP and creative director for the world's largest advertising agency, J. Walter Thompson and sat on the board of directors at Leo Burnett Advertising in the United States and Europe. His work has won major awards worldwide in virtually every marketing media, including direct mail, television, radio and magazines. Current clients include Fortune 500 companies and start-ups that want to be.

Levinson's small business expertise has also been demonstrated in his *Earning Money Without a Job*, *555 Ways to Earn Extra Money* (Holt, Rinehart & Winston, 1979 and 1982) and *Quit Your Job!* (Dodd, Mead, 1987).

He has one child and lives north of San Francisco.

Elly Valas

"Dynamic," "down-to-earth," "genuine," "practical ideas I can use right away." These are just a few of the superlatives clients use to describe Elly Valas. Author, speaker, consultant and a respected industry leader, Elly is a co-author of *Guerrilla Retailing*, part of the legendary *Guerrilla Marketing* series, with more than 14 million books in print. She shows retailers large and small how to beat the big box stores by using unconventional marketing and sales tactics that are simple, inexpensive and devastatingly effective.

Elly is the former President and CEO of the North American Retail Dealers Association. Since 1992, she has provided educational programming and services to help independent retailers grow their businesses in the consumer electronics, home appliance and furniture industries. Ms. Valas has served in many capacities on the NARDA Board of Directors including President and Chairman of the Board. She is also responsible for the association's advocacy programs that represent retailer's interests in setting industry standards and policies with manufacturers and suppliers. She works to influence government agencies and Congress on issues affecting the retail marketplace.

She has worked with retailers throughout the U.S., Canada, New Zealand, Australia and Fiji. In addition to in-store consultations, Ms. Valas presents keynotes, seminars and multi-day workshops on business planning, relationship selling, family business management and marketing.

Elly grew up in retail and is a decorated veteran of the box-store wars. She served more than twenty years in the grocery, sporting goods, consumer electronics and home appliance industries. In 1984, she became President of Valas Stores, Inc. and led it to become an early pioneer of rent-to-own, with a unique model that included retail, rental and in-store financing options in a single selling venue.

Ms. Valas is a regular contributor to *The Independent Retailer* and the Consumer Electronics Association's publication *Visions*. She has received the *Editorial Excellence* award from the American Society of Business Press Editors. She is a Senior Consultant with The Guerrilla Group, a graduate of the University of Colorado and a professional member of the National Speakers Association.

Orvel Ray Wilson, CSP

An internationally acclaimed author, trainer, motivational speaker and small-business guru, he as worked with clients in thousands of cities in more than 40 countries around the world, in a career spanning more than 25 years, and every continent except Antarctica.

His content-packed programs will transform your business and your life. They're entertaining, motivating and devastatingly effective. His take-no-prisoners approach gives you practical skills that you can *use right now* to produce extraordinary results.

In 2001, Meeting Professionals International, San Diego voted him their "Speaker of the Year."

He is a co-author of five books in the legendary *Guerrilla Marketing* series, with more than 14 million copies in print, including *Guerrilla Selling, Guerrilla TeleSelling, Guerrilla Trade Show Selling, Guerrilla Negotiating* and *Guerrilla Retailing.* When he's not on the platform, his team produces state-of-the art Internet-based sales and product training programs for clients like IBM, Ingram Micro, HP, Fujitsu, and others.

Already in its fifteenth printing, *Guerrilla Selling* stands as a "classic" in the field, published in English, Spanish, German, Korean and even Romanian. It was featured as "one of the 10 most important business books of the decade" in the July 1994 issue of *Sell!ng* magazine. His articles appear regularly in dozens of industry and trade magazines.

He started his career early, selling garden seeds door-to-door when he was twelve years old, and started his first business at nineteen. More than 30 years of real-world sales experience spans the range from advertising to automobiles, from encyclopedias to Internet middleware. He's taught closing techniques to Xerox field reps and job search skills to Indochinese refugees.

In 1980, he founded the Boulder Sales Training Institute, and his client list has since grown to include industry leaders like Choice Hotelst, Marriott, United Airlines, and Century 21. He has taught in the management development programs for the University of Colorado and the University of Denver, and created innovative business courses for Harbridge House, the University of Toledo, the Spring Institute for International Studies and Australia's Canberra College of Advanced Education. He has even pioneered workshops on capitalism for the Tyumen School of Management in the Russian Republic.

Recognized as a leader by his peers as well, Orvel Ray was elected President of the Colorado Chapter of the National Speakers Association in 1986, and served two additional terms on their Board of Directors. In 1997, the National Speakers Association bestowed upon him the highest level of certification recognized worldwide by the speaking profession: the Certified Speaking Professional, an honor held by fewer 300 professional speakers worldwide.

He's led hundreds of large-audience seminars and on-site workshops including "How to Give Exceptional Customer Service," "Managing Multiple Demands," "Taking Control of Your Workday," "Effective Collection Strategies," "Power Presentation Skills," and "Dealing with Difficult People." He has collaborated with best-selling authors to develop seminar versions of *Guerrilla Marketing* by Jay Conrad Levinson, *The Time Trap* by Alec McKenzie and *Don't Do, Delegate!* by Jack Kelly and John Jenks. He is also the author of several audiotape albums and videos.

Orvel Ray is a Senior Partner with The Guerrilla Group, Inc., a training and consulting firm serving clients worldwide. He lives with his wife, Denise in the mountains of Colorado.

Increase Your Profits Now

We coach companies how to increase their sales with unconventional weapons and tactics.

Call us toll free at **800-247-9145** to learn more about how we can help build your people and your profits.

If you need a custom-built breakout session for your next sales meeting, or a product-specific Internet based video program available on-demand for your dealers and distributors, we can help. You can expect fully customized on-site training programs and seminars in formats ranging from a 30-minute standing-ovation keynote to a multi-day intensive boot camp, from sales interventions to long-term consulting.

Our clients tell us that they choose us because, instead of woo-woo theory and psychobabble models, we deliver proven "how-to-do-it" tactics that work.

And please, share your success stories. We love hearing from you. Call today.

THE GUERRILLA GROUP inc

1002 Walnut Street
Suite 101
Boulder, CO 80302
800-247-9145
www.guerrillagroup.com
postmaster@guerrillagroup.com